0150181

D1686112

HARROLD BRIDGES LIBRARY
S. MARTIN'S COLLEGE
LANCASTER

This book is due for return on or before the last date shown below.

13 JAN 1999
CANCELLED
08 DEC 99
21 NOV 2000
CANCELLED
CANCELLED
04 MAR 2001
30 APR 2003
12 JAN 2004
17 FEB 2004
20 OCT 2004
29 NOV 2004
27 MAY 2005
05 OCT 2005
3 JAN 2007
19 FEB 2007
20 FEB 2008
17 MAR 2008
29 SEP 2009
19 MAR 2010

Don Gresswell Ltd., London, N.21 Cat. No. 1208 DG 02242/71

0415176638

The International Library of Sociology

DELINQUENCY AND OPPORTUNITY

Founded by KARL MANNHEIM

THE SOCIOLOGY OF YOUTH AND ADOLESCENCE
In 12 Volumes

I	Adolescence	*Fleming*
II	Adolescents and Morality	*Eppel*
III	Caring for Children in Trouble	*Carlebach*
IV	Casework in Child Care	*Kastell*
V	Children in Care	*Heywood*
VI	Delinquency and Opportunity	*Cloward et al*
VII	Family Environment and Delinquency	*Glueck*
VIII	German Youth: Bond or Free	*Becker*
IX	The Psychoanalytical Approach to Juvenile Delinquency	*Friedlander*
X	Studies in the Social Psychology of Adolescence	*Richardson et al*
XI	Working with Unattached Youth	*Goetschius*
XII	Youth and the Social Order	*Musgrove*

DELINQUENCY AND OPPORTUNITY

A Theory of Delinquent Gangs

by

RICHARD A. CLOWARD and LLOYD E. OHLIN

ROUTLEDGE

First published in 1961 by
Routledge and Kegan Paul Ltd

Reprinted in 1998 by
Routledge
11 New Fetter Lane, London EC4P 4EE

Printed and bound in Great Britain

© 1960 The Free Press, a Corporation

All rights reserved. No part of this book may be reprinted or reproduced or utilized in any form or by any electronic, mechanical, or other means, now known or hereafter invented, including photocopying and recording, or in any information storage or retrieval system, without permission in writing from the publishers.

The publishers have made every effort to contact authors/copyright holders of the works reprinted in *The International Library of Sociology*. This has not been possible in every case, however, and we would welcome correspondence from those individuals/companies we have been unable to trace.

British Library Cataloguing in Publication Data
A CIP catalogue record for this book
is available from the British Library

Delinquency and Opportunity
ISBN 0-415-17663-8
The Sociology of Youth and Adolescence: 12 Volumes
ISBN 0-415-17828-2
The International Library of Sociology: 274 Volumes
ISBN 0-415-17838-X

To

Robert K. Merton and

Edwin H. Sutherland

Contents

		PAGE
	INTRODUCTION	*ix*
1	DELINQUENT SUBCULTURES	*1*
	Deviance and Delinquency	*2*
	Delinquent Acts and Delinquent Subcultures	*7*
	Delinquent Norms	*13*
	Varieties of Delinquent Subculture	*20*
	The Distribution of Delinquent Subcultures	*27*
2	QUESTIONS A THEORY MUST ANSWER	*31*
	The Origin of Pressures Toward Deviance	*34*
	The Evolution of Delinquent Subcultures	*40*
	Change and Persistence of Delinquent Subculutres	*43*
3	SOME CURRENT THEORIES OF DELINQUENT SUBCULTURES	*47*
	Masculine Identification and Delinquent Subcultures	*48*
	Adolescence and Delinquent Subcultures	*54*
	Lower-class Culture and Delinquent Subcultures	*65*

4 GOALS, NORMS, AND ANOMIE 77
The Regulation of Goals: Durkheim 78
The Regulation of Goals and Norms: Merton 82
Success Values in American Life 86
Barriers to Legitimate Opportunity 97
Alternative Avenues to Success-Goals 104

5 THE EVOLUTION OF DELINQENT SUBCULTURES 108
The Process of Alienation 110
Collective vs. Individual Solutions 124
Techniques of Defense Against Guilt 130
The Collective Problem-Solving Process 139

6 ILLEGITIMATE MEANS AND DELINQUENT SUBCULTURES 144
The Availability of Illegitimate Means 145
Learning and Performance Structures 148
Differential Opportunity: A Hypothesis 150
Illegitimate Opportunities and the Social Structure of the Slum 152
Slum Organization and Subcultural Differentiation 159

7 SUBCULTURAL DIFFERENTIATION 161
The Criminal Subculture 161
The Conflict Subculture 171
The Retreatist Subculture 178

8 PERSISTENCE AND CHANGE IN DELINQUENT SUBCULTURES 187
Patterns of Persistence in Delinquent Subcultures 188
Patterns of Change in Delinquent Subcultures 193

INDEX 213

Introduction

THIS BOOK is an attempt to explore two questions: (1) Why do delinquent "norms," or rules of conduct, develop? (2) What are the conditions which account for the distinctive content of various systems of delinquent norms—such as those prescribing violence or theft or drug-use?

The first question involves a shift in emphasis from the traditional concern of the field—the analysis of delinquent acts or of the careers of individual delinquents. Detailed studies have been undertaken to explain why particular individuals are likely to become delinquent or why delinquent acts of various types are committed with varying frequencies in different social locations. Such studies take as their object of inquiry the careers of individuals or the delinquent act itself rather than the rules of conduct in delinquent gangs that require the commission of delinquent acts. Our emphasis on delinquent norms permits us to raise new questions and to offer new explanations which we believe may have both theoretical and practical significance.

The second problem to which this book is devoted is the distinction between pressures toward deviance and the outcome of these pressures. An explanation of the forces that lead individuals to depart from conventional norms does not necessarily explain the form of deviance that will result. There are, for example, several different types of delinquent gang. Whatever problem of adjustment a person may experience, there are several alternative deviant solutions that he might follow. How, then, may we account for the selection and evolution of different adaptations? This is an important problem which has generally been overlooked in previous explanations of delinquency or other modes of deviance. In this book we shall suggest that the milieu in which actors find themselves has a crucial impact upon the types of adaptation which develop in response to pressures toward deviance.

In addressing these themes, we have drawn principally upon two theoretical perspectives. The first, initiated by Emile Durkheim and greatly extended by Robert K. Merton, focuses largely upon the sources of pressure that can lead to deviance. The second, developed by Clifford R. Shaw, Henry D. McKay, and Edwin H. Sutherland, contains germinal ideas about the way in which features of social structure regulate the selection and evolution of deviant solutions. In this book we attempt to integrate these two streams of thought as they apply to the problem of delinquency. The task of consolidating them required that we redefine the unique contribution of each, that we reconceptualize elements in both, and that we develop linking concepts. The result is what we call the theory of differential opportunity systems. It is our hope that the differential opportunity systems theory provides a new and useful way of thinking about deviancy.

Many of the ideas expressed in this book stemmed from research projects supported by The Ford Foundation, whose sympathetic support we would like to acknowledge. We are also indebted to Mobilization for Youth, Inc., which provided us with an opportunity to formulate material on subcultural differentiation. The manuscript has benefited immeasurably from the insightful editorial work of Gladys Topkis. We appreciate the interest shown in this book by Jeremiah Kaplan, our publisher, and the care with which it was designed by Sidney Solomon. Our indebtedness to Leona Simmons, our secretary, is well known to her.

RICHARD A. CLOWARD
LLOYD E. OHLIN

New York School of Social Work
Columbia University, June 1960

HAROLD BRIDGES LIBRARY
S. MARTIN'S COLLEGE
LANCASTER

CHAPTER 1

Delinquent Subcultures

THIS BOOK is about delinquent gangs, or subcultures, as they are typically found among adolescent males in lower-class areas of large urban centers. It is devoted to an exposition of how delinquent subcultures arise, develop various law-violating ways of life, and persist or change. In particular, it is about three more or less distinctive kinds of delinquent subculture. One is what we call the "criminal subculture"—a type of gang which is devoted to theft, extortion, and other illegal means of securing income. A second is the "conflict subculture"—a type of gang in which the manipulation of violence predominates as a way of winning status. The third is the "retreatist subculture"—a type of gang in which the consumption of drugs is stressed. These three patterns of subcultural delinquency not only involve different styles of life for their members but also present very different problems for social control and prevention. They arise by different processes and in different parts of the social structure. They impose distinctive beliefs, values, and prescriptions for action on their members. But all three are alike in that the norms which guide the behavior of members run counter to the norms of the larger society. Later in this chapter we shall describe these three delinquent subcultures in greater detail. First, however, we shall discuss some of our reasons for devoting so much attention to them and some of the problems involved in defining them as objects of inquiry.

Deviance and Delinquency

SINCE the terms "deviance," "delinquency," and "delinquent subculture" have been given a variety of meanings, both in the theoretical literature and by field workers, we wish to make our own usage clear at the outset.

THE DELINQUENT ACT

Delinquent acts are a special category of deviant acts. Every deviant act involves the violation of social rules that regulate the behavior of participants in a social system. It is a behavioral transaction in which an actor violates the rights of a victim as defined by the system of legitimate social expectations of which the role behavior of the victim is a part. The principal feature of a deviant act, in other words, is that it is not consistent with the behavior which the victim has been led to expect from others on the basis of the social position he occupies. The deviant does not abide by the accepted rules of the game that the victim is playing. In effect, his act challenges the legitimacy and authority of these rules. It represents a departure from the system of norms to which the victim has given his consent and trust.

Delinquent acts are distinguished from this larger class of deviant acts by the fact that officials engaged in the administration of criminal justice select them, from among many deviant acts, as forms of behavior proscribed by the approved norms of the society. These acts acquire their deviant character by being violations of social rules; they acquire their specifically delinquent character by being typically treated as violations of official norms by representatives of the official system.

Systems of rules regulate the interaction of participants in social enterprises which represent investments of varying importance to the dominant power groups in the society. No great harm is done to the basic interests of these groups by manifestations of "bad manners," such as using profanity in public, refusing to welcome a guest (unless, perhaps, he is the titular head of a rival nation), or carrying on a noisy conversation during a musical performance. For the social control of such deviant conduct, various types of informal sanction, such as ridicule, criticism, or scorn, are customarily invoked. It is a different matter, however, if an act interferes with the achievement of the general welfare as defined by the controlling interest groups in a society. For example, the rules that protect persons, reputation, property, and contractual agreements regulate interests of both individuals and groups which are regarded as important to the maintenance and stability of the existing social order. A violation of these rules not only threatens a particular individual or group but is seen as a challenge to the legitimacy of the basic institutions of the society. Delinquent acts, in contrast to other violations of social rules, constitute an actual or a potential threat to the legitimacy and security of these basic institutions in the judgment of officials representing the agencies of criminal justice. *The delinquent act,* then, *is defined by two essential elements: it is behavior that violates basic norms of the society, and, when officially known, it evokes a judgment by agents of criminal justice that such norms have been violated.*

"OFFICIAL" DEFINITIONS OF DELINQUENCY

Many attempts have been made to define delinquent activity independently of the official response to it. Some investigators, sensitive to the possibility of "class bias" in law enforcement, are reluctant to treat official statistics as representative of the actual distribution of delinquent behavior throughout the social-class structure.[1] Furthermore, it is well known that only a small fraction of offenses is detected; even if no class bias operates in delinquency proceedings, official statistics would still not reveal the extent of delinquent behavior in our society. Finally, investigators who are interested in studying trends in delinquent behavior are faced with the problem of determining whether a particular trend reflects a change in official policies (*e.g.*, as regards arresting practices) or in the actual rates of delinquent behavior. For these reasons, many investigators have tended to avoid the use of official statistics and have tried to develop other ways of studying the distribution of delinquent conduct.

Such efforts have invariably failed, since delinquent acts are distinguished from other deviant acts by the very fact that they result, or are likely to result, in the initiation of official proceedings by agents of criminal justice. The norms which are challenged by acts of delinquency are backed by official sanctions. To define delinquency, one must discover the criteria that control decisions to invoke or withhold these official sanctions.

The law confers broad discretion upon officials to define many types of youthful activity as delinquent. In fact, statutory definitions of delinquency are ordinarily so broad that all children at one time or another are likely to engage in behavior that could be defined as delinquent. The New York statute, for example, includes in its definition of delinquent

> . . . children who are "incorrigible, ungovernable, or habitually disobedient," those who are "habitually truant," who desert their homes or places of abode without consent of parents or guardians,

1. For an analysis of the difficulties involved in arriving at an objective definition of delinquency which will not suffer from the inherent biases in official statistics, see P. W. Tappan, *Comparative Survey on Juvenile Delinquency,* Part I: *North America* (New York: United Nations, Division of Social Welfare, 1952), and Tappan's earlier article, "Who Is the Criminal?" *American Sociological Review,* Vol. 12 (Feb. 1947), pp. 96-102.

who associate "with immoral or vicious persons," frequent places "the existence of which is a violation of the law," habitually use obscene language, solicit alms in public places, or who so deport themselves as willfully to injure or endanger the morals or health of themselves or others.[2]

Obviously, if all instances of such behavior resulted in the institution of delinquency proceedings, the agencies of criminal justice would be hopelessly swamped and legal sanctions would lose their force as devices of social control. But such statutory definitions are permissive rather than mandatory; it is not incumbent on the officials to treat all acts subsumed by the criminal code as delinquent. Instead, the enforcement, judicial, and correctional agencies are expected to act when, *in their judgment,* the interests of the child and of the community compel legal intervention. The broad discretion officials possess to define acts as delinquent highlights the importance of the criteria they employ and of the processes by which these standards develop. The authority delegated to officials to exercise judgments that regulate the types and amount of juvenile misconduct subjected to legal proceedings adds to the variations in the nature and rates of delinquency from one time and place to another.[3]

If we understood more clearly the nature of official criteria, it might be possible to separate the effects of official action from variations in the actual rates of misconduct. We could define the characteristics of the various types of offense which, if detected, would probably lead to the initiation of delinquency proceedings. Through appropriate sampling procedures, we could then isolate a representative population of

2. H. A. Bloch and F. T. Flynn, *Delinquency: The Juvenile Offender in America Today* (New York: Random House, 1956), p. 8. The passage quoted is a summarization of certain provisions of the New York State Children's Court Act, Article I, Section 2, Subsection 2.

3. We do not mean to suggest that criminal-justice officials are wholly arbitrary in defining particular acts as delinquent. The more serious types of offense, such as robbery, burglary, violent assault, and adolescent drug use, with which we are primarily concerned here, are commonly defined as delinquent acts by officials in all jurisdictions. Official actions in these cases vary principally in the manner and vigor with which the cases are prosecuted from one jurisdiction or time period to another.

youngsters and conduct interviews designed to reveal the rates of different types of misconduct, whether known to officials or not. Although several studies have attempted to estimate hidden delinquencies,[4] the value of the results is limited because we do not know the likelihood of delinquency proceedings if these acts had been detected by officials in the jurisdictions surveyed. Systematic investigation of the conditions under which a delinquent definition of youthful rule violation is imposed and those under which it is withheld would considerably enhance both theoretical understanding and practical management of the delinquency problem.[5]

It is our opinion, then, that the anticipated official response to deviant actions is an extremely important element in the definition of delinquency. A deviant act that is frowned upon but otherwise ignored by officials will not mean the same thing either to the community or to the offender as an act that would ordinarily result in delinquency proceedings. The fact that official responses vary from one community to another does not mean that they are of little importance in conditioning the occurrence and content of the delinquent act. To the offender, the anticipated official response is a highly significant element of the total situation, one that gives different meanings as well as different risks to various delinquent acts. Acts that do not ordinarily lead to the initiation of delinquency proceedings

---

4. See F. J. Murphy, M. M. Shirley, and H. L. Witmer, "The Incidence of Hidden Delinquency," *American Journal of Orthopsychiatry*, Vol. 16 (Oct. 1946), pp. 686-96; William McCord and Joan McCord, with Irving Zola, *Origins of Crime* (New York: Columbia University Press, 1959); F. I. Nye, J. F. Short, Jr., and V. J. Olson, "Socioeconomic Status and Delinquent Behavior," *American Journal of Sociology*, Vol. 63 (Jan. 1958), pp. 381-89; J. F. Short, Jr., "A Report on the Incidence of Criminal Behavior, Arrests, and Convictions in Selected Groups," *Proceedings of the Pacific Sociological Society*, 1954, pp. 110-18; and A. L. Porterfield, *Youth in Trouble* (Fort Worth, Texas: Leo Rotishman Foundation, 1946).

5. A study of the criteria, policies, and practices which result in the imposition of a criminal definition in the case of *adult* law violators has been initiated by the American Bar Foundation as part of a research project on "The Administration of Criminal Justice in the United States." No comparable undertaking, however, has been launched in the area of juvenile offenses.

may constitute deviance from the norms of some group or organization, such as church, school, social agency, family, and peer groups; but these acts are not delinquent unless they are likely to be defined as such by agents of criminal justice.

THE DELINQUENT SUBCULTURE

The delinquent subculture is a special category of deviant subculture. The latter term is generic, encompassing all subculturally supported behavior that violates some conventionally sanctioned set of social expectations or rules of conduct. Such behaviors as truancy, profanity, property destruction, petty theft, illicit sexual experiences, disorderly conduct, and drunkenness, for example, are deviant; indeed, when they occur among adolescents they are often dealt with as delinquent acts by criminal-justice authorities. However, we would not necessarily describe as delinquent a group that tolerated or practiced these behaviors unless they were the central activities around which the group was organized. In a nondelinquent group, all roles within the group can be performed successfully without resorting to delinquent behavior. Members of the group may tolerate such behavior, but they do not require it as a demonstration of eligibility for membership or leadership status. *A delinquent subculture is one in which certain forms of delinquent activity are essential requirements for the performance of the dominant roles supported by the subculture.* It is the central position accorded to specifically delinquent activity that distinguishes the delinquent subculture from other deviant subcultures.

Delinquent Acts and Delinquent Subcultures

DELINQUENT ACTS occur in many different social contexts and take many different forms. Before we can explain them, we must try to classify them in some meaningful way. There are many aspects of delinquency that might be used as a basis of classification. For example, one could devise a set of categories based on various characteristics of the delinquents themselves, such as age, sex, social class, school achievement, family relationships, emotional stability, intelligence, relationship to other delinquents, personal aspirations, and the like. One might also classify delinquencies in terms of various characteristics of the victim, whether a person, a group, or an institution. Alternatively, one might classify certain features of the behavioral transaction between the delinquent and the victim. For example, did it involve property destruction, assault, theft, or fraud? What was the relative cost to the victim or to the more general interests of dominant power groups in the society?

The way in which one chooses to classify the complex social events that are delinquent acts depends upon what it is that one is interested in doing about these acts. People usually attend particularly to those features of delinquency that seem most relevant to the accomplishment of their objectives. For example, the policeman, interested in controlling crime, will tend to be concerned about the seriousness of the offense, the cost to the victim, the threat of a repetition by the offender, the likelihood of securing a conviction, and the effect of all these upon the public's definition of the police department. The judge, charged with such additional tasks as making an appropriate disposition of the offender, will be concerned about the social background of the delinquent, the motivation and circumstances of the act, the likelihood of a favorable response to different forms of treatment, and so forth. The social worker or psychiatrist concerned with rehabilitation will try to identify the sources of the behavior and its susceptibility to treatment. The research scientist committed to developing explanations of delinquency will seek to establish causal connections or correlations between elements of the total problem: for example, the relationship between various types of act and the social conditions that attend or precede them, or the connections between offenders and their victims.

Clearly there will be considerable overlapping among these classifications of the facts about delinquents and their offenses by persons charged with these different tasks. However, the classifications of greatest value for one purpose may not be suited to another. Legal codes represent efforts to define and to classify those facts which facilitate the determination of responsibility for illegal acts with the minimal error or cost to the innocent. Although these classifications are essential to the legal definition of persons as delinquents or criminals, they are not necessarily the only categories that might be employed in developing an understanding of the processes which generate the prohibited behavior. The same applies to the distinctions of greatest relevance to the action interests of policemen, judges, and treatment therapists. The research scientist must develop classifications that enable him to understand and explain the events he is investigating without regard to their immediate implications for action, official or otherwise.

In this book, as we have suggested, we are concerned with those forms of delinquent activity which result from the performance of social roles *specifically provided and supported by delinquent subcultures*. There are many thefts, assaults, and other delinquent acts which do not depend upon the prescriptions of a delinquent subculture but are, rather, secondary or incidental to the performance of essentially lawful social roles. The deaths, injuries, or destruction which occasionally result from fraternity initiations are of this sort; they are unintended consequences rather than expected or prescribed consequences. They may occur in the course of carrying out other expected forms of activity but are not the essential types of action upon which the social definition of the role has been constructed. Student pranks following athletic contests, to cite another example, may result in injury and property destruction, but they are not activities which are essential to being a loyal supporter of one's favorite team; one can fully perform this role without committing delinquent acts. Similarly, neurotic or psychotic youngsters often perform acts of violence, sexual assault, or property destruction without involvement in a delinquent subculture. Such youngsters are not necessarily acting out social roles sanctioned and shared by their peers. In fact, severely neurotic and psychotic adolescents are usually estranged from their peers.[6] It sometimes happens that the "lone" offender is able to maintain a role in a conventional group whose members are totally unaware that they have a delinquent in their midst. Many adolescent shoplifters fall into this category, for they sometimes succeed in concealing their delinquencies from their peers for long periods of time.

THE SOCIAL COSTS OF DELINQUENT SUBCULTURES

In this study, we focus on delinquent subcultures because in our opinion those forms of delinquent activity that are rooted in the prescriptions of a delinquent subculture represent the most costly and difficult problem in the field of delinquency control and prevention. First, acts of delinquency that reflect subcultural support are likely to recur with great frequency. In the delinquent subculture, habitual delinquent behavior is defined as a prerequisite for acceptance and status in the group. The fighting member of the street gang can lay claim to a "rep" only if he continually exhibits skill in the use of violence. The thief must persist in making big "scores" in order to maintain his reputation for dexterity and audacity and thus his social position. The drug addict wins deference by his mastery of the resources and knowledge for maintaining or increasing the esoteric experience of his "kick."

Secondly, access to a successful adult criminal career sometimes results from participation in a delinquent subculture. Delinquent subcultures, as we shall have occasion to note in later chapters, are often integrally linked to adult criminal groups. Through these age-graded relationships, the young are sometimes afforded an opportunity to acquire the values and skills that are prerequisite to competent performance of adult criminal roles. If they excel in criminal learning,

6. For example, Fritz Redl has observed that some mentally disturbed youngsters are unlikely to be tolerated by delinquent gangs because of their erratic and unreliable performances. (Helen L. Witmer and Ruth Kotinsky, eds., *New Perspectives for Research on Juvenile Delinquency,* United States Children's Bureau [Washington, D.C.: Government Printing Office, 1956], pp. 60, 64-65.)

they may subsequently be recruited into the adult world of crime. By thus furnishing continuity between juvenile and adult illegal activities, the delinquent subculture promotes careers in crime which might otherwise be successfully controlled. It therefore greatly increases the long-run social costs of juvenile misconduct.

Finally, the delinquent subculture imparts to the conduct of its members a high degree of stability and resistance to control or change. Delinquent activity is an essential feature of the social role which a member must perform in order to maintain his acceptance by other members of the group. As long as he finds satisfaction in these associations, the delinquent behavior can be expected to continue. His actions are integrated with the actions of other members who rely on him to carry out his role. A division of labor is readily apparent in the operation of the three types of delinquent group that we have identified. The member who refuses to perform further delinquencies must expect expulsion from the group. Because of this network of expectations and obligations, it is difficult to change or control one member's behavior without first changing the character of the entire group. Furthermore, efforts to induce a member to feel shame or guilt are blocked by the rationalizations and reassurances which the group provides (see Chap. 5).

A distinction between acts that are supported by delinquent subcultures and those that are not is implicit in many research investigations and official decisions, although it is seldom recognized. Law-enforcement officials must continually assess the relative social costs of offenses by different types of offender. They tend to regard the occasional or accidental delinquencies of lone offenders as less serious than the aberrant acts of those who have connections with an established delinquent group. Solitary offenders, as we have suggested, appear less likely to pursue adult criminal careers and are more easily encouraged to develop alternative solutions to their adjustment problems. In general, the delinquencies of adolescents who are not members of a delinquent subculture seem to be more transitory phenomena, more susceptible to social control.

Earlier (p. 4) we alluded to the tendency among officials of criminal justice to respond differentially to similar acts of delinquency committed by members of different social classes. This disposition to "bear down" upon lower-class offenders has been interpreted as "class bias."[7] In our opinion, however, it may also reflect a judgment that lower-class delinquency involves greater long-run social costs—at least partly because lower-class offenders are more likely to be enmeshed in a delinquent subculture.[8] The apparent class bias of law-enforcement officials may stem from their feeling that lower-class delinquencies are therefore more likely to recur, to become patterned systems of action, and perhaps even to eventuate in adult criminal careers, since the subculture constitutes a fertile criminal learning environment as well as a source of powerful social controls over the behavior and attitudes of participants. The isolated offender—as the middle-class offender more often is—is not likely to evoke serious

7. It has been noted consistently in the criminological literature that officials do not view middle-class and lower-class delinquency with the same degree of alarm. Glaser, for example, points out: "It has been well established that official agencies take a more punitive attitude towards misbehavior by low-status youth than towards the same behavior in higher status youth. The son of a highly respected family who is caught stealing or in less serious misbehavior often is merely reprimanded or taken to his parents by the victim, or even by police, where similar activity by a youth from 'across the tracks' would lead to official arrest and classification as a delinquent. In general, where the social status of the youth and his family is lower than that of the complainant, the greater the difference between their statuses, the more likely it is that the youth's activities will be called 'delinquency' " (Glaser, *op. cit.*, p. 9).

8. We do not wish to suggest that delinquent subcultures never arise in the middle class. Evidence is accumulating that they do exist but that they are organized principally for relatively petty delinquencies, such as the illicit consumption of alcohol or marijuana, sexual experiences, petty larceny, and auto theft for joy-riding. This behavior seems to occur less frequently, to be more responsive to control and change, and to be less likely to continue in the form of adult criminal careers. See, *e.g.*, A. K. Cohen and J. F. Short, Jr., "Research in Delinquent Subcultures," *Journal of Social Issues*, Vol. 14, No. 3 (Summer 1958), p. 28.

concern on the part of law-enforcement officials, who recognize that delinquent behavior tends to be less stable when peer supports are weak or absent. We shall have more to say later in this chapter about the relative frequency and social cost of delinquent behavior among the various classes.

Delinquent Norms

EVERY CULTURE provides its members with appropriate beliefs, values, and norms to carry out required activities. This is equally true of the subculture, which is distinguished by the prefix "sub" only to focus attention on its connection with a larger environing culture from which it has become partially differentiated. While he is being inducted into the subculture, the new member encounters and learns ways of describing the world about him which equip him to engage in these prescribed activities, enabling him to understand, discriminate, predict, and interpret the actions of others in relation to himself as a member of the subculture. These characteristic descriptions acquire the force of beliefs which are passed on as part of the subcultural tradition. The new member is also encouraged to adopt a set of evaluations which guide his judgments, comparisons, and preferential choices. These values are integrated with the beliefs that he has acquired. The beliefs and values that the subculture provides are in turn mobilized to support its prescriptions, which become elaborated as a set of norms for directing and controlling the behavior of its members. Descriptions, evaluations, and prescriptions, then, are provided by the subculture and shared as common property by its members.[9]

The most crucial elements of the delinquent subculture are the prescriptions, norms, or rules of conduct that define the activities required of a full-fledged member. Every delinquent

9. For a more detailed discussion of the terminology employed in these distinctions, see H. L. Zetterberg, "Compliant Actions," *Acta Sociologica*, Vol. 2 (Copenhagen, 1957), pp. 179-201.

subculture, we have said, is based upon a set of dominant roles which involve the performance of delinquent acts. Members of the subculture share a knowledge of what is required for the competent performance of these roles, which give the subculture its distinctiveness. What we have called the criminal subculture prescribes disciplined and utilitarian forms of theft; the conflict subculture prescribes the instrumental use of violence; the retreatist subculture prescribes participation in illicit consummatory experiences, such as drug use. Thus the delinquent norms that govern these activities are the primary identifying and organizing elements of delinquent subcultures.

The prescriptions of delinquent subcultures are supported, ordered, and closely integrated with appropriate values and beliefs, which serve to buttress, validate, and rationalize the different types of prescription in the various delinquent subcultures. Members of the criminal subculture, for example, believe that the world is populated by "smart guys" and "suckers"; members of the conflict gang see their "turf" as surrounded by enemies; retreatists regard the world about them as populated by "squares." Similarly, each subculture is characterized by distinctive evaluations: criminals value stealth, dexterity, wit, "front," and the capacity to evade detection; street-warriors value "heart"; retreatists place a premium on esoteric "kicks." The integration of beliefs and values with norms provides stability for the essential activities of the subculture.

DELINQUENT AND OFFICIAL NORMS

Official norms are implicit or explicit in all court proceedings. Sometimes they are formally stated in official statutes and rules or in other traditionally acknowledged guides for official judgments. Court action involves a demonstration that the delinquent has violated official norms. Officials must decide whether or not his acts are to be tolerated; that is, they must make distinctions between behavior that is permissible and behavior that is forbidden.

In making these decisions, it is customary for officials

to distinguish between the behavior of the delinquent and his attitude in relation to the system of social rules which he has violated: a person may violate the rights of persons or property through ignorance or carelessness or by accident and nevertheless fully support the existing rules and be willing to abide by them. A delinquent act, in short, is not necessarily an indication of the offender's attitude toward official norms. When delinquent behavior is supported by delinquent attitudes, however, the offender challenges the authority of the social expectations which he has violated; his sentiments and behavior are not in conflict but reinforce each other.

This distinction is a most significant one in criminal law. There are a small number of crimes, known as "absolute liability" offenses, in which the only requirement for establishing guilt is proof that the defendant committed the forbidden act. For example, a mistaken belief concerning the age of a minor is generally not a defense against the crime of selling liquor to a minor or having carnal knowledge of a female under the legal age of consent. However, for most offenses the demonstration of some kind of culpability is usually required. An effort is made to discover the grounds for deviation. It is not enough to have committed the crime; the offender must have acted "purposely, knowingly, recklessly or negligently, as the law may require, with respect to each material element of the offense."[10]

This attempt to identify the attitude underlying the act reflects an interest in establishing the existence and degree of the offender's commitment to a set of norms in opposition to those of the official system. The delinquent act that springs from a well-organized set of delinquent norms to which the offender fully subscribes is generally viewed as more serious by agents of criminal justice than a careless or unwitting law violation. Similar acts of deviation from existing rules mean quite different things depending upon the orientation toward conventional rules implicit in them. That orientation, in turn, reflects the nature of the norms to which the offender tenders allegiance.

---

10. American Law Institute, *Model Penal Code: Tentative Draft No. 4* (April 25, 1955), p. 12; see also pp. 123*ff*.

THE LEGITIMACY OF NORMS

A person attributes legitimacy to a system of rules and corresponding models of behavior when he accepts them as binding on his conduct.[11] If a system of rules is defined as legitimate, this means that the rules are accepted as an authoritative set of directives for action. Conversely, any pattern of social action may be regarded as illegitimate if participants in a group feel that no member should accept it as an authoritative model of behavior. The acceptance or rejection of a system of rules gives the system an imperative quality so that the group member perceives it as a set of rules that he *must* or *must not* follow.

This definition of legitimacy contains an essential subjective element, since it depends on the existence of a group member's readiness to obey a particular set of rules, whether or not he consciously recognizes this attitude. Under this definition, simple compliance with rules is not sufficient to establish that the actor defines them as legitimate. Just as rule violation may occur accidentally or through negligence, so conformity may be unpremeditated or coincidental. Behavioral compliance must be coupled with an attitude of acceptance to allow us to say that the rules are invested with legitimacy.

This usage is somewhat broader than that contemplated in criminal law, for we are interested in the attitude toward the rules implied in behavior that conforms to the rules as well as in behavior that violates them. Criminal-justice officials search for the underlying attitude toward the rules only in the case of behavior that violates them. In the study of subcultural development, however, lack of consent to the authority of the rules may pose a serious threat to the stability of the social system even though behavior is conforming.

People attribute legitimacy to a system of norms for a variety of reasons—perhaps because the rules facilitate certain

11. The discussion of legitimacy in this section draws heavily on Max Weber, *The Theory of Social and Economic Organization,* trans. by A. M. Henderson and Talcott Parsons (New York: Oxford University Press, 1947), esp. pp. 124-32.

emotional satisfactions; because of respect for the traditional place they have occupied in the life of the group; because of a belief in their ultimate relation to some moral, aesthetic, or other type of standard; because of a belief in their legality in the sense that they conform to the terms of a voluntary agreement between interested persons, have been established by an authority previously accepted as legitimate, or are consistent with another set of rules viewed as legitimate; or because of a belief that acceptance of the rules would be expedient. Groups tend to be characterized by the predominance among their members of certain of these motives for attributing legitimacy to group norms. For example, in family groups a mixture of affectual, moral, and traditional motives may predominate; in business groups, contractual and legal authority generates the dominant sentiments in support of the system. Similarly, group members may have different motives for upholding group norms, and these may change over time. Rules that were once accepted as a moral obligation may come to be upheld for reasons of expediency. The adolescent who abstains from drug use because he regards it as sinful may lose his moral convictions and still abstain to avoid the risk of becoming addicted or getting caught.

In technical usage, the concept of legitimacy has implied an element of "rightness" or moral validity.[12] However, we feel that the failure to draw a distinction between the legitimacy of a pattern of conduct and its ethical or moral validity can cause and has caused confusion in the literature. Unless the attribution of authority is distinguished from moral evaluations that may or may not be ascribed at the same time, it becomes impossible to understand how a person can attribute legitimacy to a set of norms that he regards as morally inferior to some alternative set of action prescriptions. Indeed,

---

12. It has been common in the sociological literature to associate a moral element with the attribution of legitimacy. See, *e.g.*, Talcott Parsons, *The Structure of Social Action* (Glencoe, Ill.: Free Press, 1949), p. 669; or, more recently, S. M. Lipset, "Political Sociology," in R. K. Merton, Leonard Broom, and L. S. Cottrell, Jr., eds., *Sociology Today: Problems and Prospects* (New York: Basic Books, 1959), pp. 108-10.

there are many occasions when men give allegiance to norms that they recognize as morally inferior to other norms. In highly competitive business situations, for example, people often accept as necessary such normative practices as misleading advertising claims for products, kickbacks, and fee-splitting at the same time that they morally condemn them. The concepts we use must permit us to reflect these distinctions between norms and moral values in our analysis of behavior.

When there is a discrepancy between the norms accepted as legitimate and those viewed as morally desirable, the system is likely to be rather unstable. Under these conditions pressures may develop to bring them back in line with one another. Nevertheless, it is possible for persons faced with such a discrepancy to function effectively, especially if they manage to develop means of discounting, de-emphasizing, or neutralizing[13] the significance of the moral issues related to the pattern of conduct to which they have given allegiance. The delinquent who accepts subcultural prescriptions for theft, street fighting, or drug use as guides to his conduct and who simultaneously views such conduct as sinful will experience severe strain unless he can find a way of coping with his moral problems—for example, by defining his delinquency as a response to an amoral situation, and so reducing his normative conflict.

The distinction we are making between the legitimacy of social norms and their moral validity is similar in many respects to Sorokin's distinction between "law norms" and "moral norms."[14] The essential characteristic of the law norm is that it "establishes a definite two-sided, imperative-attributive relationship between two parties through an indication of what one party is entitled to demand from the other and what

13. Techniques of neutralization are described in G. M. Sykes and David Matza, "Techniques of Neutralization: A Theory of Delinquency," *American Sociological Review*, Vol. 22 (Dec. 1957), pp. 664-70, and are discussed in more detail in Chap. 5, *infra*.

14. P. A. Sorokin, *Society, Culture, and Personality: Their Structure and Dynamics* (New York: Harper & Bros., 1947), pp. 71-85.

the other party is obliged to do to meet this demand."[15] The moral norm, in contrast, is one-sided. It is imperative in the sense that it urges someone to pursue a particular form of conduct, but it is not attributive since there is no one rightfully entitled to demand it. "Regardless of content," Sorokin notes, "any norm that is only imperative and not attributive, that only recommends a certain conduct but does not ascribe a right to demand it to any subject of right, is a *moral* norm, and is a very different thing from law norms."[16] When a person becomes a member of a group he is required to accept its law norms. He is obliged to perform the duties and receive the dues to which his position entitles him. Violation of these norms exposes him to appropriate sanctions. He is free, however, to apply or not to apply the moral norms of the system. Law norms and moral norms usually support each other, as in the case of laws against murder and theft and moral injunctions not to kill or steal, but even then they carry different types of authority and ability to invoke sanctions. Maintaining a distinction between what Sorokin calls "law norms" and "moral norms" enables us to consider the case of the delinquent who regards theft as legitimate under the rules of conduct he follows and yet at the same time morally wrong.

It is our view that members of delinquent subcultures have withdrawn their attribution of legitimacy to certain of the norms maintained by law-abiding groups of the larger society and have given it, instead, to new patterns of conduct which are defined as illegitimate by representatives of official agencies. Most of the behavior of delinquents conforms to conventional expectations; their violations of official norms are selective, confined to certain areas of activity and interest. However, those norms of delinquent subcultures which require the practice of theft, street warfare, and drug use are in direct opposition to official norms. Delinquents have withdrawn their support from established norms and invested officially forbidden forms of conduct with a claim to legitimacy in the

15. *Ibid.*, pp. 72-73.
16. *Ibid.*, p. 83.

light of their special situation. They recognize that law-abiding persons regard their behavior as illegitimate and they accept the necessity of secrecy and circumspection.

It should be noted that the attitude toward official norms, the imputation of legitimacy to officially prohibited conduct, and the rationalizations that make this conduct acceptable to the delinquent are best exemplified by the fully indoctrinated member of the subculture. Members may waver from time to time in the relative degree of legitimacy they attribute to official and delinquent norms. Nevertheless, the delinquent subculture calls for the withdrawal of sentiments supporting official norms and the tendering of allegiance to competing norms. To the extent that members waver in their allegiance to delinquent norms, the subculture comes to lack stability and validity as a style of life.

Varieties of Delinquent Subculture

As we have noted, there appear to be three major types of delinquent subculture typically encountered among adolescent males in lower-class areas of large urban centers. One is based principally upon criminal values; its members are organized primarily for the pursuit of material gain by such illegal means as extortion, fraud, and theft. In the second, violence is the keynote; its members pursue status ("rep") through the manipulation of force or threat of force. These are the "warrior" groups that attract so much attention in the press. Finally, there are subcultures which emphasize the consumption of drugs. The participants in these drug subcultures have become alienated from conventional roles, such as those required in the family or the occupational world. They have withdrawn into a restricted world in which the ultimate value consists in the "kick." We call these three subcultural forms "criminal," "conflict," and "retreatist," respectively.[17]

17. It should be understood that these terms characterize these delinquent modes of adaptation from the reference position of conventional

These shorthand terms simply denote the *principal* orientation of each form of adaptation from the perspective of the dominant social order; although one can find many examples of subcultures that fit accurately into one of these three categories, subcultures frequently appear in somewhat mixed form. Thus members of a predominantly conflict subculture may also on occasion engage in systematic theft; members of a criminal subculture may sometimes do combat in the streets with rival gangs. But this should not obscure the fact that these subcultures tend to exhibit essentially different orientations.

The extent to which the delinquent subculture organizes and controls a participant's allegiance varies from one member to another. Some members of the gang are almost totally immersed in the perspectives of the subculture and bring them into play in all their contacts; others segregate this aspect of their lives and maintain other roles in the family, school, and church. The chances are relatively slight, however, that an adolescent can successfully segregate delinquent and conforming roles for a long period of time. Pressures emanate from the subculture leading its members to adopt unfavorable attitudes toward parents, school teachers, policemen, and other adults in the conventional world. When he is apprehended for delinquent acts, the possibility of the delinquent's maintaining distinctly separate role involvements breaks down, and he is confronted with the necessity of choosing between law-abiding and delinquent styles of life. Since family, welfare, religious, educational, law-enforcement, and correctional institutions are arrayed against the appeal of his delinquent associates, the decision is a difficult one, frequently requiring either complete acceptance or complete rejection of one or the other system of obligations.[18]

society; they do not necessarily reflect the attitudes of members of the subcultures. Thus the term "retreatist" does not necessarily reflect the attitude of the "cat." Far from thinking of himself as being in retreat, he defines himself as among the elect.

18. Tannenbaum summarizes the community's role in this process of alienation by the phrase "dramatization of evil" (Frank Tannenbaum,

At any one point in time, however, the extent to which the norms of the delinquent subculture control behavior will vary from one member to another. Accordingly, descriptions of these subcultures must be stated in terms of the fully indoctrinated member rather than the average member. Only in this way can the distinctiveness of delinquent styles of life be made clear. It is with this understanding that we offer the following brief empirical characterizations of the three main types of delinquent subculture.

THE CRIMINAL PATTERN

The most extensive documentation in the sociological literature of delinquent behavior patterns in lower-class culture describes a tradition which integrates youthful delinquency with adult criminality.[19] In the central value orientation of youths participating in this tradition, delinquent and criminal behavior is accepted as a means of achieving success-goals. The dominant criteria of in-group evaluation stress achievement, the use of skill and knowledge to get results. In this culture, prestige is allocated to those who achieve material gain and power through avenues defined as illegitimate by the larger society. From the very young to the very old, the successful "haul"—which quickly transforms the penniless into a man of means—is an ever-present vision of the possible and desirable. Although one may also achieve material success through the routine practice of theft or fraud, the "big score" remains the symbolic image of quick success.

Crime and the Community [New York: Columbia University Press, 1938], pp. 19-21). For a more detailed account of this process, see Chap. 5, *infra.*

19. See esp. C. R. Shaw, *The Jack Roller* (Chicago: University of Chicago Press, 1930); Shaw, *The Natural History of a Delinquent Career* (Chicago: University of Chicago Press, 1940); Shaw and H. D. McKay, *Juvenile Delinquency and Urban Areas* (Chicago: University of Chicago Press, 1942); E. H. Sutherland, ed., *The Professional Thief* (Chicago: University of Chicago Press, 1937); Sutherland, *Principles of Criminology,* 4th ed. (Philadelphia: J. P. Lippincott Co., 1947); and Sutherland, *White Collar Crime* (New York: Dryden Press, 1949).

The means by which a member of a criminal subculture achieves success are clearly defined for the aspirant. At a young age, he learns to admire and respect older criminals and to adopt the "right guy" as his role-model. Delinquent episodes help him to acquire mastery of the techniques and orientation of the criminal world and to learn how to cooperate successfully with others in criminal enterprises. He exhibits hostility and distrust toward representatives of the larger society. He regards members of the conventional world as "suckers," his natural victims, to be exploited when possible. He sees successful people in the conventional world as having a "racket"—*e.g.*, big businessmen have huge expense accounts, politicians get graft, etc. This attitude successfully neutralizes the controlling effect of conventional norms. Toward the in-group the "right guy" maintains relationships of loyalty, honesty, and trustworthiness. He must prove himself reliable and dependable in his contacts with his criminal associates although he has no such obligations toward the out-group of noncriminals.

One of the best ways of assuring success in the criminal world is to cultivate appropriate "connections." As a youngster, this means running with a clique composed of other "right guys" and promoting an apprenticeship or some other favored relationship with older and successful offenders. Close and dependable ties with income-producing outlets for stolen goods, such as the wagon peddler, the junkman, and the fence, are especially useful. Furthermore, these intermediaries encourage and protect the young delinquent in a criminal way of life by giving him a jaundiced perspective on the private morality of many functionaries in conventional society. As he matures, the young delinquent becomes acquainted with a new world made up of predatory bondsmen, shady lawyers, crooked policemen, grafting politicians, dishonest businessmen, and corrupt jailers. Through "connections" with occupants of these half-legitimate, half-illegitimate roles and with "big shots" in the underworld, the aspiring criminal validates and assures his freedom of movement in a world made safe for crime.

THE CONFLICT PATTERN[20]

The role-model in the conflict pattern of lower-class culture is the "bopper" who swaggers with his gang, fights with weapons to win a wary respect from other gangs, and compels a fearful deference from the conventional adult world by his unpredictable and destructive assaults on persons and property. To other gang members, however, the key qualities of the bopper are those of the successful warrior. His performance must reveal a willingness to defend his personal integrity and the honor of the gang. He must do this with great courage and displays of fearlessness in the face of personal danger.

The immediate aim in the world of fighting gangs is to acquire a reputation for toughness and destructive violence. A "rep" assures not only respectful behavior from peers and threatened adults but also admiration for the physical strength and masculinity which it symbolizes. It represents a way of securing access to the scarce resources for adolescent pleasure and opportunity in underprivileged areas.

Above all things, the bopper is valued for his "heart." He does not "chicken out," even when confronted by superior force. He never defaults in the face of a personal insult or a challenge to the integrity of his gang. The code of the bopper is that of the warrior who places great stress on courage, the defense of his group, and the maintenance of honor.

Relationships between bopping gang members and the adult world are severely attenuated. The term that the bopper

---

20. For descriptions of conflict groups, see Harrison Salisbury, *The Shook-up Generation* (New York: Harper & Bros., 1958); *Reaching the Unreached,* a Publication of the New York City Youth Board, 1952; C. K. Myers, *Light the Dark Streets* (Greenwich, Conn.: Seabury Press, 1957); Walter Bernstein, "The Cherubs Are Rumbling," *The New Yorker,* Sept. 21, 1957; Sam Glane, "Juvenile Gangs in East Side Los Angeles," *Focus,* Vol. 29 (Sept. 1959), pp. 136-41; Dale Kramer and Madeline Karr, *Teen-Age Gangs* (New York: Henry Holt, 1953); S. V. Jones, "The Cougars—Life with a Brooklyn Gang," *Harper's,* Vol. 209 (Nov. 1954), pp. 35-43; P. C. Crawford, D. I. Malamud, and J. R. Dumpson, *Working with Teen-Age Gangs* (New York Welfare Council, 1950); Dan Wakefield, "The Gang That Went Good," *Harper's,* Vol. 216 (June 1958), pp. 36-43.

uses most frequently to characterize his relationships with adults is "weak." He is unable to find appropriate role-models that can designate for him a structure of opportunities leading to adult success. He views himself as isolated and the adult world as indifferent. The commitments of adults are to their own interests and not to his. Their explanations of why he should behave differently are "weak," as are their efforts to help him.

Confronted by the apparent indifference and insincerity of the adult world, the ideal bopper seeks to win by coercion the attention and opportunities he lacks and cannot otherwise attract. In recent years the street-gang worker who deals with the fighting gang on its own "turf" has come to symbolize not only a recognition by conventional adult society of the gang's toughness but also a concession of opportunities formerly denied. Through the alchemy of competition between gangs, this gesture of attention by the adult world to the "worst" gangs is transformed into a mark of prestige. Thus does the manipulation of violence convert indifference into accommodation and attention into status.

THE RETREATIST PATTERN

Retreatism may include a variety of expressive, sensual, or consummatory experiences, alone or in a group. In this analysis, we are interested only in those experiences that involve the use of drugs and that are supported by a subculture. We have adopted these limitations in order to maintain our focus on subcultural formations which are clearly recognized as delinquent, as drug use by adolescents is. The retreatist preoccupation with expressive experiences creates many varieties of "hipster" cult among lower-class adolescents which foster patterns of deviant but not necessarily delinquent conduct.

Subcultural drug-users in lower-class areas perceive themselves as culturally and socially detached from the life-style and everyday preoccupations of members of the conventional world. The following characterization of the "cat" culture, observed by Finestone in a lower-class Negro area in Chicago, describes drug use in the more general context of "hipsterism."[21] Thus it should not be assumed that this description in every respect fits drug cultures found elsewhere. We have drawn heavily on Finestone's observations, however, because they provide the best descriptions available of the social world in which lower-class adolescent drug cultures typically arise.

The dominant feature of the retreatist subculture of the "cat" lies in the continuous pursuit of the "kick." Every cat has a kick—alcohol, marijuana, addicting drugs, unusual sexual experiences, hot jazz, cool jazz, or any combination of these. Whatever its content, the kick is a search for ecstatic experiences. The retreatist strives for an intense awareness of living and a sense of pleasure that is "out of this world." In extreme form, he seeks an almost spiritual and mystical knowledge that is experienced when one comes to know "it" at the height of one's kick. The past and the future recede in the time perspective of the cat, since complete awareness in present experience is the essence of the kick.

The successful cat has a lucrative "hustle" which contrasts sharply with the routine and discipline required in the ordinary occupational tasks of conventional society. The many varieties of the hustle are characterized by a rejection of violence or force and a preference for manipulating, persuading, outwitting, or "conning" others to obtain resources for experiencing the kick. The cat begs, borrows, steals, or engages in some petty con-game. He caters to the illegitimate cravings of others by peddling drugs or working as a pimp. A highly exploitative attitude toward women permits the cat to view pimping as a prestigeful source of income. Through the labor of "chicks" engaged in prostitution or shoplifting, he can live in idleness and concentrate his entire attention on organizing, scheduling, and experiencing the esthetic pleasure of the kick. The hustle of the cat is secondary to his interest in the kick. In this respect the cat differs from his fellow delinquents in

21. Harold Finestone, "Cats, Kicks and Color," *Social Problems,* Vol. 5 (July 1957), pp. 3-13.

the criminal subculture, for whom income-producing activity is a primary concern.

The ideal cat's appearance, demeanor, and taste can best be characterized as "cool." The cat seeks to exhibit a highly developed and sophisticated taste for clothes. In his demeanor, he struggles to reveal a self-assured and unruffled manner, thereby emphasizing his aloofness and "superiority" to the "squares." He develops a colorful, discriminating vocabulary and ritualized gestures which express his sense of difference from the conventional world and his solidarity with the retreatist subculture.

The word "cool" also best describes the sense of apartness and detachment which the retreatist experiences in his relationships with the conventional world. His reference group is the "society of cats," an "elite" group in which he becomes isolated from conventional society. Within this group, a new order of goals and criteria of achievement are created. The cat does not seek to impose this system of values on the world of the squares. Instead, he strives for status and deference within the society of cats by cultivating the kick and the hustle. Thus the retreatist subculture provides avenues to success-goals, to the social admiration and the sense of well-being or oneness with the world which the members feel are otherwise beyond their reach.

The Distribution of Delinquent Subcultures

EVIDENCE is available to justify the assumption that these various types of delinquent subculture can be expected to arise at different locations in the social structure. Unfortunately, this evidence is fragmentary, impressionistic, and uncoordinated, consisting essentially of a large number of discrete observations and personal impressions by research, law-enforcement, education, welfare, and journalistic personnel. We have not been sufficiently alert to the significance of group affiliations to insist on systematic and comprehensive surveys of available data on them. Official statistics on delinquency are not helpful, for the administration of criminal justice is organized to prosecute misconduct on an individualistic, case-by-case basis. The diffuse connections which the offender maintains with groups are obscured when he is taken out of his social world and processed as an individual law-violator. The result is that we lack a way of linking statistics on individual acts of delinquency to the various subcultural contexts within which these acts may have occurred. For example, it is difficult to tell from statistics on felonious assault whether these are the acts of individuals or of participants in a criminal- or conflict-oriented gang. We need to know much more about the distribution of the various delinquent subcultures by age, sex, class, nationality, and race and about changes in distribution over time in order to develop an understanding of the processes and forces promoting their growth, patterning, and persistence.

The descriptions available in lay and professional literature and judgments of law-enforcement and welfare personnel do suggest, however, that the three types of delinquent subculture are found most commonly in lower-class areas of large cities, although, as we have pointed out, delinquent subcultures sometimes arise in middle-class areas as well. In the lower class they seem to exhibit more distinctive and highly integrated forms of organization than in the middle class. For this reason, we suggested, lower-class patterns of delinquency present the most costly and difficult problems in the area of delinquency control and prevention.

To recognize the higher social costs of lower-class delinquencies does not mean, however, that more punitive measures of control and treatment for lower-class delinquents are justifiable. It simply suggests that the tasks of control, deterrence, reformation, and especially prevention must take a different direction for these youth. It appears that the middle-class offender, whether alone or involved with a group, is more amenable to the various individualized forms of control and therapy which parents or the community can provide. Once alerted to the problem, the parents of the middle-class offender seem to be better able to exploit successfully the greater social visibility of his behavior and the more varied career alternatives open to him in contrast to the lower-class youngster, whose behavior is characterized by anonymity and whose opportunities are limited. If the delinquent subculture, as we suggest, plays a crucial role in the development and persistence of criminal forms of activity among the lower class, it becomes highly important, theoretically and practically, to deal directly with this phenomenon. We must understand how such subcultures arise, develop, and persist if we wish to lessen the influence they exercise over their members. This book represents a theoretical inquiry directed toward these ends.

Very little evidence is currently available on the distribution of these three types of delinquent subculture in lower-class areas, but certain types seem to be especially prevalent among certain racial and ethnic groups.[22] In New York City, for example, criminal groups oriented toward "the rackets," such as gambling, vice, narcotics peddling, etc., tend to be found most often in Italian neighborhoods, while criminal groups oriented toward professional burglary, robbery, and theft are most likely to be found in areas of mixed nationality. Conflict and retreatist groups appear to be especially prevalent in Negro and Puerto Rican neighborhoods.

Unfortunately, we lack adequate accounts of the types of delinquent subculture to be found in small towns and rural areas. However, judging from available descriptions and expressions of public concern, well-developed collective patterns of delinquent activity seem to be a product of the conditions of life in large metropolitan centers and particularly in those inner-city areas that have traditionally exhibited many other kinds of social problem. As yet there appear to be only slight tendencies for these delinquent subcultures to diffuse outward from the inner metropolitan areas to suburban communities or

---

22. We regard the ethnic and racial differences as consequences of the stage of assimilation which the various racial and nationality groups have reached and the forms of neighborhood organization to which they are exposed. This point is developed in Chaps. 7 and 8, *infra*.

smaller urban centers.[23] Thus far the conflict pattern seems to show the strongest tendencies toward diffusion. Former gang members displaced by slum-clearance projects to outer areas carry their conflict subculture with them and seek to establish their old reputations in the new areas. The conflict pattern also seems to lend itself most readily to imitation because of its relative autonomy and lack of dependence on adult connections for self-maintenance.

Delinquent subcultures in lower-class urban areas may be observed in clearest form among adolescent males. Occasionally gangs of delinquent girls have been noted, but they are likely to be affiliated in some subordinate relationship with a group of delinquent boys (*e.g.*, the society of "debs" affiliated with the fighting street gang of male adolescents).[24] Preadolescent or early-teen-age gangs of delinquents have also been observed, but these groups are usually closely related to a group of older delinquents whose behavior their members emulate and whose ranks they aspire to join.[25] There appears to be general consensus in the literature that the most consistently serious problems of delinquency, considering the social cost to the individual and to society, are to be found in the organized delinquent activities of boys in late adolescence. This does not mean that other delinquent groups should be ignored, but for the purpose of understanding the growth and persistence of different types of delinquent subculture it seems desirable to start by studying the most visible and well-articulated forms.

Clearly we need much better data on the social and ecological distribution of these subcultures. For the present we can only conclude, in the absence of contradictory information, that our current indications as to their location among urban, lower-class, male adolescents are accurate. In the following chapters we shall consider the sources, growth, and persistence of delinquent subcultures.

---

23. Although Salisbury (*op. cit.*, pp. 104-17) suggests that such diffusion is taking place, it is not clear that the behavior of suburban adolescent groups is of the same type as is found in the inner-city areas.

24. *Ibid.*, pp. 32-35.

25. *Ibid.*, pp. 20-21.

CHAPTER 2

Questions a Theory Must Answer

THE OUTCOME of any scientific undertaking is determined in large part by the nature of the questions with which the inquiry begins; in a sense, the process of inquiry itself may be understood as an effort to frame questions more precisely. This chapter is devoted to an exposition and clarification of the questions which we regard as crucial to an understanding of delinquent subcultures.

Generally speaking, we are interested in knowing why delinquent subcultures arise in certain locations in the social structure. But this is a very broad and crudely stated question. It subsumes a sequence of at least five distinct classes of question, all of which must be answered by a comprehensive theory. Before stating these questions, however, it should be noted that efforts to distinguish between them result in a measure of artificiality. Although the various classes of question are analytically distinct, they refer to empirical processes and conditions which are integrally related to one another. With this caution in mind, then, we may state the questions briefly as follows:

1. What is the precise nature of the delinquent adaptation which is to be explained?

2. How is this mode of adaptation distributed in the social structure? How is it located in terms of age, sex, socioeconomic position, and other social variables?

3. To what problems of adjustment might this pattern be a response? Under what conditions will persons experience strains and tensions that lead to delinquent subcultures?

4. Why is a particular mode of delinquency selected rather than others? Several delinquent adaptations are conceivably available in any given situation; what, then, are the determinants of the process of selection? Among delinquents who participate in subcultures, for example, why do some become apprentice criminals rather than street fighters or drug addicts? These are distinctive subcultural adaptations; an explanation of one may not constitute an explanation of the others.

5. What determines the relative stability or instability of a particular delinquent pattern? Why, for example, is the conflict subculture so much less stable than either the criminal or the retreatist subculture? Why is it that some persons shift from one subcultural adaptation to another, as in the case of street fighters who become drug addicts? These and other problems lie within the area of social equilibrium and social change, and they generate important theoretical issues that must be resolved if our explanation of delinquent subcultures is to be complete.

All five of these questions figure prominently in the way we think about delinquent subcultures and, therefore, in the way in which we have organized this book. In Chapter 1 we dealt with the first two questions, which have to do with the definition of our object of inquiry and its distribution in the social structure. A few more remarks on these matters may be in order before we take up the remaining questions in detail.

Definition of the object of inquiry is perhaps the most difficult task to which we address ourselves, and one to which little attention is given in the literature on delinquency. This neglect is particularly frustrating since the term "delinquency," as it is commonly used, subsumes an enormous range of quite disparate behavior. Indeed, almost every kind of violation by juveniles of adult expectations has at one time or another been labeled "delinquent," with the result that the term has become meaningless. If theorists fail to delineate the boundaries of the type of delinquency they are seeking to explain, their explanations are of little value. It is our belief that many of the current disputes regarding the adequacy of apparently conflicting theories are actually irrelevant, for often the theorists are not talking about the same kinds of delinquency.

In Chapter 1, we stated that this inquiry will focus upon delinquent *subcultures*. That is, we shall exclude from our purview acts of delinquency that are committed by isolated individuals, or by members of groups in which delinquent acts are not prescribed. We dealt in some detail with the definition of delinquent subcultures and with their distinction from other deviant subcultures.

We also asked how these subcultures were distributed in the social structure. We suggested that they are usually (but not exclusively) associated with the male sex role, that they tend to be concentrated in the lower class, that they emerge during adolescence, and that they are most likely to be found in urban areas. These and similar matters regarding location or distribution provide clues to the sources of a pattern. If we know that a particular type of adaptation is more characteristic of lower-class than of middle-class persons, we can investigate features of lower-class life that might conceivably help to explain the origins of the adaptation. If we know that an adaptation occurs disproportionately among males, we may wish to inquire about the influence of sex roles upon the emergence of such a pattern. Locational data, in short, provide guides to potentially fruitful lines of inquiry, for we assume that variations in the rates of an adaptation from one position in the social structure to another are significantly related to variations in the features of the corresponding social environments.

The Origin of Pressures Toward Deviance

PERHAPS the largest area of conceptual confusion in the literature on delinquency is the failure to distinguish clearly among questions regarding the origin of pressures toward delinquency, the selection and evolution of different solutions, and the persistence and change of these various solutions. These questions must be analytically distinguished from one another in order to avoid ambiguity; in practice, however, they are usually merged, so that an answer to one is taken to be an answer to all three.

The sense in which these questions are different needs to be stressed. To account for the development of pressures toward deviance does not sufficiently explain why these pressures result in one deviant solution rather than another. Furthermore, forces that account for the selection of one rather than another solution may have little to do with whether the resulting pattern will be stable or unstable. And, conversely, the social pressures that help to maintain or alter a particular form of deviance may not be identical with the pressures that gave rise to the initial problem of adjustment. Although these questions are integrally related to one another, they must nevertheless be kept analytically distinct.

In Chapter 3 we shall review several current theories of delinquency, noting the problems that arise when these distinctions are not clearly drawn. Two brief illustrations will suffice to make our point here.

Sociological no less than psychological theorists commonly —and erroneously—assume that an explanation of the motivational basis for a deviant pattern also explains the resulting response. That is, they assume an identity between pressures toward deviance and the subsequent solution. In a recent essay, for example, Milton L. Barron seeks to explain delinquency by reference to a set of ideas developed by Émile Durkheim[1] and extended by Robert K. Merton.[2] After discussing these ideas, Barron concludes:

> . . . many children in American society center their emotional convictions heavily upon objectives, with far less emotional support for the prescribed processes of reaching out for them. Given such a differential emphasis upon goals on the one hand and norms on the other, the latter becomes so weakened as to lead to the behavior of the children being limited solely by considerations of efficiency. *The result is delinquency.*[3]

Whether or not we accept the theory of motivation expressed in this quotation, the final statement is anything but self-evident. Why do persons who expect to fall short of realizing their aspirations and who have incompletely internalized cultural norms *necessarily* become delinquent rather than, say, suicidal? Even if we admit the possibility that delinquency is a plausible response under such conditions, how are we to account for the evolution of a particular delinquent adaptation? Some delinquents engage in essentially private, individual forms of deviance; others band together, forming subcultures. Furthermore, there are, as we have suggested, at least three distinctive subcultural variations; the criminal, the "bopper," and the "cat" are not all alike. Hence several crucial questions remain: Why do adolescents orient themselves toward one rather than another adaptation? How do subcultural solutions arise? And what are the forces that make for the persistence or disintegration of various delinquent adaptations? Barron's analysis is directed solely to the origin of pressures toward delinquency; it cannot be taken as an answer to the remaining questions.

Much the same criticism can be directed against the well-known works of the "Chicago school," notably of Clifford R.

1. See Émile Durkheim, *Suicide: A Study of Sociology,* trans. by J. A. Spaulding and George Simpson, ed. by George Simpson (Glencoe, Ill.: Free Press, 1951), esp. Chap. 5.

2. See R. K. Merton, *Social Theory and Social Structure,* Rev. and Enl. Ed. (Glencoe, Ill.: Free Press, 1957), esp. Chaps. 4 and 5.

3. M. L. Barron, *The Juvenile in Delinquent Society* (New York: Alfred A. Knopf, 1956), p. 41. Emphasis added.

Shaw, Henry D. McKay, and Edwin Sutherland.[4] In this intellectual tradition—roughly denoted by the terms "cultural transmission" and "differential association"—a specialized deviant system of action, the criminal culture, has been described and analyzed. The bulk of the materials emanating from this group bears primarily upon the persistence of criminal cultures: the development of internal organization, the emergence of stabilizing connections with other groups in the society, the recruitment and induction of new members, and the like. Proponents of this tradition often define it as a "complete" explanation of delinquency. However, it falls short of this mark on two counts. First, we are told very little about the kinds of pressure that impinge upon the motivational systems of individuals leading to delinquent subcultures; secondly, we are told very little about why the result is a criminal way of life rather than some alternative deviant pattern. The Chicago school has greatly enhanced our understanding of the way in which deviant adaptations can become persisting, stable, often institutionalized features of the larger social structure of our society. But it does not provide us with answers to the other questions that must also be of interest to us.

With these conceptual distinctions in mind, we may now return to the specific objective of this section—namely, to define the class of questions related to the origins of adjustment problems which lead to a readiness to engage in delinquent adaptations. Our approach to this task is based on several general assumptions. Foremost among these is the notion that deviance is not simply an asocial or primitive reaction. People sometimes "explain" the law-violating patterns of juvenile delinquents by suggesting that these youngsters have been improperly socialized, poorly trained at home or school. The delinquent, they say, has simply not learned the "rights" and "wrongs" of conduct in a civilized society. For but one of many

4. See C. R. Shaw, *The Jack-Roller* (Chicago: University of Chicago Press, 1930); Shaw, *The Natural History of a Delinquent Career* (Chicago: University of Chicago Press, 1931); Shaw *et al.*, *Delinquency Areas* (Chicago: University of Chicago Press, 1940); and Shaw and H. D. McKay, *Juvenile Delinquency and Urban Areas* (Chicago: University of Chicago Press, 1942). See also Chap. 6, *infra*.

examples of this point of view, note the following remarks by Elliott and Merrill:

The normal child is individualistic, egoistic, thoughtless, and selfish. Only by patient effort, by precept and example, does the child learn to be unselfish, obedient, kind and altruistic, and to respect private property. . . . The delinquent child, on the other hand, is one who has not been trained to control his normal impulses according to the dictates of social convention.[5]

We do not subscribe to explanations of this kind, for we do not view the delinquent as untouched or unreached by the society of which he is a part. It has been our experience that most persons who participate in delinquent subcultures, if not lone offenders, are fully aware of the difference between right and wrong, between conventional behavior and rule-violating behavior. They may not care about the difference, or they may enjoy flouting the rules of the game, or they may have decided that illegitimate practices get them what they want more efficiently than legitimate practices. But to say this is not quite the same as to say that they do not understand the rules. Furthermore, this "explanation" ignores some well-established facts about the participants in delinquent subcultures, particularly the fact that they are ordinarily quite capable of subordinating their individual interests to the larger interests of the group. Delinquent subcultures are not simply aggregates of impulsive, egoistic, individualistic, and selfish persons. The capacities of participants to conform to the norms of their subcultures seem to be neither less nor greater than the abilities of other persons in our society to conform to the dictates of the groups to which they belong. The strategic difference lies, of course, in the nature of the norms to which these delinquents conform as opposed to the more conventional norms to which nondelinquents usually conform.

We believe that deviance and conformity generally result from the same kinds of social condition. As Cohen has pointed out: "People are prone to assume that those things which we define as evil and those which we define as good have their

5. Mabel A. Elliott and F. E. Merrill, *Social Disorganization,* Rev. Ed. (New York: Harper & Bros, 1941), pp. 114-15.

origins in separate and distinct features of society. Evil flows from poisoned wells; good flows from pure and crystal fountains. The same sources cannot feed both. Our view is different."[6] The idea that deviance and conformity can arise from the same features of social life is based on a further assumption: that efforts to conform, to live up to social expectations, often entail profound strain and frustration. For example, a boy of fourteen may desperately wish to become a man, and certainly we should agree that this is a proper goal for him. Yet the very fact that he wants so much what the society at large wants for him produces problems of adjustment, for ours is not a society that eases the transition from childhood to adulthood. We have thrown up difficult obstacles to the achievement of adult status except after the young have endured long years of waiting and training. But during the years of preparation, they become more and more impatient to be what we have urged them to be. This impatience with the enforced occupancy of a half-child, half-adult status frequently bursts forth and finds expression in dissidence and protest.[7] Thus efforts to be what one is supposed to be sometimes lead to aberrant behavior. Reaching out for socially approved goals under conditions that preclude their legitimate achievement may become a prelude to deviance. Conformity, taking cultural mandates seriously, is thus a crucial step in the process by which deviance is generated.

Finally, deviance ordinarily represents a search for solutions to problems of adjustment. As we noted above, deviance may be understood as an effort to resolve difficulties that sometimes result from conformity. In this sense deviance is not purposeless, although it may be random and disorganized. It may not result in a successful solution (in fact, deviant solutions may even bring on additional and more serious problems of adjustment), but action need not be rational in order to be purposeful. The person who gropes blindly for a way of re-

---

6. A. K. Cohen, *Delinquent Boys: The Culture of the Gang* (Glencoe, Ill.: Free Press, 1955), p. 137.

7. See Herbert Bloch and Arthur Niederhoffer, *The Gang: A Study in Adolescent Behavior* (New York: Philosophical Library, 1958).

solving a problem of adjustment is engaging in purposeful action even if the solutions he reaches are senseless and self-defeating.

In summary, it is our contention that problems of adjustment are engendered by acts of social conformity performed under adverse circumstances. The result is a search for solutions which may or may not turn out to be nonconforming or delinquent. In Chapter 4, we shall point to a major problem of adjustment which, we believe, helps to explain why delinquent subcultures arise among lower-class adolescent males in urban areas.

There are, of course, a variety of problems of adjustment that might seem, at first glance, to have some relation to the emergence of delinquent subcultures. In deciding which of these problems best accounts for the phenomena we wish to explain, we have used the following criteria: (1) the *distribution* of the problem in relation to the distribution of delinquent subcultures; (2) the *significance* of the problem; and (3) its *permanence.*

DISTRIBUTION

If, as we have suggested, delinquent subcultures are concentrated among lower-class male adolescents, then the problem of adjustment that accounts for the emergence of these subcultures must also occur among lower-class male adolescents. This does not mean that there must be perfect correlation between the distribution of problems of adjustment and the distribution of delinquent subcultures. We have noted that the existence of a problem of adjustment never fully explains the resulting adaptation. One must, however, at least be able to show that where delinquent subcultures occur, the problem of adjustment also occurs. If a particular adjustment problem is distributed more widely than delinquent subcultures are, we then have the additional task of showing why solutions to this problem vary from one part of the social structure to another. This may require that we identify certain intervening variables and show how they tend to channel adjustment difficulties into one or another mode of adaptation.

SIGNIFICANCE

Participation in a delinquent subculture ordinarily entails rather weighty personal and social costs. For an individual to shoulder these costs, he must be faced with a problem of adjustment that threatens activities and investments which are significant in his psychological and social economy. It is not enough, therefore, to show that the delinquent individual experiences a given problem of adjustment; we must also show that the problem has great significance for him.

PERMANENCE

A problem of adjustment may be more crucial if it is relatively permanent rather than transitory, and if it is so perceived by the actor. If the problem can be resolved by enduring adverse circumstances for a short time, it is probably not so likely to result in a delinquent solution. On the other hand, a problem to which there appears to be no legitimate solution may generate acute pressures for the emergence of a delinquent one.

The Evolution of Delinquent Subcultures

AT THIS JUNCTURE, it might be appropriate to reiterate a point that was made earlier: *the pressures that lead to deviant patterns do not necessarily determine the particular pattern of deviance that results.* A given problem of adjustment may result in any one of several solutions. In other words, we cannot predict the content of deviance simply from our knowledge of the problem of adjustment to which it is a response. In any situation, alternative responses are always possible. We must therefore explain each solution in its own right, identifying the new variables which arise to direct impulses toward deviance into one pattern rather than another and showing how these variables impinge upon actors in search of a solution to a problem of adjustment. Failure to recognize the need for this task is, as we have noted, a major weakness of many current theories of delinquency. All too often, a theory that explains the origin of a problem of adjustment is erroneously assumed to explain the resulting deviant adaptation as well.[8]

Several questions must be considered in connection with the evolution of delinquent subcultures. Under what conditions are sentiments supporting the legitimacy of conventional norms withdrawn or qualified? Under what conditions do pressures toward deviance result in shared rather than solitary solutions? Finally, what are the conditions that result in the differentiation of collective solutions?

IMPUTATIONS OF LEGITIMACY

As we noted in Chapter 1, this inquiry focuses upon aberrant behavior which is supported by norms that conflict with conventional norms. People may attribute legitimacy to rules which are in conflict with official norms—even when they regard the official norms as morally superior. For our purposes, then, a theory of "pressures leading to aberrant acts" is not sufficient; we must also identify the social conditions that lead to the attribution of legitimacy to officially proscribed norms. Thus the question of legitimacy occupies a place of crucial importance in this inquiry. It will be discussed in Chapter 5.

INDIVIDUAL AND COLLECTIVE DEVIANCE

The great bulk of delinquent behavior appears to occur in association rather than isolation from other like-minded persons. In the 1930's Shaw found that of all male delinquents

8. We do not argue that there is no relationship between problems of adjustment and the resulting deviant adaptation, but we contend that there is no *necessary deterministic* relationship between them. The problem of adjustment may limit the range of satisfactory outcomes, but which alternative will emerge remains problematical. As long as there are at least two conceivable deviant outcomes to a given problem of adjustment, the problem of adjustment cannot be said to determine the outcome.

brought before the Juvenile Court of Cook County (Chicago) during a given period, only 19 per cent "always committed their offenses alone."[9] No evidence that modifies this general finding has since been reported. It is clear, therefore, that we must inquire into the conditions under which pressures toward delinquency result in collective rather than individual responses.

Most theories of delinquent behavior as a subcultural phenomenon deal with one of two questions: (1) why are certain individuals motivated to belong to a delinquent subculture? and (2) why do delinquent subcultures tend to persist? Neither of these questions accounts for the origins of subcultural patterns. This point has been made by Cohen:

> Now we come to a curious gap in delinquency theory. Note the part that the existence of the delinquent subculture plays in the cultural-transmission theories. It is treated as a *datum,* that is, as something which already exists in the environment of the child. The problem with which these theories are concerned is to *explain how that subculture is taken over by the child.* Now we may ask: Why is there such a subculture? Why is it "there" to be "taken over"? . . . Why does it arise?[10]

Our question, in short, refers to the development of *collective* patterns. Our theory must specify the conditions which result in subcultural rather than individualistic solutions to problems of adjustment. This problem will also be taken up in Chapter 5.

TYPES OF DEVIANT SUBCULTURE

Delinquency, we have said, tends to be largely a collective phenomenon. However, we cannot rest with simply determining when delinquency is likely to take a collective rather than an individual form, for not all delinquent subcultures are alike. As we noted in Chapter 1, there appear to be three more or less distinctive delinquent styles of life commonly found among

---

9. C. R. Shaw, "Juvenile Delinquency—A Case History," *Bulletin of the State University of Iowa,* No. 24, N. S. no. 701, 1933, pp. 1-3.
10. Cohen, *op. cit.,* p. 18.

lower-class boys. It is true that the criminal, the conflict, and the retreatist patterns are seldom found in "pure" form; a given delinquent subculture frequently exhibits elements drawn from all three orientations. However, it also appears to be true that, over time, one orientation tends to become somewhat more prominent than the others in a given group. The literature, in fact, contains descriptive accounts of subcultures that are virtually "pure" cases of one or another of these styles of life. Thus we are faced with a further question: How can we account for the distinctive styles of life that characterize these various subcultures?

It is our view that these subcultural patterns can be explained only by combining several systems of variables. Some variables help us to explain why predispositions to deviate from accepted norms arise; other variables tell us why delinquent rather than other types of deviance are selected; and still other variables tell us why collective solutions of various kinds evolve. In previous theories, as we have noted, there has been a tendency to emphasize variables which explain one but not all of these phases in the development of the delinquent subculture, although it is often asserted that they explain the entire phenomenon. This has led to considerable confusion. What we must show is how different classes of variables, in combination, produce delinquent subcultures. Although we shall discuss these sets of variables separately, they comprise an integrated system of forces.

Change and Persistence of Delinquent Subcultures

THE EXTENT to which deviant adaptations exhibit stability raises two further sets of questions: (1) How can we account for the persistence of some forms of delinquent adaptation? (2) How can we account for changes in other forms of delinquent adaptation?

THE PERSISTENCE OF DEVIANT ADAPTATIONS

Delinquent subcultures, once formed, often develop a capacity to persist even when the forces that gave rise to them are no longer fully or directly operative. Thus a theory which accounts for the emergence of delinquent subcultures may not necessarily explain how these subcultures are maintained.

The question of the persistence of delinquent subcultures is of especial interest because there appear to be variations in stability among the subcultural types. There is considerable evidence, for example, that criminal systems exhibit relatively great stability. One source of stability is the degree to which various age-levels of offender are linked. Adolescents who participate in such systems generally know and are associated with more mature and sophisticated young adult offenders; the latter, in turn, are often linked with persons who occupy permanent positions in the adult criminal occupational structure. These bonds between age-levels, as we shall see in later chapters, have a stabilizing effect and contribute markedly to the persistence of adolescent criminal subcultures. The conflict subculture, on the other hand, does not appear to develop these age-graded bonds. Conflict orientations appear to be limited to adolescents. Once the adolescent reaches young adulthood, he tends to relinquish violent modes of behavior. There is no directly continuous adult counterpart of the adolescent conflict adaptation, and thus the conflict adaptation is eventually abandoned. In this sense, it is unstable. Differences between subcultures in the degree of integration of age-levels are but one source of relative stability. There are many others, some of which will be discussed in Chapter 8.

If we are to develop an understanding of various delinquent subcultures, we must identify and explain the social conditions that make for stability or instability in each. If differences in the integration of age-levels influence stability, for example, we must ask why some subcultures develop this form of integration while others do not. The same question, in turn, must be raised in considering each of the forces that impinge upon delinquent subcultures: how do these forces contribute to the persistence of the various subcultural adaptations?

CHANGE IN DELINQUENT ADAPTATIONS

When we speak of subcultural instability, of the disintegration of delinquent adaptations, we are posing a question of social change. Certain delinquent adaptations change with such recurrent regularity as to suggest that highly patterned forces are at work. For example, sequences of delinquent adaptations may be observed as a result of the transition from adolescence to adulthood, which constitutes a major turning point in the lives of many delinquents. If we look at the criminal pattern we can identify a number of these sequences. There are some persons who, having participated in a criminal subculture during adolescence, move into stable criminal roles upon reaching adulthood. This is a sequence in which there is considerable continuity in role preparation and performance from one age-level to another. Other persons, however, shift to a law-abiding adjustment upon reaching adulthood. This is a sequence involving discontinuity between role preparation and performance. Still others shift from a criminal adaptation during adolescence to some other form of deviance during adulthood—for example, to drug addiction or alcoholism. This is a sequence involving substitution of deviant roles. Each of these sequences may be observed in analyzing the careers of members of the criminal subculture, and similar role changes may be identified in the other two delinquent subcultures. Our theory must tell us not only why these patterned shifts or sequences occur but also what categories of persons will be most likely to follow a particular sequence. Here, then, is one type of problem of social change.

Other significant problems of change pertain to alteration in the prevalence and distribution of delinquent subcultures—for example, the apparent increase in conflict adaptations during the past several decades. Assuming that violence in general has been on the increase, how can we account for this historical change? Changes in delinquent adaptations also seem to be associated with stages of assimilation of immigrant groups. In the first stage, conflict adaptations abound; in later stages, criminal adaptations appear to be more prominent; finally, as assimilation is completed, violence again tends to break out among those residual adolescent males whose families have failed to rise from the old immigrant slum community. Our theory must help us to account for these and other forms of social change in delinquent subcultures. In the final pages of this book, we shall discuss hypotheses regarding some of these problems of social change.[11]

---

11. A sixth class of question might pertain to the social functions of deviant behavior. Any deviant adaptation may be examined from the standpoint of the functions it performs for the participants, for the larger society, and so forth. One function of crime, for example, is the redistribution of income. Throughout our analysis, many social functions of illegitimate patterns will be noted. We have not, however, taken up the matter of social functions systematically. In a "complete" exposition of deviance, attention would have to be given to this problem.

HAROLD BRIDGES LIBRARY
S. MARTIN'S COLLEGE
LANCASTER

CHAPTER 3

Some Current Theories of Delinquent Subcultures

A THEORY of the development of the delinquent subculture must specify some problem of adjustment that is common to those who contribute to the formation of the group. As we have indicated, delinquent subcultures appear to arise principally among lower-class adolescent males. Current sociological theories tend to single out one or another of these structural attributes—class, age, or sex—and treat it as the principal source of the adjustment problem shared by the innovators of delinquent subcultures. Some theorists say, for example, that delinquent subcultures represent a response to a conflict in cultural codes, one form of which is represented in the clash between lower- and middle-class values. Middle-class standards of conduct are implicit in legal statutes; conformity to lower-class values therefore results automatically in behavior defined unfavorably by official agents of criminal justice. Other theorists suggest that delinquent subcultures are a response to the acute stresses engendered during the transition from adolescence to adulthood. Finally, there are theorists who claim that certain features of the nuclear family in Western society—especially its tendency toward female-centered households—make it difficult for a boy to develop a masculine identification. He may compensate by engaging in "compulsively masculine" behavior, of which delinquent conduct is an exaggerated form.

We should say at the outset that we are not inclined to accept these explanations of the pressures which give rise to delinquent subcultures. Our own point of view will become evident as we describe the problems that these theories leave unresolved, basing our critique on the five classes of question which we outlined in Chapter 2. The theoretical approaches we are about to examine have been advanced as complete explanations; none of them, however, actually provides answers to all five classes of question.

Masculine Identification and Delinquent Subcultures

SEX DIFFERENCES are not just biological; they also reflect differences in social definitions of masculinity and femininity. Part of "growing up" entails learning the social roles prescribed for the members of each sex. Sometimes young people seeking to make an appropriate sex identification encounter serious obstacles; tendencies toward aberrant behavior may result. This problem of adjustment arises from efforts to conform to cultural expectations under conditions in which conformity is hampered or precluded.

A number of observers have suggested that "ganging," especially among adolescent males in our society, and particularly "compulsive masculinity" may be understood as reactions to obstacles to masculine identification. Talcott Parsons, for example, asserts that certain features of the American kinship system and the relatively sharp segregation of kinship and occupational roles create barriers to masculine identification. Our kinship system tends to be female-centered. In the middle class, adult males feel compelled to invest great energy in their occupational roles. This reduces the amount of their involvement in kinship activities. Since the occupational tasks of the father are almost invariably performed outside the home, he is not readily available as a masculine model for his sons. In some sectors of the lower class, particularly among Negro families, female-centered households result from the great occupational instability and familial transience of adult males. The problem is intensified among all social classes by the fact that occupations are becoming highly specialized, complex, and esoteric. Since occupational activity is an important component of the masculine role, boys have trouble forming a clear masculine self-image.

Under such conditions, boys presumably gravitate toward the mother as the central object of identification. When they reach adolescence, and encounter especially strong cultural expectations that they behave as males, they experience the most acute strain. Engulfed by a feminine world and uncertain of their own identification, they tend to "protest" against femininity. This protest may take the form of robust and aggressive behavior, and even of malicious, irresponsible, and destructive acts. Such acts evoke maternal disapproval and thus come to stand for independence and masculinity to rebellious adolescents. This is the process designated by such terms as "masculine protest" or "compulsive masculinity":

> Our kinship situation, it has been noted, throws children of both sexes overwhelmingly upon the mother as *the* emotionally significant adult. In such a situation, "identification" in the sense that the adult becomes a "role model" is the normal result. For a girl this is normal and natural, not only because she belongs to the same sex as the mother, but because the functions of housewife and mother are immediately before her eyes and are tangible and relatively easily understood by a child. . . . Thus the girl has a more favorable opportunity for emotional maturing through positive identification with an adult model, a fact which seems to have much

to do with the well-known earlier maturity of girls. The boy, on the other hand, has a tendency to form a direct feminine identification, since his mother is the model most readily available and significant to him. But he is not destined to become an adult woman. Moreover, he soon discovers that in certain vital respects women are considered inferior to men, that it would hence be shameful for him to grow up to be like a woman. Hence when boys emerge into what Freudians call the "latency period," their behavior tends to be marked by a kind of "compulsive masculinity." They refuse to have anything to do with girls. "Sissy" becomes the worst of insults. They get interested in athletics and physical prowess, in the things in which men have the most primitive and obvious advantage over women. Furthermore, they become allergic to all expression of tender emotion; they must be "tough." This universal pattern bears all the earmarks of a "reaction formation." It is so conspicuous, not because it is simply "masculine nature," but because it is a defense against a feminine identification.[1]

INADEQUACIES OF THE THEORY

Exponents of the theory that problems of masculinity generate delinquency have concentrated on the dynamics of the adjustment problem rather than on its relation to delinquent conduct. As a result, their explanations fail to take explicit account of the five questions that we believe a theory of delinquent subcultures must answer.

Definition—In the first place, this theory provides no clear definitions of the types of deviant behavior that are supposedly explained by problems of masculine identification. Parsons, for example, is concerned principally with the relations between *aggressive* behavior and various features of Western family and social organization. He does not claim explicitly that the problem of masculinity explains delinquency; he simply observes that female-centered family systems result in "a strong tendency for boyish behavior to run in antisocial if not directly destructive directions, in striking contrast to that of pre-adolescent girls."[2] Other theorists, principally Cohen and Miller, explicitly claim that problems of masculine

1. Talcott Parsons, *Essays in Sociological Theory,* Rev. Ed. (Glencoe, Ill.: Free Press, 1954), pp. 304-05.

2. *Ibid.,* p. 306.

identification can be a source of delinquent behavior. However, neither Cohen nor Miller defines the precise forms of delinquency to which problems of masculine identification lead. Cohen relates these problems to the emergence of "malicious, non-utilitarian, negativistic, and hedonistic behavior" among middle-class boys whereas Miller relates them to tough, aggressive, and irresponsible acts among lower-class boys. Neither writer relates the problems simultaneously to *delinquent* and *collective* conduct. But it is not enough to suggest that problems of masculine identification produce deviant acts; it must also be shown that they generate collective patterns that are normally construed by officials as transgressions of legal prohibitions.

Distribution—The relative diffuseness of the behavior which the masculine-identity crisis is said to explain makes it difficult to use this crisis as a basis for describing the distribution of delinquency. An emphasis upon toughness, aggressiveness, and hedonism may or may not result in delinquent acts or norms. Toughness may be displayed in many ways that are not subject to legal sanctions; the same may be said of aggressiveness and hedonism. Thus a description of the distribution of values stressing toughness would not necessarily provide a description of the distribution of delinquent acts or norms. Proponents of the masculine-identity-crisis theory have not as yet been able to show a correspondence between the distribution of values emphasizing masculinity and the distribution of norms prescribing delinquent acts. Indeed, there is considerable doubt as to the distribution of the masculine-identity crisis itself, as we shall presently see.

The Problem of Adjustment—Difficulties arise in defining masculine identification as the problem of adjustment underlying the development of delinquent subcultures when we apply our three criteria of relevance—distribution, significance, and permanence. As we have noted, there is no firm agreement among theorists as to where in the social structure this problem occurs most frequently or in most acute form. Theorists even differ concerning the distribution of the female-centered family, which, it is claimed, gives rise to the masculinity crisis.

Parsons apparently feels that it can be found at both middle- and lower-class levels. There is, he claims, "a strong tendency to instability of marriage and a 'mother-centered' type of family structure . . . both in Negro and white population elements [of the lower class]."[3] He also notes the existence of a "suburban matriarchy": "In certain suburban areas, especially with an upper-middle-class population, the husband and father is out of the home a very large proportion of the time. He tends to leave by far the greater part of responsibility for children to his wife."[4] Other theorists, however, regard the female-centered household as a more prominent feature of one class than of the other. Cohen, for example, says:

It should be emphasized that Parsons advances this view as an explanation of delinquency *in general;* however, it seems to us that the circumstances to which he attributes delinquency are most marked in the middle class.[5]

Miller, on the other hand, asserts:

The genesis of the intense concern over "toughness" in lower-class culture is probably related to the fact that a significant proportion of lower-class males are reared in a predominantly female household and lack a consistently present male figure with whom to identify and from whom to learn essential components of a "male" role. Since women serve as a primary object of identification during the pre-adolescent years, the almost obsessive lower-class concern with "masculinity" probably resembles a type of compulsive reaction-formation.[6]

The distribution of female-centered households is, of course, important to establish. If such households are equally prevalent in the middle and lower classes, then the theorist is confronted with the problem of explaining why delinquent subcultures arise in one stratum but not in the other.

---

3. *Ibid.*, p. 185.
4. *Ibid.*, p. 13.
5. A. K. Cohen, *Delinquent Boys: The Culture of the Gang* (Glencoe, Ill.: Free Press, 1955), p. 162.
6. W. B. Miller, "Lower Class Culture as a Generating Milieu of Gang Delinquency," *Journal of Social Issues,* Vol. 14, No. 3 (1958), p. 9.

Evidence is lacking as to the significance and the permanence of problems of masculinity. Plausible arguments may be advanced to support or reject the proposition that this problem intimately engages the major concerns of adolescents and strikes them as a permanent threat to the achievement of long-range personal goals.

The Evolution of Subcultural Solutions—The formation of a delinquent subculture, as we have pointed out, involves the emergence of delinquent norms. Disaffected persons partially withdraw sentiments supporting the legitimacy of official norms and draw together in a new group. There is little doubt that barriers to masculine identification may produce a tendency for adolescent males to assert their fundamental maleness by engaging in aggressive deviant conduct. But there is an important difference between deviant acts and delinquent acts. Furthermore, the masculine-crisis theory fails to explain why delinquent *norms* are a logical outcome of barriers to masculine identification.

Failure to specify the relation between problems of masculine identification and the emergence of delinquent norms leads to a further theoretical difficulty: it makes it impossible to identify the conditions that result in the differentiation of delinquent subcultures. Delinquent subcultures, as we have said, vary in significant respects. Nothing in the masculinity-crisis theory helps us to specify the intervening variables that determine the outcome of generalized pressures resulting from this problem of adjustment.

Persistence and Change—No effort has been made to show the relevance of problems of masculine identification to the persistence or change of different types of delinquent subculture. If the theory is valid, changes in delinquent patterns would be related to changes in problems of masculine identification. If delinquency rates are increasing, the theorist would have to show that boys are experiencing greater difficulty developing a sense of masculinity; if the rates are decreasing, he would have to show that problems of masculine identity are diminishing. Data in confirmation of these hypothesized relationships are not available.

In summary, we are inclined to think that the masculine-identity theory, although it explains "compulsive masculinity," is not an adequate explanation of the formation of delinquent norms. It may be that problems of masculine identification have a reinforcing effect on other motivations leading to the development of delinquent subcultures or play a part in motivating individuals to become actively involved in *established* delinquent subcultures. However, we do not feel that these problems are central to an explanation of the origins or differentiation of delinquent subcultures among lower-class male adolescents.

Adolescence and Delinquent Subcultures

THE TRANSITION from adolescence to adulthood poses many problems of adjustment for boys in our society. Attempts to explain delinquency as a product of these difficulties have usually been based on three related propositions: (1) any major change in status constitutes a crisis in the life of the individual; (2) the severity of the crisis depends on the availability of socially institutionalized means to facilitate the change; (3) aberrant behavior may result from this crisis.

Passage from childhood to adulthood is generally regarded as one of the most prominent instances of status transition in human society. Although the achievement of adulthood is a stressful period in most societies, it is generally acknowledged to be especially difficult in Western societies because of the extreme complexity of the occupational structure. A young man usually cannot take over an adult occupation simply because he wants to do so or because his father wishes him to be his successor. Our occupational system is technical and specialized; the successful pursuit of many occupational roles requires years of formal training and preparation. Furthermore, until young males acquire the values, knowledge, and skills that are prerequisite to adult occupational activities, they ordinarily must forego other adult roles. Since they usually cannot support a wife and children during this period, they are forced to postpone participation in the roles of husband and father despite their biological and emotional readiness to discharge these roles. Thus male adolescents are cut off from adult roles and relegated to a prolonged preparatory status in which they are no longer children but are not yet adults.

Although the adolescent is barred from immediate access to adult roles, every effort is made to ensure that he does not relinquish his aspirations for eventual adult status. Even though he is formally deprived of the major rewards of adult status—money, personal autonomy, sexual relations, and the like—he is at the same time imbued with the belief that these are rewards worth having. He is thus led to orient himself toward ends which are not immediately available to him by socially approved means. Despite his aspirations and his physical and emotional readiness, he is forced to remain in a state of social, economic, and legal dependency.

The frustrations that build up under these conditions exert constant pressure for deviant behavior. A common reaction is the boisterous ganging tendency of male adolescents, voicing their protests against the adult world in all manner of aberrant acts. Among his compeers, the adolescent can play semi-adult roles free from the disapproving and depriving attitudes of the adult world. Here he can "act the adult"—even if the resulting behavior is awkward and exaggerated, recognized as adult only by his contemporaries.

One of the most detailed expositions of this adjustment problem as a source of delinquent subcultures can be found in *The Gang: A Study in Adolescent Behavior,* by Bloch and Niederhoffer. They summarize their position as follows:

The adolescent period in all cultures, visualized as a phase of striving for the attainment of adult status, produces experiences which are much the same for all youths, and certain common dynamisms for expressing reaction to such subjectively held experiences. The intensity of the adolescent experience and the vehemence of external expression depend on a variety of factors, including the general societal attitudes towards adolescence, the duration of the adolescent period itself, and the degree to which the society tends to facilitate entrance into adulthood by virtue of institutionalized patterns, ceremonials, rites, and rituals, and socially supported emotional and intellectual preparation. When a society does not make adequate preparation, formal or otherwise, for the induction of its adolescents to the adult status, equivalent forms of behavior arise spontaneously among adolescents themselves, reinforced by their own group structure, which seemingly provides the same psychological content and function as the more formalized rituals found in other societies. This the gang structure appears to do in American society, apparently satisfying deep-seated needs experienced by adolescents in all cultures. Such, very briefly, is our hypothesis.[7]

INADEQUACIES OF THE THEORY

Definition—Like the masculine-identification theory, the theory that conflict in the transition to adulthood is the source of delinquent subcultures fails to identify clearly the pattern of deviant behavior to be explained. Bloch and Niederhoffer consistently equate "adolescent gangs" with "delinquent gangs." It is true that most delinquent gangs are composed of adolescents, but one can hardly say that all adolescent groups are composed of delinquents. Nevertheless, Bloch and Niederhoffer do not distinguish between adolescent groups whose behavior is within the limits of conventional tolerance and delinquent groups as such.

Distribution—Failure to delimit the object of inquiry inevitably confounds the task of describing its distribution in the social structure. This is clearly apparent in the somewhat ambiguous assertions by Bloch and Niederhoffer regarding the distribution of delinquency. At the outset, they argue that delinquency is rather widely diffused throughout the social structure and, furthermore, that it is extremely difficult to distinguish middle-class from lower-class delinquency.

It became extremely difficult upon occasion to draw a clear line of distinction between . . . lower- and middle-class groups. If, for example, conflict or hostility to the out-group is one of the criteria of gang behavior, middle-class groups are certainly not exempt from such characterization. . . . As far as the commission of delinquent

7. Herbert Bloch and Arthur Niederhoffer, *The Gang: A Study in Adolescent Behavior* (New York: Philosophical Library, 1958), p. 17.

acts is concerned, middle-class adolescents, singly or in groups, participate in a variety of delinquent episodes, including such illegal activities as auto theft, operating a motor vehicle without a license, disorderly conduct. . . . In respect to the type of organization structure, there is little to distinguish, in one sense, between middle- and lower-class adolescent groups. Although middle-class groups of teen-agers are not as apt to have the formal, almost military structure characteristic of certain lower-class "war gangs" . . . they do have similar and well-defined informal patterns of leadership and control.[8]

Despite these apparent class similarities, Bloch and Niederhoffer appear to agree with the majority of observers that the problem of delinquency is more serious in the lower class. They base their belief on the observation that delinquent acts in the lower class tend to develop strong subcultural supports.

. . . [I]n recognizing the group nature of delinquent acts, it is significant to note that the lower-class youth, exposed to powerful instigating forces of his own milieu and subcultural setting, does tend to develop a unique delinquent subculture of his own. . . . Differences in the qualitative nature of delinquency, as well as the character of the psychological and sociological reinforcement of the delinquent act, would appear to follow as a result of . . . class and cultural differences. In this sense, therefore, *viz.* that delinquent acts in a lower-class setting receive strong sanctioned support and approval, [the] view that the locus of much delinquency is in the lower-class gang may not be seriously disputed.[9]

The assertion that lower-class delinquency receives "strong sanctioned support and approval" identifies a difference that goes to the heart of the problem of defining and locating delinquent subcultures. Indeed, it is principally this difference that permits us to say, with Bloch and Niederhoffer, that the most serious delinquency problem exists in the lower class. Whether or not delinquent norms are part of the structure of the group is, it seems to us, a crucial criterion in distinguishing between delinquent and nondelinquent subcultures. If members of a group have not qualified or partially withdrawn their support of the legitimacy of conventional norms, then we would not call the group a delinquent subculture.

8. *Ibid.*, pp. 7-9.
9. *Ibid.*, p. 15.

Having alluded to this crucial distinction, however, Bloch and Niederhoffer do not then incorporate it in their analysis of delinquent behavior. Rather than focus upon the forces which transform adolescent groups into specifically delinquent gangs, they attempt to account for the features that are common to all adolescent groups, delinquent and otherwise:

From the foregoing discussion, it would appear that many of the . . . features which distinguish the [lower-class] gang from middle-class cliques are primarily a matter of degree. Actually, what we are concerned with here are the general characteristics of the adolescent group process itself. May we assume that there are certain common features of this grouping process which appear to function irrespective of class, ethnic, and cultural level? Examination of the evidence of group behavior, characteristic of adolescents not only on different class levels within the same culture but even within widely divergent cultures, would seem to suggest that adolescence produces certain remarkable similarities in the group behavior of the young person striving for adulthood.[10]

Our objection to statements of this kind is based not on the assertion that "adolescence produces certain remarkable similarities," whatever the individual's society or position within a given society, but on the implication of this assertion, that delinquency, being a manifestation of adolescence, is also more or less the same wherever it arises. Indeed, Bloch and Niederhoffer also have difficulty with this point, for, as we noted, they seem to agree that lower-class delinquency is different from delinquency elsewhere in the social structure principally because it is rooted in subcultural norms. Their failure to define the object of inquiry thus leads to considerable confusion regarding its distribution.

The Problem of Adjustment—According to Bloch and Niederhoffer, adolescent cultures arise because the young encounter barriers in access to adult status. This status crisis is a significant one which produces a great deal of discontent and frustration. It appears to result in marked tendencies toward ganging and unruly behavior, particularly among males.

10. *Ibid.*, p. 10.

The adolescent culture is one "of negation in which the positive values of the prevailing culture are distorted and inverted for uses best suited to a philosophy of youthful dissidence and protest."[11] Probably few people would question this general explanation of turbulence during adolescence. It is, however, a rather long step from "youthful dissidence and protest" to systematic, recurrent thievery, organized street warfare, and habitual drug use. Treating "youthful dissidence" and these other phenomena as if they were similar is rather like lumping the social drinker and the chronic alcoholic under the same rubric. The theory of adolescent protest may help to explain the emergence of "youth culture," but it does not explain the conditions under which *delinquent* subcultures develop.

The experience of frustration in adolescent strivings toward adulthood seems to be so widespread in our society that it is hard to decide where it is most frequent and acute. In the absence of definitive data to show that this adjustment problem is concentrated among lower-class males in large cities, plausible arguments can be advanced for either a middle- or a lower-class concentration. For example, one might argue that the middle-class adolescent experiences more conflict because he generally has to delay much longer than the lower-class boy before assuming adult roles. His expected occupational roles as an adult generally require much longer periods of preparatory training. The lower-class boy is permitted to participate in adult roles and rewards much closer to the time when he is physically and emotionally ready to do so. On the other hand, it might be argued that the lower-class boy feels more frustrated because he has not been trained to delay gratification as has the middle-class boy, who has been led to anticipate a prolonged period of training as essential and encouraged to accept intermediate substitutes for eventual adult rewards.

The problem of the transition to adulthood is obviously not a permanent one. Although the adolescent crisis is acute,

11. *Ibid.*, p. 13.

adult status is bound to come in time. Given the temporary quality of this problem of adjustment, current theories of adolescent frustration as explanations of delinquent subculture do not seem convincing to us.

The Evolution of Subcultural Solutions—How does the theory of adolescent status crisis account for the origin of delinquent norms? The "adolescent protest," like the "masculine protest," may lead to delinquent acts—assaults, vandalism, and the like—in many adolescent groups, but these acts may or may not be supported by specifically delinquent norms. In our opinion, most adolescents who engage in such acts acknowledge the legitimacy of the conventional norms from which their behavior departs. Most adolescent groups in which delinquent acts occur, therefore, cannot properly be called delinquent subcultures. Thus the adolescent status-crisis theory does not provide an answer to the critical question of how delinquent norms originate.

Indeed, Bloch and Niederhoffer themselves do not seem wholly certain that the problem of adolescent status transition is the chief source of lower-class delinquent norms, for they introduce a further problem of adjustment experienced by lower-class youth—namely, discontent arising from a marked discrepancy between aspirations and opportunities for upward social mobility.

> The lower-class boy . . . absorbs dominant *middle-class values* which set goals for him, *but sees on every hand that he is unable to pursue these ends.* To many a lower-class boy, the socially approved objectives for desired manhood are so far-fetched, so unattainable, that they constitute a sort of chimera, a never-never land about which he can dream but actually not hope to achieve. The patterns of living of his father and other adult male figures in his environment appear to offer testimony as to the futility of achieving the goals which the popular cult of American success so stridently affirms in the classroom, the movies, TV, and other popular channels of mass enlightenment. What models are offered in the lives of parents and others in his environment, who are closely bound to a limited and constricted routine of seemingly unrewarded toil, appear uninspired and, for many youths, hardly worth the effort. Recognizing the limitations on his strivings, the values of the working-class youth may be an actual negation of the very things

which the calculated prudence of the middle class hopes to foster among its own young.[12]

Where previously these authors stressed barriers to adult status, they now point to barriers to *middle-class* adult status. The problem of the lower-class adolescent, they say, is not simply one of becoming a lower-class adult. Rather, it is a problem of leaving his class of origin and becoming affiliated with a class higher in the social structure. Pressures toward deviance arise because legitimate routes to success-goals are limited or closed to lower-class youth. As a result, frustrated adolescents may seek higher status by alternative, though illegal, paths. In their analysis of a lower-class gang known as the Pirates, for example, Bloch and Niederhoffer note that the members engaged in "glorification of racketeers." Anticipating lack of access to middle-class status, these lower-class boys apparently withdrew sentiments supporting the legitimacy of conventional norms, for they developed "contempt for the doctrine that hard work leads to success and happiness. The gang stopped reading Horatio Alger long ago. The squalor of the lower-class worker's life compared to the glamour of the racketeer leaves no choice. The big man, the big shot, is the realistic ideal from which to shape life."[13] Rejecting the goal of conventional lower-class adult status but cut off from middle-class adult status, potential delinquents orient themselves toward an illegitimate opportunity structure—the rackets.

It appears, then, that Bloch and Niederhoffer, while explicitly suggesting that delinquent subcultures arise from adolescent strivings toward immediate adult gratifications, have in fact advanced a theory based on the discrepancy between aspirations for culturally defined success-goals and the realistic possibilities of achieving those goals by legitimate means. It is the latter problem of adjustment that they use to account for the withdrawal of sentiments supporting official norms. This analysis may be presented graphically as shown in Table 1.

A test of the explicit Bloch-Neiderhoffer hypothesis would require a comparison of the propensities toward delinquency

12. *Ibid.*, p. 109. Emphasis added.
13. *Ibid.*, p. 170.

exhibited by persons in categories (a) and (c)—that is, by lower-class youth who wish to become lower-class adults and by middle-class youth who wish to become middle-class adults. If such a comparison showed that lower-class youth experience greater stress, it might then be said that the distribution of the adolescent crisis parallels the class distribution of delinquent subcultures. Unfortunately, Bloch and Niederhoffer do not provide the necessary data for such a comparison, nor do we find supporting data elsewhere in the literature on adolescence. But whatever we may eventually discover with respect to this comparison, it remains true that the Bloch and Niederhoffer account does not rest exclusively on the hypothesis that adolescent role strains are responsible for delinquency. Instead they imply that the dual problem of achieving adult status *and* middle-class status—*i.e.,* category (b)—is the adjustment dilemma to which delinquent subcultures in the lower class are a response.

Table 1

Relation of Class of Orientation to Class of Origin

		Class of Orientation	
		Same	Higher
Class of Origin	Lower	(a)	(b)
	Middle	(c)	(d)

When we consider the adolescent-crisis theory as a basis for identifying the conditions accounting for the emergence of the three types of subculture among lower-class youth, statements found in the literature prove somewhat confusing. Bloch and Niederhoffer assert that most lower-class delinquency is rational, disciplined, and utilitarian:

The present authors' investigations of literally hundreds of juvenile crimes, including burglaries and robberies, expose the overwhelming number committed by lower-class gangs. Inevitably, money or valuable property was taken. If the scene of the crime was ransacked, it was because the perpetrators turned the place over in their search for the hiding place of the money. It is true that often other articles in addition to the money were taken. But these, too, were apt to be useful to the gang in some way. . . . Rarely was there evidence to corroborate the non-utilitarian motives which Cohen ascribes to lower-class crime. Perhaps with boys younger than twelve, this may be true, reflecting their immaturity and lack of social intelligence rather than class membership.[14]

They do not, of course, deny the existence of the conflict and retreatist forms of delinquent subculture; they simply assert the primacy of the criminal pattern. (They do, however, note historical changes in the rates of each pattern, suggesting that the conflict pattern is tending to become ascendent.)

This emphasis on utilitarian delinquency does not seem to be consistent with their theoretical analysis. It is not clear why the frustrations of adolescence should yield disciplined, utilitarian behavior. In fact, one might expect the reverse: that negativistic, aggressive, destructive—*i.e.,* "conflict"—behavior would result from the stresses of adolescence. As a matter of fact, this is precisely what the cross-cultural comparisons presented by Bloch and Niederhoffer show, as witness the following examples:

Manus: In the study of the Manus people, it has been demonstrated that rites are inadequate in preparing adolescents in that society for the abrupt transition from a happy childhood to the anxiety-ridden life they lead as adults. This should be fertile territory for the growth of gangs. Here again we find evidence of the formation of groups of dissident and roistering adolescent males . . . *"the terror of their own village girls, the scourge of neighboring villages."*

Comanche: There were deviant individuals who by their depredations and reckless courage earned the sobriquet of "the contrary ones." Both Herbert Bloch and Abraham Kardiner point out that while such gangs or individuals represent a definite threat to the peace and harmony of the community, they are tolerated because this same reckless behavior is demanded of the "contrary ones" in war. In this, non-conforming "delinquent" activity, whether gang or individual, is channeled into constructive paths.[15]

14. *Ibid.,* p. 178.
15. *Ibid.,* pp. 134-35. Emphasis added.

Their illustrations of delinquency from the American scene, by contrast, stress utilitarian behavior: "In gangs dedicated to burglaries, robberies and larcenies, there are careful preparations involving 'casing the job,' practicing rehearsals, coordination of efforts according to a master plan. Long hours are spent acquiring mechanical and electrical skills, checking the patrol habits of the policeman on the post. Surely this is not short-run hedonism!"[16] With this last statement we must agree. But how, then, are we to reconcile these accounts of utilitarian behavior among many lower-class gangs with the unruly behavior of the Manus and Comanche adolescents, or with accounts of urban "fighting gangs"?

Persistence and Change—Bloch and Niederhoffer present a discussion of the "rising trend of modern delinquency." However, instead of using their theory of the adolescent crisis to account for this development, they invoke psychological explanations: "Considerable recent evidence suggests rather strongly that the rising trend of modern delinquency is characterized by pathological states of minds. The frequency of psychopathies and emotional disturbances among young offenders may be reaching significant proportions."[17] Whatever the merits of this explanation, it seems unrelated to the general theory that delinquent subcultures—and changes in them—result from the status deprivations of adolescence.

Logically, proponents of the adolescent-crisis theory of delinquency must account for changes in delinquency rates on the basis of changes in the relationship of adolescent and adult roles. If delinquency rates are increasing, has there been a corresponding increase in the difficulties associated with the transition from adolescence to adulthood? Unfortunately, Bloch and Niederhoffer do not pursue this line of inquiry, nor have relevant data been reported elsewhere in the literature on adolescence.

---

16. *Ibid.,* p. 180.
17. *Ibid.,* p. 148.

Lower-class Culture and Delinquent Subcultures

AMERICAN CRIMINOLOGISTS have frequently attributed the emergence of delinquent and criminal subcultures to value conflicts. Briefly, this point of view asserts that societies often contain several value systems which vary in their relative dominance so that conformity with a subordinate value system evokes sanctions from the agents of the dominant value system. One variant of the traditional "value conflict" or "culture conflict" theory has recently been advanced by Walter B. Miller. Unfortunately, Miller has not concerned himself with many of the theoretical issues raised by former proponents and critics of this tradition, so that many unresolved problems remain in his work.

Miller's thesis may be reduced to three main propositions: (1) The lower class is characterized by distinctive values. (2) These vary markedly from the middle-class values which undergird the legal code. (3) The result is that conformity with certain lower-class values may automatically result in violation of the law. As Miller puts it, "Engaging in certain cultural practices which comprise essential elements of the total life pattern of lower-class culture automatically violates certain legal norms. Examples of this may be seen in the use of profanity, in hanging around or loitering, and in the serial-mating pattern characteristic of many homes." In other words, the lower-class way of life as such is intrinsically law-violating; it runs counter to the definitions of conformity that prevail in other sectors of the society.[18] This view is clearly implied in Miller's statement: "Many school [personnel] tend to see the future lives of [lower-class youth] in terms of only two major alternatives—an essentially lower-class or an essentially middle-class

18. See Miller's remarks in W. C. Kvaraceus and W. B. Miller, *Delinquent Behavior: Culture and the Individual* (Washington, D. C.: National Education Association, 1959), pp. 68-69.

way of life. A third alternative—and one which is far more feasible in a large proportion of cases—is to train and prepare the youngsters for a *law-abiding lower-class way of life.*"[19] The task of the school in this perspective is to help youngsters to overcome the general propensities toward law-violating behavior which are a "normal" consequence of socialization in the lower class.

The "focal concerns," values, or preoccupations which characterize the lower class and which predispose its members to law-violating behavior are defined by Miller as follows:

Trouble: Concern over "trouble" is a dominant feature of lower-class culture. . . . "Trouble" in one of its aspects represents a situation or a kind of behavior which results in unwelcome or complicating involvement with official authorities or agencies of middle-class society. . . . For men, "trouble" frequently involves fighting or sexual adventures while drinking; for women, sexual involvement with disadvantageous consequences. Expressed desire to avoid behavior which violates moral or legal norms is often based less on an explicit commitment to "official" moral or legal standards than on a desire to avoid "getting into trouble," *e.g.*, the complicating consequences of the action.

Toughness: The concept of "toughness" in lower-class culture represents a compound combination of qualities or states. Among its most important components are physical prowess, evidenced both by demonstrated possession of strength and endurance and athletic skill; "masculinity," symbolized by a complex of acts and avoidance (bodily tattooing, absence of sentimentality; non-concern with "art," "literature"; conceptualization of women as conquest objects, etc.); and bravery in the face of physical threat. The model for the "tough guy"—hard, fearless, undemonstrative, skilled in physical combat—is represented by the movie gangster of the thirties, the "private eye," and the movie cowboy.

Smartness: "Smartness" . . . involves the capacity to outsmart, outfox, outwit, dupe, "take," "con" another or others, and the concomitant capacity to avoid being outwitted, "taken," or duped oneself. In its essence, smartness involves the capacity to achieve a valued entity—material goods, personal status—through a maximum use of mental agility and a minimum of physical effort.

Excitement: For many lower-class individuals the rhythm of life fluctuates between periods of relatively routine or repetitive ac-

19. *Ibid.*, pp. 74-75.

tivity and sought situations of great emotional stimulation. Many of the most characteristic features of lower-class life are related to the search for excitement or "thrill." Involved here are the widespread use of gambling of all kinds. . . . The quest for excitement finds . . . its most vivid expression in the . . . recurrent "night on the town" . . . a patterned set of activities in which alcohol, music, and sexual adventuring are major components.

Fate: Related to the quest for excitement is the concern with fate, fortune, or luck. Here also a distinction is made between two states—being "lucky" or "in luck," and being unlucky or jinxed. Many lower-class persons feel that their lives are subject to a set of forces over which they have relatively little control. These are not equated directly with the supernatural forces of formally organized religion, but relate more to a concept of "destiny" or man as a pawn of magical powers. . . . This often implicit world view is associated with a conception of the ultimate futility of directed effort toward a goal. . . .

Autonomy: The extent and nature of control over the behavior of the individual—an important concern in most cultures—has a special significance and is distinctively patterned in lower-class culture. . . . On the overt level there is a strong and frequently expressed resentment of the idea of external controls, restrictions on behavior, and unjust or coercive authority. . . . Actual patterns of behavior, however, reveal a marked discrepancy between expressed sentiment and what is covertly valued. Many lower-class people appear to seek out highly restrictive social environments wherein stringent external controls are maintained over their behavior. . . . Lower-class patients in mental hospitals will exercise considerable ingenuity to insure continued commitment while voicing the desire to get out; delinquent boys will frequently "run" from a correctional institution to activate efforts to return them; to be caught and returned means that one is cared for.[20]

Proponents of culture-conflict theories have differed in their views regarding the relation of such conflict to delinquency. For example, Wirth says that culture conflict is relevant to delinquency only when two conflicting value systems are simultaneously internalized; this produces feeling of anxiety and insecurity which may result in delinquent behavior.[21] Miller, however, seems to view delinquency among lower-class youth

20. Miller, *op. cit.*, pp. 8-13.

21. Louis Wirth, "Culture Conflict and Misconduct," *Social Forces*, Vol. 9 (June 1931), pp. 484-92.

as the outcome of an *external* clash of cultural codes. He asserts that delinquents have internalized only the distinctive code of the lower class but that the power structure of the society enforces the middle-class code. Their efforts to conform to their own values thus bring them into conflict with the agents of middle-class norms, with the result that lower-class youngsters are defined as delinquent. This point of view is strongly reminiscent of Sellin's classic discussion of "external cultural conflict":

> A few years ago, a Sicilian father in New Jersey killed the sixteen-year-old seducer of his daughter, expressing surprise at his arrest since he had merely defended his family honor in a traditional way. In this case a mental conflict in the sociological sense did not exist. The conflict was external and occurred between cultural codes or norms. We may assume that where such conflicts occur, violations or norms of one cultural group or area migrate to another and that such conflict will continue so long as the acculturation process has not been completed.[22]

Although it seems unlikely that there are many lower-class persons today so completely unacculturated to the "core" values of American society as this Sicilian father, Miller nevertheless adheres closely to the position implied by this incident with respect to certain lower-class values:

> A large body of systematically interrelated attitudes, practices, behaviors, and values characteristic of lower-class culture are designed to support and maintain the basic features of the lower-class way of life. In areas where these differ from features of middle-class culture, action oriented to the achievement and maintenance of the lower-class system may violate norms of the middle class and be perceived as deliberately non-conforming or malicious by an observer strongly cathected to middle-class norms. This does not mean, however, that violation of the middle-class norm is the dominant component of motivation; *it is a byproduct of action primarily oriented to the lower-class system.*[23]

Yet the lower class is now composed principally of persons who are at least one generation removed from foreign-

22. Thorsten Sellin, *Culture Conflict and Crime* (New York: Social Science Research Council, 1938), p. 68.
23. Miller, *op. cit.*, p. 19.

born ancestors. These people, in common with middle-class persons, have been exposed to the cultural impact of universal public education and the mass media of our society. Although middle- and lower-class value systems are not identical, they are nevertheless parts of the same society and thus have much in common. This is a point to which we will return later in this discussion, for it bears directly on the adequacy of the theory of culture conflict.

INADEQUACIES OF THE THEORY

Definition—The culture-conflict theory, like the adolescent-status and masculine-identity theories, is an attempt to explain *all* types of delinquent act, whether or not these acts are supported by subcultural norms. Thus there is a tendency to classify as delinquent any group in which delinquent acts occur. Miller defines delinquency as *"behavior by nonadults which violates specific legal norms or the norms of a particular societal institution with sufficient frequency and/or seriousness so as to provide a firm basis for legal action against the behaving individual or group."*[24] He notes, further, that the members of all lower-class adolescent "street-corner" groups commit acts which fit this definition as part of their ordinary activities:

> The customary set of activities of the adolescent street-corner group includes activities which are in violation of laws and ordinances of the legal code. Most of these center around assault and theft of various types (the gang fight; auto theft; assault on an individual; petty pilfering and shoplifting; "mugging"; pocketbook theft).[25]

It would appear that for Miller the only basis for differentiating delinquent and nondelinquent groups is that members of the former engage in delinquent acts more frequently. Thus Miller says that "delinquent gangs" are simply a variant of street-corner groups:

> What has been called the "delinquent gang" . . . defined on the basis of frequency of participation in law-violating activity . . .

24. Kvaraceus and Miller, *op. cit.*, p. 54.
25. Miller, *op. cit.*, p. 17.

should not be considered a legitimate unit of study per se, but rather as one particular variant of the adolescent street-corner group.[26]

The problem with a definition that focuses exclusively upon delinquent acts is that it encompasses many street-corner groups whose core members generally disapprove of, or at best merely tolerate, the delinquencies of other members. In such groups, delinquent acts are not a requirement or a desideratum for membership. By Miller's definition, a social or athletic group which becomes involved in a delinquent episode is no less delinquent than are groups which are organized specifically for theft, street warfare, or other illegal activities. Failure to recognize the relationship between a delinquent act and the social and cultural structure of the group in which it occurs thus leads to serious problems of definition.

Distribution—Miller's concept of delinquency also can be criticized on the ground that an extraordinarily wide range of adolescents are caught in the net. Delinquent subcultures, as we have said, tend to be confined to adolescent males in lower-class urban areas, but this certainly cannot be said of delinquent acts. Delinquent acts, as such, occur throughout the social structure; although the rates differ, they are committed by females, middle-class adolescents, and residents in rural areas. It is unreasonable to assume that a single theory can account for such diverse behavior. If we focus on delinquent norms, by contrast, the theoretical task becomes much more manageable, for the emergence of delinquent norms tends to be restricted to certain social locations. Furthermore, an emphasis on supporting norms—that is, on the cultural structure of the delinquent group—makes it possible to draw meaningful distinctions among various types of gang, which cannot be done when the act alone is taken as the criterion of delinquency.

The Problem of Adjustment—How, then, are we to account for delinquent acts which are so widely dispersed throughout the social structure? Miller suggests that conformity with lower-class values in a middle-class world is such an ad-

---

26. *Ibid.*, p. 14.

justment problem. But what of middle-class adolescents who commit delinquent acts? Miller offers the rather unconvincing answer that middle-class adolescent groups are taking over many of the focal concerns of the lower class and thus are finding themselves at odds with the values of their own class. Miller feels that the preoccupation with the diffusion of middle-class values in our society has caused us to underestimate the upward diffusion of lower-class values, particularly with the development of mass media of communication.[27] It is certainly a debatable question whether the mass media disseminate middle-class or lower-class values. In any case, middle-class groups embraced by Miller's definition of delinquent gang present a major problem for theories based on the culture-conflict theme.

Miller's theory can also be challenged on the ground that the conflict between lower-class and middle-class values is not so significant and persistent a problem in the life experience of delinquents as he supposes. Serious delinquencies, such as burglary, robbery, assault, gang killings, and drug addiction, violate lower-class as well as middle-class values. Miller's examples of deviance arising from culture conflict—"the use of profanity, . . . hanging around or loitering, . . . the serial-mating pattern characteristic of many homes"—tend to be relatively innocuous forms of conduct from the standpoint of both lower- and middle-class norms. Furthermore, the focal concerns of lower-class groups as outlined by Miller—trouble, toughness, smartness, excitement, fate, and autonomy—do not seem to differ from middle-class preoccupations so much that simple conformity to these values would "automatically" lead to serious law violations. Miller's analysis suggests a degree of cultural independence of the two classes that has probably not prevailed since the mass immigrations of the nineteenth and early twentieth centuries.

The Evolution of Subcultural Solutions—Perhaps the most serious defect of the culture-conflict theory of delinquent gangs lies in its failure to account for the origins of delinquent norms. Under what conditions do the focal concerns of lower-class

27. Kvaraceus and Miller, *op. cit.,* Chap. 10.

youngsters become transformed into specifically delinquent prescriptions? Miller, like earlier theorists in the culture-conflict tradition, has concentrated on explaining delinquent as opposed to nondelinquent acts. This leaves the problem of identifying the conditions under which delinquent acts come to be buttressed by a stable set of delinquent norms. In order to explain how patterned delinquent subcultures emerge—how lower-class "focal concerns" become sufficiently "intensified," "maximized," or "distorted" to lead to subcultural delinquency —Miller turns to two additional problems of adjustment.

He first explores the consequences of socialization in the female-centered household and introduces a version of the problem of masculine identification. In order to assert their masculinity, he contends, lower-class boys from female-centered households tend to exaggerate delinquent aspects of the lower-class value system.[28] Miller also points to discrepancies between the aspirations of lower-class youth and the realistic possibilities for achievement as a source of frustration and anxiety. It should be noted that this second problem runs counter to his frequent emphasis on the relative isolation of lower- and middle-class value systems. Success themes are at the core of the middle-class value system in America, and there is much in Miller's work to indicate that lower-class youth are exposed to these themes and take them quite seriously. In this connection, Miller suggests a typology of lower-class youth based on the gap between aspirations and possibilities of achievement:

1. *"Stable" lower class.* This group consists of youngsters who, for all practical purposes, do not aspire to higher status or who have no realistic possibility of achieving such aspirations.
2. *Aspiring but conflicted lower class.* This group represents those for whom family or other community influences have produced a desire to elevate their status, but who lack the necessary personal attributes or cultural "equipment" to make the grade, or for whom cultural pressures effectively inhibit aspirations.
3. *Successfully aspiring lower class.* This group, popularly assumed

28. See *ibid.*, Chap. 11, and Miller, *op. cit.*, pp. 13-14.

to be the most prevalent, includes those who have both the will and the capacity to elevate their status.[29]

The first two categories in this typology are marked by internal contradictions. With respect to the stable lower class (type 1), there is a considerable difference between those "who do not aspire to higher status" and those who do aspire but "have no realistic possibility of achieving such aspirations." Those who do not aspire avoid frustrations arising from position discontent; those who aspire but are cut off from appropriate avenues to higher status experience acute frustrations. To preserve this distinction it might be preferable to describe type 1 as follows:

This group consists of youngsters who, for all practical purposes, do not aspire to higher status or who, because of expectations of failure, have revised their aspirations downward.

The definition of type 2 also blurs important distinctions. Miller says that persons in this category "desire to elevate their status" but that various "cultural pressures effectively inhibit aspirations." Thus it is not clear what he intends to convey about the aspiration levels of this category. It would appear from other elements in the definition that this type should properly consist of lower-class youth who aspire to but are cut off from success, either because they "lack the necessary personal attributes or 'cultural equipment' to make the grade" or because opportunity is objectively limited. To the extent that their aspirations persist under conditions limiting achievement, acute frustrations would be experienced. This group, then, should be clearly distinguished from type 1 and type 3. Type 3 includes those who aspire and who possess traits and abilities that are likely to bring them success.

According to Miller, discrepancies between aspirations and possibilities of achievement are a major source of pressures toward delinquent behavior: "The lower-class youngster who is 'stalled' in regard to his achievement aspiration is . . . likely to become delinquent."[30] This statement and others that call at-

29. Kvaraceus and Miller, *op. cit.*, p. 72.
30. *Ibid.*, p. 136.

tention to social and cultural dislocations within lower-class environments obviously conflict with Miller's hypothesis that delinquency is basically a consequence of conformity to lower-class values. It is perhaps sufficient at this point for us to note that the theory of culture conflict does not prove adequate by itself to account for the emergence of delinquent subcultures. It is necessary to introduce other types of adjustment problem to differentiate the responses of lower-class youngsters to their living conditions.

Nothing in Miller's account of lower-class life helps to explain the differentiation of delinquent subcultures. Even if his definition of lower-class values were accepted, it is not at all clear why this conflict would result alternatively in criminal, conflict, or retreatist adaptations.

Persistence and Change—The culture-conflict theory addresses the problem of the persistence of delinquent norms more directly than the problem of their origins. Delinquent norms are regarded as "given"; Miller, for example, is concerned primarily with how these norms are taken over by the child. His theory assumes the existence of delinquent norms whose dictates must be followed by new members as the price of admission to the group:

> The *demanded* response to certain situations recurrently engendered within lower-class culture may call for the commission of illegal acts. For many youngsters the bases of prestige are to be found in toughness, physical prowess, skill, fearlessness, bravery, ability to con people, gaining money by wits, shrewdness, adroitness, smart repartee, seeking and finding thrills, risk, danger, freedom from external constraint, and freedom from superordinate authority. These are the explicit values of the most important and essential reference group of many delinquent youngsters. These are the things he respects and strives to attain. The lower-class youngster who engages in a long and recurrent series of delinquent behaviors that are sanctioned by his peer group is acting so as to achieve prestige within his reference system.[31]

31. *Ibid.*, p. 69. Miller's statement that "the *demanded* response to certain situations recurrently engendered within lower-class culture may call for the commission of illegal acts" sounds very much as though he were referring to *delinquent norms* as such—that is, to norms that prescribe the commission of various delinquent acts. Here

It is apparent, however, that a theory of the persistence of a cultural tradition is not a sufficient explanation of the origin of that tradition. To maintain that delinquent norms are an exaggeration of aspects of the lower-class value system simply shifts the original question to the problem of accounting for the development of different value systems within the same society and of the relative dominance of one over the others. Miller alludes to a historical continuity between contemporary lower-class values in the United States and the traditional values of depressed groups in other parts of the world, asserting that "lower-class culture is a distinctive tradition many centuries old with an integrity of its own."[32] But at some juncture the theorist must identify the social conditions from which these values develop as a solution to the adjustment problems of everyday life. The historical-continuity theory of lower-class values as a source of delinquent norms can be attacked on many points. We should like to point out here that it ignores the extent to which lower-class and delinquent cultures today are predictable responses to conditions in our society rather than persisting patterns taken over from foreign cultures. This is a matter to which we shall devote considerable attention in the next chapter.

The culture-conflict hypothesis poses special problems when one considers the sources of change in the patterns of delinquent activity. Culture-conflict theorists typically account for a reduction in delinquency by referring to acculturation—a process in which serious value conflicts are gradually elim-

---

again we find an ambiguity in Miller's work, for the distinction between lower-class norms in general and delinquent norms is unclear. Furthermore, it should be noted that lower-class focal concerns, such as the emphasis upon masculinity, are not delinquent or criminal. Miller has not shown why efforts to be masculine result in delinquent or criminal behavior. There are many ways of exhibiting masculinity that do not entail legal violations. If ways are chosen that entail law violations, then these *choices* require explanation.

In this connection, Miller's work has similarities to that of Shaw, McKay, and Sutherland, who were also very much in the culture-conflict tradition. They, too, took delinquent codes as *given* and focused on the transmission of these codes from one generation to another.

32. Miller, *op. cit.*, p. 19.

inated. It is somewhat harder, however, for culture-conflict theorists to explain an increase in the amount of delinquency and a change in its content. Logically these changes must be explained by the infusion of new value conflicts into the system or by some type of breakdown in the diffusion of existing values, although no account of such a breakdown has been offered. In conclusion, therefore, we are not disposed to accept the hypothesis that culture conflict is the most characteristic and significant adjustment problem underlying the development of delinquent subcultures.

In the chapters that follow, we shall take as our starting point the adjustment problems that arise when there are serious discrepancies between aspirations toward success goals and opportunities for achieving them. It is our view that problems of this type have a more direct and powerful influence on the emergence of various types of delinquent subculture than any that we have reviewed in this chapter.

CHAPTER 4

Goals, Norms, and Anomie

IN THIS CHAPTER, we shall be engaged in a search for causes. What pressures lead the young to form or join delinquent subcultures? To what problem of adjustment is alienation from conventional styles of life a response? There are, of course, no simple answers to these questions. Lacking many kinds of data, we can offer only tentative explanations, in the hope that others will also reflect upon them and undertake new lines of inquiry suggested by them. It should be borne in mind that we distinguish between the question of the problem of adjustment to which delinquent behavior is a response and the question of the conditions under which such behavior comes to be buttressed by delinquent norms. In this chapter, we shall be concerned with the first of these questions. In Chapter 5 we shall discuss the second.

The Regulation of Goals: Durkheim[1]

It is our view that pressures toward the formation of delinquent subcultures originate in marked discrepancies between culturally induced aspirations among lower-class youth and the possibilities of achieving them by legitimate means. This hypothesis owes a great deal to the work of the nineteenth-century sociologist Émile Durkheim. We shall be especially concerned with his use of the concept "anomie"—which means lawlessness, or normlessness. According to Durkheim, anomie results from a breakdown in the regulation of goals such that men's aspirations become unlimited. Unlimited aspirations create a constant pressure for deviant behavior—that is, for behavior that departs from social norms. "Anomie" thus refers to a state in which social norms no longer control men's actions.

Durkheim distinguished between two kinds of need: physical and social. He observed that these two categories of need depend upon quite different sources of regulation. Physical needs are automatically regulated by man's organic structure. Once satiated, for example, the body rejects additional food. But this is not the case with social needs, such as the desire for wealth, prestige, or power; man's capacity to want social gratification is "an insatiable and bottomless abyss." Nothing in the organic structure is capable of regulating these social desires once they have been stimulated. If aspirations are to be kept within reasonable bounds, therefore, some other agency must exert control. This regulatory function is performed, according to Durkeim, by the social order.

A stable society is one in which men throughout the social hierarchy are more or less content with their lot in life or aspire to achieve only what it is realistically possible for them to achieve. "Each person is then . . . in harmony with his condition, and desires only what he may legitimately hope for as the normal reward of his activity." In other words, a

1. See Émile Durkheim, *Suicide: A Study in Sociology,* trans. by J. A. Spaulding and George Simpson, ed. by George Simpson (Glencoe, Ill.: Free Press, 1951), esp. Chap. 5. Quotations in this section are from pp. 247-57.

stable order is one in which men ascribe legitimacy to the criteria for the distribution of social rewards and do not challenge the socially defined relationship between personal worth and location in the social hierarchy.[2] This stability tends to break down, says Durkheim, when men's aspirations become unlimited. When there is no restraint upon their aspirations, "their very demands make fulfillment impossible. . . . Nothing gives satisfaction . . . agitation is uninterruptedly maintained."

Durkheim identified several states of social organization that tend to result in unrestrained aspiration. Economic crises, he thought, can have this effect, for the abrupt changes in social position that they produce generate a sense of disorientation such that "the limits are unknown between the possible and impossible, what is just and what is unjust, legitimate claims and hopes and those which are immoderate." He also pointed out that the industrial world is marked by a tendency toward unlimited goals—an observation that has especial pertinence for this inquiry, since delinquency tends to be a pronounced characteristic of industrial societies. "The sphere of trade and industry . . . is actually in a chronic state [of anomie]." Rapid technological developments and the existence of vast unexploited markets excite the imagination by presenting apparently infinite possibilities for the accumulation of wealth.

> Now that [the manufacturer] may assume to have almost the entire world as his customer, how could [his aspirations] accept their former confinement in the face of such limitless prospects? Such is the source of excitement predominating in this part of society . . . [that] the state of crisis and anomie [are] constant and, so to speak, normal. From top to bottom of the ladder, greed is aroused without knowing where to find ultimate foothold. Nothing can calm it, since its goal is far beyond all it can attain.

These unlimited aspirations and expectations for the ac-

2. The question of how society succeeds in imposing these definitions of legitimacy, of how it persuades the poor man to accept his station in life as just, is a very important one, but it is much beyond the scope of this book. For our immediate purposes, the processes that result in a widespread sense of contentment with the social order are of less interest than the processes that lead to a diminution of this state of mind.

quisition of wealth, prestige, and power, generated by a burgeoning industrialism, come to be buttressed by ideologies in which man is defined as inherently restless and ambitious: "It is everlastingly repeated that it is man's nature to be eternally dissatisfied, constantly to advance, without relief or rest, toward an indefinite goal. The longing for infinity is daily represented as a mark of moral distinction." It is precisely these cultural emphases upon "infinite" or "receding" goals that, in Durkheim's opinion, put a strain upon the regulatory apparatus of the society. For if men are never satisfied with their position in the social hierarchy, if they are driven by unrealistic desires to improve their lot in life, then they may cease to be bound by the prevailing rules of the society.

But why, we might ask, is an emphasis on achievement, on upward striving in the occupational world, so pronounced a characteristic of industrial societies? What is the origin of ideologies that say it is man's "nature" to be dissatisfied? Obviously such ideologies do not exist in all societies. Something in the organization of industrial life must therefore require that the members of industrial societies make a virtue of dissatisfaction, of discontent with their present position in life. If we can identify this "something," we shall be on our way to understanding an important feature of American life, and, furthermore, we shall have taken another step toward an explanation of delinquency, for one of the distinctive features of delinquent subcultures is the acute dissatisfaction of their members with the prospects life holds for them.

All societies, including the industrial order, must solve the problem of maintaining themselves or else disintegrate. Societies differ, however, in the devices that are required to cope with the problem of survival. In many societies it is enough that the young work alongside their parents, acquiring through these intimate associations the values and skills that will enable them to engage successfully in adult occupational and kinship activities. The occupational systems in such societies are relatively simple and undifferentiated; most of the major work roles can be passed directly from father to son. The transmittal of occupational skills is a more difficult problem in our society, with its vastly proliferated structure of extremely technical work roles. We cannot depend upon the vagaries of birth to determine who will occupy each role, for we cannot assume that the son of a physicist will automatically be a competent successor to his father. Nor can we require the father to transmit highly specialized knowledge to his son in the context of the family, for this would divert the father's energies from the primary work role that he is supposed to perform. The family, in other words, is not a satisfactory environment for the learning of specialized occupational skills. The industrial society must organize itself in such a way that it can allocate people to roles more or less on the basis of merit and endowment rather than on the basis of social origins, and it must provide—outside the family—the formal learning experiences that are prerequisite to occupational performance.

A crucial problem in the industrial world, then, is to locate and train the most talented persons in every generation, irrespective of the vicissitudes of birth, to occupy technical work roles. Whether he is born into wealth or poverty, each individual, depending upon his ability and diligence, must be encouraged to find his "natural level" in the social order. This problem is one of tremendous proportions. Since we cannot know in advance who can best fulfill the requirements of various occupational roles, the matter is presumably settled through the process of competition. But how can men throughout the social order be motivated to participate in this competition? How can society generate the ambition and persistence that are necessary if the individual is to make his way in the occupational world? How can we persuade the young to invest their resources, time, and energies in acquiring specialized knowledge and complex skills? It is not enough for a few to make the race; all must be motivated to strive, so that the most able and talented will be the victors in the competitive struggle for higher status.

One of the ways in which the industrial society attempts to solve this problem is by defining success-goals as potentially accessible to all, regardless of race, creed, or socioeconomic position. Great social rewards, it is said, are not limited to any particular segment or segments of the population but are available to anyone, however lowly his origins. The status of a young man's father presumably does not put an upper limit on the height to which the son may aspire; in fact, he is exhorted to improve his status over that of his father. The industrial society, in short, emphasizes *common* or universal success-goals as a way of ensuring its survival. If large masses of young people can be motivated to reach out for great social rewards, many of them will make the appropriate investment in learning and preparation, and a rough correlation between talent and ultimate position in the occupational hierarchy will presumably result.

One of the paradoxes of social life is that the processes by which societies seek to ensure order sometimes result in disorder. If a cultural emphasis on unlimited success-goals tends to solve some problems in the industrial society, it also creates new ones. A pervasive feeling of position discontent leads men to compete for higher status and so contributes to the survival of the industrial order, but it also produces acute pressure for deviant behavior. Unlimited aspirations, Durkheim pointed out, exert an intense pressure toward disorder because they are, by definition, unachievable and thus constitute a source of "uninterrupted agitation."

The Regulation of Goals and Norms: Merton[3]

DURKHEIM'S pioneering work on the conditions that make for a breakdown in social control has been greatly advanced by the contemporary American sociologist Robert K. Merton. Like Durkheim, Merton set himself the task of accounting for the emergence of deviant behavior. At the outset, he distinguished between two features of organized social life: the cultural structure and the social structure. The cultural structure consists of goals and norms, the approved ends toward which

3. See R. K. Merton, *Social Theory and Social Structure*, Rev. and Enl. Ed. (Glencoe, Ill.: Free Press, 1957), esp. Chaps. 4 and 5.

men orient themselves and the approved ways in which they reach out for these ends. The social structure consists of the patterned sets of relationships in which people are involved. The division of people into social classes or strata according to wealth, power, or prestige is one important type of social structure.

Using these conceptual distinctions, Merton has extended and refined the intellectual tradition initiated by Durkheim. Durkheim, it will be remembered, emphasized the need for society to regulate the social goals of its members, to keep them within the limits of possible achievement, in order to avert tension, frustration, and consequent deviant behavior. In Merton's somewhat different view, anomie develops not because of a breakdown in the regulation of goals alone but, rather, because of a breakdown in *the relationship between goals and legitimate avenues of access to them*. A stable society is one in which there is a rough balance between goals and norms, between culturally prescribed aspirations and socially approved modes of achieving them. An unstable society is one in which these two elements of the cultural structure are out of concert with each other: "Aberrant behavior may be regarded sociologically as a symptom of dissociation between culturally prescribed aspirations and socially structured avenues of realizing these aspirations."[4]

The conceptual refinements introduced by Merton offer several distinct contributions. First, they enable us to expand our inquiry to include the results of striving for *limited* goals when the possibilities of achieving them legitimately are also limited. This is an important refinement, for probably relatively few people are afflicted with insatiable aspirations. An acute observer of the American scene, Alexis de Tocqueville, remarked on this point a century ago, and there is no reason to assume that his observations are less true now:

> The first thing that strikes a traveler in the United States is the innumerable multitude of those who seek to emerge from their original condition; and the second is the rarity of lofty ambition to be observed in the midst of the universally ambitious stir of society.

4. *Ibid.*, p. 134.

No Americans are devoid of a yearning desire to rise, but hardly any appear to entertain hope of great magnitude or to pursue very lofty aims. All are constantly seeking to acquire property, power, and reputation; few contemplate these things upon a great scale.[5]

We have little evidence regarding the heights to which Americans typically aspire. What evidence we have suggests that people are oriented, not toward the top of the social ladder, but toward the next rung—not toward a doubling or tripling of income, but toward a 25-per-cent increase. It may be true that, once having negotiated the next rung on the ladder, they tend to orient themselves to a still higher one; nevertheless, their ambitions at any given moment appear to be fixed upon limited ends.

Merton's statement of the problem also enables us to account for anomie under conditions other than economic crisis or burgeoning industrialism. These, according to Durkheim, are instances of disturbances in the collective order which result in unregulated aspirations. With Merton's position, however, we can explain pressures leading to deviance in the normal functioning of the social order. At some point, the problems of adjustment resulting from discrepancies between ambition and achievement can be expected to have an adverse effect upon conformity to social rules, whether or not conditions of economic crisis prevail. Merton's point frees us to examine the everyday processes giving rise to deviant behavior. Situations of crisis thus become special instances affecting the basic relationship between aspirations and opportunities. Some types of crisis may broaden the discrepancy; others may lessen it.[6] But it is the relationship between these components of the

5. Alexis de Tocqueville, *Democracy in America*, Vol. 2 (New York: Vintage Books, 1958), p. 256.

6. In this connection, there is some evidence that lower-class crime rates (especially offenses against property) vary depending upon conditions of prosperity or depression. Adult crime rates appear to vary directly with unemployment; juvenile crime rates, however, appear to vary inversely with unemployment. For adults, unemployment poses genuine problems of economic survival, and thus it is not difficult to understand why more property offenses occur in this group under conditions of economic hardship. Why prosperity should result in higher rates of juvenile crime is not so easy to understand. One

cultural structure upon which we now fix our attention, whatever the relative stability of particular features of the collective order.

Merton's formulation, further, permits us to make distinctions regarding the severity of pressures toward deviant behavior which originate *at different points in the social structure.* It helps us to explain, for example, why youth in the lower class are apparently more likely than middle-class youth to engage in extreme law-violating behavior. There is every reason to think that persons variously located in the social hierarchy have rather different chances of reaching common success-goals despite the prevailing ideology of equal opportunity. The middle-class person can generally take advantage of educational opportunities despite their cost; his family may be in a position to finance his beginnings in a profession or in business, or at least to put him in touch with established and successful people who can give him an "edge." In these and other ways, middle-class youth enjoy greater access to success-goals. Although the lower-class boy may yearn to rise in the social structure, the obstacles are great. Advanced education may seem a remote possibility, since the costs may easily exceed his resources. As Merton observes, "Recourse to legitimate channels for 'getting in the money' is limited by a class structure which is not fully open at each level to men of good capacity. Despite our persisting open-class ideology, advance toward the success goals is relatively rare and notably difficult for those armed with little formal education and few economic resources."[7] Later in this chapter we shall have more to say

---

explanation is that prosperity heightens the aspirations of lower-class young people wihout appreciably affecting the likelihood of their achieving their goals; hence discontent with economic position and economic prospects is intensified during prosperous times. See, for evidence on this point, Daniel Glaser and Kent Rice, "Crime, Age, and Employment," *American Sociological Review,* Vol. 24, No. 5 (Oct. 1959), pp. 679-86.

7. Merton, *op. cit.,* pp. 145-46. It should not be inferred that there is a perfect positive correlation between pressures toward deviance and rate of deviance. Other variables intervene to influence the outcome of these pressures. One such variable is the relative availability of opportunities to engage in a deviant adaptation. For a

about the differences in legitimate opportunity for persons in different parts of the social structure. Here we wish simply to establish the basic hypothesis that discrepancies between aspirations and legitimate chances of achievement increase as one descends in the class structure. The ideology of common success-goals and equal opportunity may become an empty myth for those who find themselves cut off from legitimate pathways upward. We may predict, then, that the pressure to engage in deviant behavior will be greatest in the lower levels of the society.

Our hypothesis can be summarized as follows: The disparity between what lower-class youth are led to want and what is actually available to them is the source of a major problem of adjustment.[8] Adolescents who form delinquent subcultures, we suggest, have internalized an emphasis upon conventional goals. Faced with limitations on legitimate avenues of access to these goals, and unable to revise their aspirations downward, they experience intense frustrations; the exploration of nonconformist alternatives may be the result.

Success Values in American Life

WE HAVE NOTED that the success-goals toward which Americans are enjoined to orient themselves are not class-bounded; that is, people are not, so the ideology goes, forever restricted

---

further discussion of the relationship between pressures toward deviance and the availability of illegitimate opportunity, see R. A. Cloward, "Illegitimate Means, Anomie, and Deviant Behavior," *American Sociological Review,* Vol. 24, No. 2 (April 1959), pp. 164-76, and Chap. 6, *infra.*

8. The young acquire definitions of the availability of success-goals from older persons with whom they interact. For our purposes, "actual" and "anticipated" failure to improve one's social position are functional equivalents. This point of view is entirely consonant, for example, with experimental studies showing that young Negro children become aware of invidious color distinctions in our society even though they may not have been directly exposed to discriminatory racial practices.

to the station into which they were born or even to the one above. But to what extent are success values internalized by people in different parts of the society? Precisely what is it that people aspire toward?

THE CLASS DISTRIBUTION OF ASPIRATIONS

We have hypothesized that adolescents feel pressures for deviant behavior when they experience marked discrepancies between their aspirations and opportunities for achievement. To support our assumption that delinquent subcultures arise primarily among lower-class adolescent males in large cities, we must, therefore, demonstrate that these youngsters are exposed to greater discrepancies between aspirations and opportunities than are persons located elsewhere in the social structure. Before we review some of the relevant evidence, an important distinction should be made. "Aspiration" may be defined in at least two ways. First, we may ask: How high does the individual aspire, *irrespective of his present position?* We may also ask: How high does he aspire *in relation to his present position?*

Absolute Aspirations—In a recent article, Hyman assembled an array of evidence on aspirations in American society, culled principally from public-opinion surveys.[9] In general, these data reveal differences in absolute aspiration among persons in various social strata. For example, when respondents in a national survey were asked to express their preference for one of three types of job ("a low income but secure job; a job with good pay but with a 50-50 risk of losing it; or a job with extremely high income and great risk"), the responses differed markedly by class. With each upward step in the social hierarchy, the proportion who chose the high-income but great-risk alternative increased. Only 14 per cent of youth from laboring families chose this alternative as contrasted with 31 per cent

9. H. H. Hyman, "The Value Systems of Different Classes: A Social-Psychological Contribution to the Analysis of Stratification," in Reinhard Bendix and S. M. Lipset, eds., *Class, Status and Power* (Glencoe, Ill.: Free Press, 1953), pp. 432-34.

from executive and professional families. This general finding, confirmed by the results of several other studies, led Hyman to suggest that "the poor cannot accept the risk involved in becoming less poor." The results of a study of high-school seniors conducted by Empey support this conclusion.[10] Empey asked members of his sample to state the occupations that they hoped to enter. When their choices were ranked on the basis of generally accepted criteria of occupational status in American society, the aspirations of middle- and upper-class respondents were found to be consistently higher than those of seniors from lower-class families.

It should be noted that our hypothesis does not depend upon showing that a *large proportion* of persons in the lower class exhibit a high level of aspiration; it is sufficient to show that a *significant number* of lower-class members aspire beyond their means if it can also be demonstrated that these same persons contribute disproportionately to the ranks of delinquent subcultures. In this connection, the conclusions of several studies might be cited. In a comparative study of drug-users and nonusers, Gerard and Kornetsky concluded:

> Regardless of the actual familial socioeconomic status, familial needs for high attainment in education and vocational areas play very important roles in the developmental experiences of many of the addict patients. Their families inculcated high levels of aspiration and expectation into them, yet failed to strengthen their capacities to attain their goals through realistic appraisal of their environments and acceptance of the need to work toward subordinate goals in the paths to their more final objectives. Denial of personal limitations, wish-fulfilling distortions of reality, and status-orientation at the expense of satisfaction are some of the prominent features of the family backgrounds of the adolescent addicts which are plausibly related to their aspiration-achievement discrepancies. . . . Unrealistic and excessive aspirations are likely to be a heavy burden for even the most intact ego.[11]

---

10. L. T. Empey, "Social Class and Occupational Aspiration: A Comparison of Absolute and Relative Measurement," *American Sociological Review,* Vol. 21, No. 6 (Dec. 1956), p. 706.

11. D. L. Gerard and Conon Kornetsky, "Adolescent Opiate Addiction—A Study of Control and Addict Subjects," *Psychiatric Quarterly,* Vol. 29 (April 1955), p. 483.

Finestone drew similar conclusions from studies of drug addicts in Chicago. He noted that addiction among lower-class Negro adolescents "represents a reaction to a feeling of exclusion from access to the means toward the goals of our society."[12] These observations suggest that youngsters who partipate in delinquent subcultures may experience serious discontent with their position in the social structure.

Relative Aspirations—The studies we have cited support the general conclusion that there are class differentials in absolute level of aspiration. We get a rather different picture of the relationship between social class and aspirations if we look at the height to which people aspire in relation to the point from which they start.

The results of several studies tend to confirm the hypothesis that most Americans, whatever their social position, are dissatisfied with their income. There are, however, social-class differences in the degree of dissatisfaction. In general, the poor desire a proportionately larger increase in income than do persons in higher strata. As Hyman says, "*Relatively* speaking, the wealthier need and want less of an increase. . . . As one goes up in the economic ladder, the increment of income desired decreases."[13] The absolute or dollar increase in income sought is far greater among the wealthy than among the poor, but the proportion of current income that this increment represents decreases with each upward step in the scale. Empey reports a similar finding: almost all the seniors in his sample hoped to improve their position over that of their father, but the degree of relative occupational aspiration decreased significantly with each upward step in the social scale.[14] Thus we may conclude that persons in the lower reaches of society experience a relatively greater sense of position discontent despite the fact that their absolute aspirations are less lofty.

The concept of relative aspirations gives us a better gauge of position discontent than can be derived by comparing the

12. Harold Finestone, "Cats, Kicks, and Color," *Social Problems*, Vol. 5, No. 1 (July 1957), p. 13.
13. Hyman, *op. cit.*, pp. 435-36.
14. Empey, *op. cit.*, pp. 706-07.

heights to which people in various social classes aspire. And it is position discontent that is of greatest relevance to our theory. If, as we have suggested, lower-class persons experience relatively greater dissatisfaction with their present position and also have fewer legitimate ways of changing their status, then they should experience greater pressures toward deviant behavior.

TYPES OF ASPIRATION

It is somewhat misleading to assert, as we have done, that there are class differences in level of aspiration, for this implies that all members of a given class share the same goals. In this section, therefore, we shall try to qualify this implication by developing a typology of goals within the lower class. Our typology is limited to the lower class because, as we have pointed out, this is the primary locus of delinquent subcultures.

In his classic study of life in an urban slum, William F. Whyte divided lower-class male adolescents into two broad categories: the "college boys," who are "primarily interested in social advancement," and the "corner boys," who are "primarily interested in their local community."[15] The two groups, in other words, are differentiated essentially in terms of aspirations. The college boys identify with the middle-class style of life; the corner boys, on the other hand, are relatively content with their lower-class life-style. The "social advancement" sought by the college boys therefore means rising into the middle class.

Since Whyte's study, other writers also have assumed that "ambitious" lower-class youth wish to rise into the middle class. Bloch and Niederhoffer, for example, take this view: "The lower-class boy . . . absorbs dominant middle-class values which set goals for him."[16] Cohen's recent work on

---

15. W. F. Whyte, *Street Corner Society: The Social Structure of an Italian Slum*, Enl. Ed. (Chicago: The University of Chicago Press, 1955), p. 97.

16. Herbert Bloch and Arthur Niederhoffer, *The Gang: A Study*

delinquency also assumes that many lower-class youth seek to affiliate with the middle class: "It is a plausible assumption . . . that the working-class boy whose status is low in middle-class terms cares about that status, that this status confronts him with a general problem of adjustment."[17] Indeed, Cohen suggests that delinquency results when access to this goal is limited: "The delinquent subculture, we suggest, is a way of dealing with . . . status problems: certain children are denied status in the respectable society because they cannot meet the criteria of the respectable status system. The delinquent subculture deals with these problems by providing criteria of status which these children *can* meet."[18] Using Whyte's classification of "corner boys" and "college boys" as a starting point, Cohen adds the category of "delinquent boys." He describes these three modes of adaptation as follows:

> (1) A certain proportion of working-class boys [the "college boys"] accept the challenge of the middle-class status system and play the status game by the middle-class rules. . . .
>
> (2) Another response, perhaps the most common, is what we may call the "stable corner-boy response." It represents an acceptance of the corner-boy way of life and an effort to make the best of a situation. . . .
>
> (3) The delinquent response . . . differs from the stable corner-boy response. The hallmark of the delinquent subculture is the explicit and wholesale repudiation of middle-class standards and the adoption of their very antithesis. *The corner-boy culture is not specifically delinquent* . . . ; [it] temporizes with middle-class morality; the full-fledged delinquent subculture does not.[19]

The assumption that many lower-class youth seek to affiliate with the middle class has come under sharp attack by other students of delinquency. Kitsuse and Dietrick, for example, question whether available evidence supports this contention:

---

in Adolescent Behavior (New York: Philosophical Library, 1958), p. 109.

17. A. K. Cohen, *Delinquent Boys: The Culture of the Gang* (Glencoe, Ill.: Free Press, 1955), p. 129.

18. *Ibid.*, p. 121.

19. *Ibid.*, pp. 128-30.

Cohen's image of the working-class boy . . . standing alone to face humiliation at the hands of middle-class agents is difficult to comprehend. To add to this picture of the pre-teen and teen-ager an intense desire to gain status in the middle-class system, which when frustrated provides sufficient basis for a reaction-formation response, is to overdraw him beyond recognition.[20]

Cohen's tendency to equate high levels of aspiration among lower-class youth with an orientation toward the middle class implies that lower-class youth who are dissatisfied with their position (1) internalize middle-class values and (2) seek to leave their class of origin and affiliate with the carriers of middle-class values. We submit, however, that this may be true of *some* discontented lower-class youth but not of all. It is our view that many discontented lower-class youth do not wish to adopt a middle-class way of life or to disrupt their present associations and negotiate passage into middle-class groups. The solution they seek entails the acquisition of higher position in terms of lower-class rather than middle-class criteria.

Our point may be illustrated by referring again to Miller's typology of lower-class adolescents (pp. 72-73). He describes boys of type 1 as " 'stable' lower-class [members] who, for all practical purposes, do not aspire to higher status." This category thus seems to be identical with what Whyte and Cohen refer to as "corner boys."[21] According to Miller, "There is evidence that type 1, the 'nonaspiring' lower-class youngster, is far more common than generally supposed, and that this group does not seem to be getting smaller, and may be getting larger."[22] As it turns out, however, Miller's own data raise serious question about whether a category of stable, nonaspiring lower-class youth exists at all. Consider only the following description of this category:

---

20. J. I. Kitsuse and D. C. Dietrick, "*Delinquent Boys:* A Critique," *American Sociological Review*, Vol. 24, No. 2 (April 1959), pp. 211-12.

21. See Miller's comments in W. C. Kvaraceus and W. B. Miller, *Delinquent Behavior: Culture and the Individual* (Washington, D. C.: National Education Association, 1959), p. 72.

22. *Ibid.*, p. 73.

In common with most adolescents in American society, the lower-class corner group manifests a dominant concern with "status." What differentiates this type of group from others, however, is the particular set of criteria and weighting thereof by which "status" is defined. In general, status is achieved and maintained by demonstrated possession of the valued qualities of lower-class culture. . . . It is important to stress once more that the individual orients to [success-goals] as they are defined within lower-class society.[23]

Thus Miller, despite his clear recognition of the importance of status striving among corner boys, tends to classify lower-class youth as "nonaspiring" if they do not orient themselves toward the middle class. Once we recognize that lower-class youngsters may experience intense position discontent without being oriented toward the middle class, we can classify lower-class youth to distinguish between boys who define success-goals in essentially lower-class terms and those who define them in essentially middle-class terms.

Evidence from studies of social stratification suggests that the criteria people use to rank one another vary depending upon social-class position.[24] That is, there is not uniform agreement throughout the class structure as to the basis for invidious distinctions. The upper-class person tends to rank others primarily in terms of style of life and ancestry; the middle-class person, in terms of money and morality; the lower-class person, in terms of money alone. Except for the lower class, money is a significant but not a sufficient criterion of high rank; it must be translated into a way of life that symbolizes such things as "respectability." The lower class,

23. W. B. Miller, "Lower Class Culture as a Generating Milieu of Gang Delinquency," *Journal of Social Issues,* Vol. 14, No. 3 (1958), p. 15.

24. See, *e.g.,* W. L. Warner and P. S. Lunt, *The Social Life of a Modern Community* (New Haven: Yale University Press, 1941), Vol. 1, Yankee City Series, p. 91. The fact that socioeconomic position influences perceptions of the number of ranks and the criteria distinguishing ranks is evident from the data gathered by Warner and Lunt, although they did not stress this point. It remained for various critics of the Yankee City Series to emphasize the importance of class differentials in perceptions of social divisions. For a summary of these criticisms, see Ruth Rosner Kornhauser, "The Warner Approach to Social Stratification," in Bendix and Lipset, eds., *op. cit.,* pp. 224-55.

by contrast, appears to make fewer distinctions in terms of life-style and social reputation. For many lower-class members, society is divided into two general categories of persons: those who have money, and those who do not. In this respect as in others, however, the lower class is extremely heterogeneous: money may be an important criterion of success for some but not for all. To many, the middle-class style of life may be the controlling model; the goal of such persons would be to rise into the middle class. Success within the lower-class world is doubtless the chief goal for many others, however; these persons are interested in maintaining their general membership affiliations but wish to rise within that structure.

What we are here suggesting is that types of aspiration can be classified on the basis of whether or not the aspirer envisages a change in membership group. For the lower-class boy who seeks to change his economic position without shifting his style of life or associations, his membership group—the lower class—continues to be his primary reference group. However, lower-class youth in the "college boy" category envisage a definite change in membership group. They take the style of life of the middle-class world as a frame of reference and are oriented toward eventual affiliation with the carriers of middle-class values. Furthermore, for some of these boys the anticipated shift in membership group may assume greater importance than potential shifts in economic position. There are doubtless many "college boys" who, if faced with a choice between a high-paying position as a master craftsman (or a racketeer) and a low-paying position as a teacher, would choose the latter, for these youngsters are seeking a new way of life, a new definition of reputability, a new set of associations. Hence they tend to devalue their membership group and to seek acceptance in a group that is less invidiously defined, if less well remunerated. Members of lower-middle-class professions—teachers, for example—probably accord higher value to respectability and life-style than to money as such. This is not to say that they would not like to improve their financial positions, but they probably would not relinquish their style of life and social position in order to maximize financial gain (for example, by entering a manual occupation that is more highly remunerated than teaching).

Once we recognize that level of aspiration may entail a change in economic position or in reference group or both, we can then classify lower-class youth as follows:

	ORIENTATION OF LOWER-CLASS YOUTH	
CATEGORIES OF LOWER-CLASS YOUTH	Toward Membership in Middle Class	Toward Improvement in Economic Position
Type I	+	+
Type II	+	−
Type III	−	+
Type IV	−	−

Types I and II are composed of the "college boys" so vividly portrayed by Whyte. Those of type I place *equal* emphasis on change in economic position and in reference group. Youth of type II regard a change in membership group as a more important goal than a change in economic position. Youth of type III are oriented toward a definition of success that stresses a change in economic position, but they do not seek to change their style of life or to affiliate with the carriers of middle-class values. Those of type IV are genuinely nonaspiring, for they do not exhibit serious distress about remaining in their present membership-group position *and* their present economic status. These four categories, then, are distinguished by the criteria of success that they employ. All these criteria define ends that come within the scope of "culturally approved goals," although the particular goals vary.

One potential value of this typology is that it may correlate with a typology of delinquent behavior. Youngsters of types I and II may react to status discontent differently from those of type III. For example, it may be that property destruction is a type of delinquency that is characteristic of types I and II, according to Cohen's contention that youngsters who are thwarted in the quest for middle-class status may, by a process of reaction-formation, come to devalue what they secretly prize (see Chap. 5). The members of certain esoteric adolescent cults, such as the "hipster" groups which emphasize jazz and sex, may also be frustrated aspirants for middle-class status; although not specifically delinquent, these cults are on the borderline between tolerated and illegal behavior. However, we do not think that the seriously delinquent constituents of the criminal, conflict, and retreatist subcultures are drawn from types I and II. It is our view that they are more likely to be from type III, and that the process by which such persons become delinquent has less to do with reaction-formation than with the selective withdrawal or qualification of sentiments supporting the legitimacy of institutional norms (see pp. 16-20). The literature on lower-class delinquent subcultures is replete with references to the conspicuous consumption of wealth: delinquents repeatedly remark that they want "big cars," "flashy clothes," and "swell dames" (see Chaps. 6 and 7). These symbols of success, framed primarily in economic terms rather than in terms of middle-class life-styles, suggest to us that the participants in delinquent subcultures are seeking higher status within their own cultural milieu. If legitimate paths to higher status become restricted, then the delinquent subculture provides alternative (albeit illegal) avenues. Our discussion in the remaining chapters of this book is therefore concerned primarily with type III youth, for these, we believe, are the principal constituents of delinquent subcultures.

This typology, it might also be noted, can also be used in respecifying the much discussed conflict between lower-class youth and carriers of middle-class values—a conflict which is often said to have a direct bearing upon the etiology of delinquency. Youth of types I and II, who aspire to enter the middle class, exhibit values that are essentially congruent with those of the middle-class carriers with whom they come in contact in school and settlement houses. Value differences are therefore not a source of conflict for these adolescents. If pressures for deviant behavior do arise among such boys, the reason may be, as Cohen argues, that many of them lack the skills and attitudes that make conformity with middle-class values possible. Hence they are led to devalue what they secretly desire but cannot achieve.

Type III youth, we contend, experience the greatest conflict with middle-class carriers, who not only devalue the lower-class style of life and seek to induce a desire for change in membership group but also devalue the materialistic success-goals toward which type III adolescents orient themselves. Type III youth, in short, are looked down upon both for what they do *not* want (*i.e.*, the middle-class style of life) and for what they *do* want (*i.e.*, "crass materialism").

Unlike type III youth, who are devalued because they want the "wrong" things, type IV youth—the "corner boys," who are not strongly oriented toward social mobility in any sphere—are criticized principally because they are "unmotivated." They doubtless resent the invidious definition of their way of life implicit in their contacts with middle-class agents, but this resentment can be largely managed by minimizing interaction. Thus the corner boy plays hookey from school and avoids the settlement house.

Note that our hypothesis challenges the view that the school participates in producing delinquency by imposing middle-class success-goals which lower-class youth cannot achieve. Type III youth are alienated from the school because of a conflict regarding *appropriate* success-goals; this conflict simply reinforces their own definitions of criteria of success. If these youngsters subsequently become delinquent, it is chiefly because they anticipate that legitimate channels to the goals they seek will be limited or closed.

Barriers to Legitimate Opportunity

"EDUCATION," Lipset and Bendix have remarked, "has become the principal avenue for upward mobility in most industrial nations," particularly in the United States. The number of nonmanual occupations that can be fruitfully pursued without extensive educational background is diminishing and will doubtless continue to do so as our occupational structure becomes increasingly technical and specialized.[25] This being the

25. S. M. Lipset and Reinhard Bendix, *Social Mobility in Industrial Society* (Berkeley and Los Angeles, Calif.: University of California Press, 1959), p. 91.

case, we might focus our discussion of barriers to opportunity on the question of barriers to education.

It should be pointed out, however, that educational attainment does not necessarily enable the lower-class person to overcome the disadvantages of his low social origins.

> Thus workers' sons with "some college" education are about as well off [financially] as a group as the sons of nonmanual fathers who have graduated from high school but not attended college. Similarly, high school graduation for the sons of workers results in their being only slightly better off than the sons of nonmanual workers who have not completed high school.[26]

To the extent that one's social origins, despite education, still constitute a restraining influence on upward movement, we may assume that other objective consequences of social position intervene, such as the ability of one's family to give one a start in a business or profession by supplying funds or influential contacts. Nevertheless, the lower-class boy who fails to secure an education is likely to discover that he has little chance of improving his circumstances. Hence acute discontent may be generated, leading in turn to aberrant behavior.

Although education is widely valued in our society, it is not equally valued among the several social classes. Hyman has summarized a national survey in which a sample of 500 youths was asked: "About how much schooling do you think most young men need these days to get along well in the world?" The results are shown in Table 2.

Table 2
Class Differentials in Emphasis on the Need for College Education
*(201 Males Aged 14 to 20)**

Socioeconomic Position of Family	*Per Cent Recommending a College Education*	*Number of Respondents*
Wealthy and prosperous	74	39
Middle class	63	100
Lower class	42	62

* H. H. Hyman, "The Value Systems of Different Classes: A Social-Psychological Contribution to the Analysis of Stratification," in Reinhard Bendix and S. M. Lipset, eds., *Class, Status and Power* (Glencoe, Ill.: Free Press, 1953), p. 432.

26. *Ibid.*, p. 99.

Table 2, like others that Hyman presents, shows that a sizable proportion of persons at each point in the social structure consider a college education desirable. Even in the lowest level of society, the proportion who emphasize the need for education is not small. But it is also true that there are strong differences from one stratum to another. In general, the proportion recommending higher education increases with each upward step in the socioeconomic hierarchy.

Given the fundamental importance of education to social advancement, how are we to account for these class differentials in emphasis on the value of education? Why is it that a substantial proportion of lower-class males aged 14 to 20 do *not* orient themselves toward acquiring higher education?

CULTURAL BARRIERS

The lower class is still influenced to some extent by the persistence of values brought to our shores by immigrants from various peasant cultures in which education was not greatly stressed or was even devalued. Toby has remarked on this point in his comparison of Jewish and Italian immigrants and their descendants.[27]

27. See Jackson Toby, "Hoodlum or Businessman: An American Dilemma," in Marshall Sklare, ed., *The Jews: Social Patterns of an American Group* (Glencoe, Ill.: Free Press, 1958), pp. 548-50, from which the excerpts that follow are taken. There are, of course, other features of lower-class socialization that inhibit mobility. Such traits as the inability to defer gratification, the unwillingness to postpone marriage and family, the lack of readiness to minimize obligations to family of orientation and to maximize investment in occupational preparation, and the inability to sever peer ties and to move easily into new groups are apparently more characteristic of the lower than of the middle class. A number of studies have shown that the capacity to defer gratification, for example, is stressed by middle-class parents to a greater extent than by lower-class parents. Similarly, middle-class youth are encouraged if not expected to minimize kinship ties and to devote their energies to occupational achievement, whereas among certain groups in the lower class young people are expected to maintain close ties with the family. These kinship obligations often interfere with occupational obligations and thus detract from occupational achievement. In these respects, then, the lower-class child is not so well prepared as his middle-class counterpart to take advantage of traditional avenues to higher position. For a review of studies bearing

Jews and Italians came to the United States in large numbers at about the same time—the turn of the century—and both settled in urban areas. There was, however, a very different attitude toward intellectual accomplishment in the two cultures. Jews from Eastern Europe regarded religious study as the most important activity for an adult male. The rabbi enjoyed great prestige because he was a scholar, a teacher, a logician. . . . Life in America gave a secular emphasis to the Jewish reverence for learning. Material success is a more important motive than salvation for American youngsters, Jewish as well as Christian, and secular education is better training for business and professional careers than Talmudic exegesis. Nevertheless, intellectual achievement continued to be valued by Jews—and to have measurable effects. Second-generation Jewish students did homework diligently, got high grades, went to college in disproportionate numbers, and scored high on intelligence tests. Two thousand years of preparation lay behind them.

Immigrants from Southern Italy, on the other hand, tended to regard formal education either as a frill or as a source of dangerous ideas from which the minds of the young should be protected. They remembered Sicily, where a child who attended school regularly was a rarity. In the United States, many Southern Italian immigrants maintained the same attitudes. They resented compulsory school-attendance laws and prodded their children to go to work and become economic assets as soon as possible. They did not realize that education has more importance in an urban-industrial society than in a semi-feudal one. . . . [Children] accepted their parents' conception of the school as worthless and thereby lost their best opportunity for social ascent.

Second-generation Italian youngsters, having failed in school, tended to quit and go to work. But employment oportunities for the uneducated do not usually afford much chance for advancement. Consequently, according to Toby, frustrations increased and the young turned to illegitimate activities.

Second-generation Italian boys became delinquent in disproportionately large numbers. In New York City, 39 per cent of the white delinquents of foreign-born parents in 1930 were of Italian origin, although less than 22 per cent of the white families with foreign-born heads were of that ethnic group. In Chicago, second-generation Italian boys in the years of 1927-33 had an appearance rate in the Cook County Juvenile Court twice as high as white boys generally.

---

upon class-related attitudes and values influencing mobility patterns, see Lipset and Bendix, *op. cit.*

The figures for Jewish adolescents were quite different:

Second-generation Jewish youths had less reason to become hoodlums . . . for their chances in the marketplace were excellent. . . . In New York City, for example, Jewish youngsters constituted in 1930 about a quarter of the white delinquents—although the Jewish population at large was estimated to be about a third of the total white population of the city. . . . Crude though these data are, they show that the probability of becoming a hoodlum was not the same for second-generation Jews and second-generation Italians.

Toby concludes that "some youths become hoodlums instead of businessmen, not because they lack the ability to succeed legitimately . . . but because they find out too late the relationship between school adjustment and [upward social mobility]."[28]

STRUCTURAL BARRIERS

Despite their importance, these cultural barriers, we contend, do not fully account for class differentials in the values placed on education. Success-themes, as we have noted, are widely diffused throughout our society. In fact, there is reason to think that lower-class persons experience a *relatively* greater sense of position discontent than persons higher in the social structure. By the same token, it is doubtful that lower-class persons are unaware of the general importance assigned to education in our society or of the relationship between education and social mobility. But they are probably also very much aware of their limited opportunities to secure access to

28. Whyte made much the same point in his study of lower-class youth (*op. cit.*, p. 273): "Our society places a high value upon social mobility. . . . To get ahead, the Cornerville man must move either in the world of business and Republican politics or in the world of Democratic politics and the rackets. He cannot rise in both worlds at once. . . . If he advances in the first world, he is recognized by society at large as a successful man, but he is recognized in Cornerville only as an alien to the district. If he advances in the second world, he achieves recognition in Cornerville but becomes a social outcast to the respectable people elsewhere. The entire course of the corner boy's training in the social life of his district prepares him for a career in the rackets or in Democratic politics."

educational facilities. Educational achievement is not just a matter of favorable attitudes; opportunities must be available to those who seek them. For many members of the lower class, struggling to maintain a minimum level of subsistence, the goal of advanced education must seem remote indeed. In a family that can scarcely afford food, shelter, and clothing, pressure is exerted upon the young to leave school early in order to secure employment and thereby help the family. In a recent study of an extensive sample of adolescents in Nashville, Tennessee, Reiss and Rhodes found that most adolescents who quit school did so not because they devalued education but because they wanted to go to work immediately. Quitting school, their data show, is not necessarily a negative or rebellious response to compulsory-attendance laws but may be a necessary response to economic pressures.[29]

In the past few decades, a variety of studies have concluded that there are marked class differentials in access to educational facilities.[30] The lower the social position of one's father, the less likely that one can take advantage of educational opportunities. Furthermore, class differentials in access to educational facilities are not explained by differences in intelligence. If children from various social classes who have the same general intelligence are compared, differentials in chances to acquire an education still obtain.

The influence of economic barriers to education can be inferred from studies of situations in which these barriers have been temporarily relaxed. Warner and his associates, for example, observed a "sharp increase in college and high school

---

29. A. J. Reiss and A. L. Rhodes, "Are Educational Norms and Goals of Conforming and Delinquent Adolescents Influenced by Group Position in American Society?" *Journal of Negro Education* (Summer 1959), pp. 262-66.

30. See W. L. Warner, R. J. Havighurst, and M. B. Loeb, *Who Shall Be Educated—The Challenge of Unequal Opportunities* (New York: Harper & Bros., 1944); Lipset and Bendix, *op. cit.;* Elbridge Sibley, "Some Demographic Clues to Stratification," *American Sociological Review,* Vol. 7 (June 1942), pp. 322-30; and George F. Zuok, "The Findings and Recommendations of the President's Commission on Higher Education," *Bulletin of the American Association of University Professors,* Vol. 35 (Spring 1949), pp. 17-22.

enrollment [resulting from] the establishing of the National Youth Administration student-aid program in 1935."[31] In a more recent study, Mulligan examined the proportions of students from various socioeconomic strata enrolled in a Midwestern university before and during the G. I. Bill of Rights educational program. Not surprisingly, his data show that as a result of the government-aid program a larger proportion of students was drawn from the lower echelons of the society. This strongly suggests that the lower class contains many persons who desire higher education but cannot ordinarily afford to acquire it.[32]

It is our view that class differentials in the value placed on education reflect in large part differentials in the availability of educational opportunities. What we are suggesting is that lower-class attitudes toward education are adaptive; that is, expectations are scaled down to accord with the realistic limitations on access to educational opportunities. Educational attainment and related forms of goal-striving are thus eschewed not so much because they are inherently devalued as because access to them is relatively restricted. Although these cultural orientations, once crystallized, persist as major obstacles to the utilization of opportunity, it should be remembered that they emerged initially as adaptive responses to socially structured deprivations.[33]

---

31. W. L. Warner *et al., op. cit.,* p. 53. Commenting on financial barriers to high-school attendance, Warner and his associates note: "There is a substantial out-of-pocket cost attached to attendance at a 'free' high school. . . . Students can go to school and spend little or no money. But [the poor] are barred from many of the school activities, they cannot even take regular laboratory courses, and they must go around in what is to high-school youngsters the supremely embarrassing condition of having no change to rattle in their pockets, no money to contribute to a party, no possibility of being independent in their dealings with their friends" (pp. 53-54). For a further discussion of these and related matters, see A. B. Hollingshead, *Elmtown's Youth* (New York: John Wiley & Sons, 1949).

32. R. A. Mulligan, "Socio-Economic Background and College Enrollment," *American Sociological Review,* Vol. 16, No. 2 (April 1951), pp. 188-96.

33. In this connection, Hyman (*op. cit.,* p. 437) summarizes data which show that there are distinct differentials by class in judgments regarding the accessibility of success-goals. Thus 63 per cent of

Alternative Avenues to Success-Goals

IF traditional channels to higher position, such as education, are restricted for large categories of people, then pressures will mount for the use of alternative routes. Studies have shown that some lower-class persons orient themselves toward occupations in the field of entertainment and sports.[34] People of modest social origins who have been conspicuously successful in these spheres often become salient models for the young in depressed sectors of the society. The heavyweight champion, the night-club singer, the baseball star—these symbolize the possibility of achieving success in conventional terms despite poor education and low social origins. The businessman, the physicist, and the physician, on the other hand, occupy roles to which the lower-class youngster has little access because of his limited educational opportunities. By orienting himself toward occupations which offer some hope of success in spite of poor social origins and education, the lower-class boy follows a legitimate alternative to traditional avenues to success-goals.

But the dilemma of many lower-class people is that their efforts to locate alternative avenues to success-goals are futile, for these alternatives are often just as resticted as educational channels, if not more so. One has only to think of the many lower-class adolescents who go into the "fight game," hoping to win great social rewards—money and glamor—by sheer physical exertion and stamina. A few succeed, but the over-

one sample of persons in professional and managerial positions felt that the "years ahead held good chances for advancement" while only 48 per cent of a sample of factory workers gave this response. Furthermore, the factory workers were more likely to think that "getting along well with the boss" or being a "friend or relative of the boss" were important determinants of mobility; professional and executive personnel were more likely to stress "quality of work" and "energy and willingness." Such findings suggest that lower-class persons perceive differentials in opportunity associated with social origins. See Chap. 5 for a further discussion of this matter.

34. *Ibid.*, p. 437.

whelming majority are destined to fail. For these lower-class youth there seems no legitimate way out of poverty. In a society that did not encourage them to hold high aspirations, to devalue their station in life, to set their sights high, they might adjust more easily to their impoverished circumstances; but since social worth is so closely identified wtih social position in our society, discontent and frustration pervade the lower reaches of the social order.[35]

When pressures from unfulfilled aspirations and blocked opportunity become sufficiently intense, many lower-class youth turn away from legitimate channels, adopting other means, beyond conventional mores, which might offer a possible route to success-goals. As Merton suggests, "It is only when a system of cultural values extols, virtually above all else, certain *common* success-goals *for the population at large* while the social structure rigorously restricts or completely closes access to approved modes of reaching these goals *for a considerable part of the same population,* that deviant behavior ensues on a large scale."[36] Discrepancies between aspirations and legitimate avenues thus produce intense pressures for the use of illegitimate alternatives. Many lower-class persons, in short, are the victims of a contradiction between the goals toward which they have been led to orient themselves and socially structured means of striving for these goals. Under these conditions, there is an acute pressure to depart from institutional norms and to adopt illegitimate alterntaives. Merton puts this theory as follows:

Of those located in the lower reaches of the social structure, the culture makes incompatible demands. On the one hand, they are asked to orient their conduct toward the prospect of large wealth . . . and on the other, they are largely denied effective opportunities to do so institutionally. The consequence of this structural inconsistency is a high rate of deviant behavior. The equilibrium between

35. Poverty alone, as Durkheim, Merton, and others have made abundantly clear, is not necessarily a source of deviant behavior. But poverty coupled with culturally approved high aspirations under conditions of limited opportunity can be an important source of pressures toward deviance.

36. Merton, *op. cit.*, p. 146.

culturally designated ends and means becomes highly unstable with progressive emphasis on attaining the prestige-laden ends by any means whatsoever.[37]

What we have been saying only points up all the more the fallacy of attributing delinquent responses in the lower class to inadequate socialization or simply to conformity with lower-class values. One can accept these perspectives only if it is assumed either that the lower class is highly disorganized and demoralized or that a large number of lower-class persons are unacculturated to the system of norms that prevails in our society generally. We contend, on the other hand, that widespread tendencies toward delinquent practices in the lower class are modes of adaptation to structured strains and inconsistencies within the social order.[38] These modes of adaptation are then passed on from one generation to another.

Although we have been focusing upon class differentials in pressures toward deviant behavior, it should also be noted that these pressures affect males more than females and adolescents more than younger or older people. It is primarily the male who must go into the marketplace to seek employment, make a career for himself, and support a family. It is during adolescence that decisions regarding occupational selection and routes to occupational success must be made. The adolescent male in the lower class is therefore most vulnerable to pressures toward deviance arising from discrepancies between aspirations and opportunities for achievement. If educational facilities appear beyond his financial reach, life may seem to hold very few prospects for him. The "permanent" quality of this dilemma makes it all the more acute. If the problem were simply one of achieving adult status, it would be less severe, for adolescents are well aware that adult status will be accorded them eventually. But improving one's lot in life constitutes a more enduring problem. We suggest that many lower-class

37. *Ibid.*

38. For a further discussion of adaptations to limited opportunity, see Oscar Handlin, *The Newcomers: Negroes and Puerto Ricans in a Changing Metropolis* (Cambridge: Harvard University Press, 1959), Chap. 4.

male adolescents experience desperation born of the certainty that their position in the economic structure is relatively fixed and immutable—a desperation made all the more poignant by their exposure to a cultural ideology in which failure to orient oneself upward is regarded as a moral defect and failure to become mobile as proof of it.

Delinquent subcultures, we believe, represent specialized modes of adaptation to this problem of adjustment. Two of these subcultures—the criminal and the conflict—provide illegal avenues to success-goals. The retreatist subculture consists of a loosely structured group of persons who have withdrawn from competition in the larger society, who anticipate defeat and now seek escape from the burden of failure. We turn now to a discussion of the processes by which these subcultures evolve.

CHAPTER 5

The Evolution of Delinquent Subcultures

WHEN A SOCIAL SYSTEM generates severe problems of adjustment for occupants of a particular social status, it is possible that a collective challenge to the legitimacy of the established rules of conduct will emerge. As we have noted, this is especially likely to occur where a democratic ideology exists, espousing equality of opportunity and universally high aspirations for success. Since discrepancies between aspiration and opportunity are likely to be experienced more intensely at some social positions than at others, persons in status locations where the discrepancy is most acute may develop a common perception and sense of indignation about their disadvantages as contrasted with the advantages of others. Interaction among those sharing the same problem may provide encouragement for the withdrawal of sentiments in support of the established system of norms. Once freed of allegiance to the existing set of rules, such persons may devise or adopt delinquent means of achieving success.

A collective delinquent solution to an adjustment problem is more likely to evolve by this process in a society in which the legitimacy of social rules can be questioned apart from their moral validity. For example, it would be relatively unlikely to develop in a tradition-bound, self-sufficient folk society where a complex network of closely integrated moral sentiments reinforce acceptance of the dominant norms. In such a society an intricate interweaving of sacred and secular motivations defines whatever is as right. In the secular, competitive, impersonal, mass society of the modern Western world, on the other hand, the necessity for highly specialized activities has enormously complicated the task of maintaining a cohesive and stable order.[1] It has become more and more difficult to identify universally shared moral sentiments which will guarantee allegiance to the dominant norms of the society. The long, complex chains of relationships required to integrate the social and economic life of the society permit the development of special beliefs, values, and norms at different social locations and the dissolution of links in the established structure of beliefs, values, and norms. What seems expedient, rational, and efficient often becomes separable from what is traditional, sacred, and moral as a basis for the imputation of legitimacy. Under such conditions it is difficult for persons at different social positions to agree about the forms of conduct that are both expedient and morally right. Once this separation takes place, the supporting structure of the existing system of norms becomes highly vulnerable. When the individual defines his commitment to the dominant system of norms on the basis of expediency rather than moral validity, his sentiments may become attached to some

1. There is an extensive body of theoretical and empirical observations in anthropological and sociological literature distinguishing the characteristics and problems of folk and urban societies. See, *e.g.*, Robert Redfield, "The Folk Society," *American Journal of Sociology*, Vol. 52 (1947), pp. 293-308; and Howard Becker, "Sacred and Secular Societies," *Social Forces*, Vol. 28 (1950), pp. 361-76.

competing set of norms more to his advantage. It is even possible that he may attribute legitimacy on the grounds of expediency to rules of conduct that he regards at the same time as morally inferior to some competing set of norms.

To understand the growth of delinquent subcultures, we must identify more explicitly the social conditions within which this alienation from established norms and acceptance of illegitimate models of behavior occurs. It seems evident that the members of a newly emerging delinquent subculture must pass through a complex process of change in attitudes toward themselves, other persons, and the established social order before such a major shift in allegiance can take place. First, they must be freed from commitment to and belief in the legitimacy of certain aspects of the existing organization of means. They must be led to question the validity of various conventional codes of conduct as an appropriate guide for their own actions before accepting a model of behavior involving forbidden acts. Secondly, they must join with others in seeking a solution to their adjustment problems rather than attempt to solve them alone. Thirdly, they must be provided with appropriate means for handling the problems of guilt and fear which new recruits to the subculture sometimes experience as a result of engaging in acts of deviance. Finally, they must face no obstacles to the possibility of joint problem-solving. In this chapter we shall consider each of these four necessary conditions for the development of collective patterns of delinquent conduct. In later chapters we shall consider the conditions that promote particular types of delinquent subculture.

The Process of Alienation[2]

A COMMON SOURCE of alienation from the dominant norms of a social group is failure, or the anticipation of failure, in achieving success-goals by socially approved means. As we have in-

2. In this chapter we use the term "alienation" to characterize a process of withdrawal of attributions of legitimacy from established social norms. The focus is on the degree of isolation from these norms

dicated, lower-class male adolescents frequently find themselves at a competitive disadvantage in gaining access to legitimate routes to success. Many of them intuitively sense or consciously perceive that they cannot "make the grade." Whether or not they will become alienated and repudiate the established organization of approved means depends in large measure on the way in which they account for their actual or potential failure.

THE EXPLANATION OF FAILURE

It is our view that the most significant step in the withdrawal of sentiments supporting the legitimacy of conventional norms is the attribution of the cause of failure to the social order rather than to oneself, for the way in which a person explains his failure largely determines what he will do about it. Some persons who have experienced a marked discrepancy between aspirations and achievements may look outward, attributing their failure to the existence of unjust or arbitrary institutional arrangements which keep men of ability and ambition from rising in the social structure. Such persons do not view their failure as a reflection of personal inadequacy but instead blame a cultural and social system that encourages everyone to reach for success while differentially restricting access to the success-goals. In contrast to this group there are individuals who attribute failure to their own inadequacies—to a lack of discipline, zeal, intelligence, persistence, or other personal quality.

Whether the "failure" blames the social order or himself is of central importance to the understanding of deviant conduct. When a person ascribes his failure to injustice in the social system, he may criticize that system, bend his efforts toward reforming it, or disassociate himself from it—in other words, he may become alienated from the established set of social norms. He may even be convinced that he is justified in

rather than on the illegitimate rules of conduct subsequently evolved. For a recent attempt to distinguish various uses of this concept, see Melvin Seeman, "On the Meaning of Alienation," *American Sociological Review,* Vol. 24 (Dec. 1959), pp. 783-91.

evading these norms in his pursuit of success-goals. The individual who locates the source of his failure in his own inadequacy, on the other hand, feels pressure to change himself rather than the system. Suffering from a loss of self-esteem, he must either develop mechanisms that will protect him from these feelings of personal inadequacy or work toward eliminating them by developing greater personal competence. By implication, then, attributing failure to one's own faults reveals an attitude supporting the legitimacy of the existing norms.

Despite the importance of this problem, relatively little is known about the conditions that lead to external rather than internal attributions of causality. The problem has received more attention in recent years, however, particularly from psychologists interested in studying social perception.[3] One of their major concerns has been to identify the types of personality that characteristically attribute causality to themselves or to the world without.[4] Ultimately, however, inquiry must

---

3. See, *inter alia,* Renato Tagiuri and Luigi Petrullo, eds., *Person Perception and Interpersonal Behavior* (Stanford: Stanford University Press, 1958), especially the paper by Fritz Heider, "Social Perception and Phenomenal Causality," pp. 1-22.

4. See, *e.g.,* Rosenzweig's classification of reactions to frustration which result in the attribution of blame to the outer world or to oneself. Each of the various types of reaction tends to dominate in a given personality type. (S. Rosenzweig, "The Experimental Measurement of Types of Reaction to Frustration," in H. A. Murray, ed., *Explorations in Personality* [Oxford: Oxford University Press, 1938], pp. 585-99.) More recent work by Rotter and his students shifts the focus slightly from explaining different forms of causal attribution to identifying the personality and situational correlates of "internal and external control of reinforcements" in the framework of learning theory. (J. B. Rotter, *Social Learning and Clinical Psychology* [New York: Prentice Hall, 1954]; and W. H. James and J. B. Rotter, "Partial and One Hundred Per Cent Reinforcement Under Chance and Skill Conditions," *Journal of Experimental Psychology,* Vol. 55 [May 1958], pp. 397-403.)

A very promising line of inquiry is being pursued by Schroder and Hunt, who employ an interactional scheme and study the response of different personality types to failure and criticism under different situational circumstances. (H. M. Schroder and D. E. Hunt, "Failure-Avoidance in Situational Interpretation and Problem Solving," *Psychological Monographs,* Vol. 71, No. 3 [1957]; and also Schroder and

also be directed toward identifying the personal and social factors that account for such personality differences. Merton has noted the need for this type of research most clearly:

> At this point, it is clear that research is needed to discover the structure of those social situations which typically elicit self-evaluations or internalized judgments—for example, where comparison with the achievements of specified others leads to invidious self-depreciation, to a sense of personal inadequacy—and the structure of those situations which typically lead to evaluations of institutions or externalized judgments—for example, where comparison with others leads to a sense of institutional inadequacies, to the judgment that the social system militates against any close correspondence between individual merit and social reward. . . . The sociological factors which lead men to consider their own, relatively low, social position as legitimate, as well as those which lead them to construe their position as a result of defective and possibly unjustified social arrangements clearly comprise a problem area of paramount theoretical and political importance. When are relatively slim life-chances taken by men as a normal and expectable state of affairs which they attribute to their own personal inadequacies and when are they regarded as the results of an arbitrary social system of mobility, in which rewards are not proportioned to ability?[5]

We should like to suggest two situational variables that seem to us rewarding approaches to an investigation of the social conditions that produce external attributions of blame for failure: (1) the relative discrepancy between institutionally induced expectations (as distinct from aspirations) and possibilities of achievement, which produces a sense of unjust deprivation; and (2) highly visible barriers to the achievement of aspirations, which give rise to feelings of discrimination.

EXPECTATIONS AND UNJUST DEPRIVATION

Everyone who maintains social relationships with others participates in a social order made up of shared definitions and expectations. Even in the multifarious fleeting contacts of

---

Hunt, "Dispositional Effects upon Conformity at Different Levels of Discrepancy," *Journal of Personality,* Vol. 26 [1958], pp. 243-85.)

5. R. K. Merton, *Social Theory and Social Structure* (Glencoe, Ill.: Free Press, 1957), p. 240.

everyday life, we are continually engaged in creating a working consensus of rules and definitions which permits us to conduct successfully our joint social endeavors.[6] In those institutionalized patterns of social relationships which constitute the major areas of our interests, such as family life, school, or work, the rules and definitions with which we must deal tend to be clearer and more firmly established. Every group develops criteria of excellence around its basic activities to which group members are encouraged to refer in framing judgments or making decisions. In school situations the task-organization and grading system encourages comparisons on the basis of reading, writing, and arithmetic skills, verbal fluency, and the like. Outside school, adolescents develop criteria around athletic prowess, physical attractiveness, skill in social repartee, and the like. These and similar definitions and criteria are part of a cultural heritage which we assimilate almost unwittingly as we grow up. It is true that the criteria change and that to some extent we can resist them or suggest new ones; yet the interests of newcomers carry little weight against the tradition-laden investments of those who have been successfully socialized. It takes collective resistance or catastrophic crises to bring about major shifts in the definitional structure of those basic social institutions which engage most of our daily effort and attention.

As individuals, we use these socially sanctioned criteria to locate ourselves and others in the social order.[7] We use

---

6. For a stimulating analysis of the consensual nature of understandings in everyday social contacts, see Erving Goffman, *The Presentation of Self in Everyday Life* (New York: Doubleday Anchor Books, 1959).

7. The choice and development of careers, both legitimate and illegitimate, in relation to the structure of social definitions and opportunities which the community provides have long been of interest to sociologists. See especially the life-history documents assembled by Clifford Shaw and his associates in C. R. Shaw, *The Jack-Roller* (Chicago: University of Chicago Press, 1930); Shaw, *The Natural History of a Delinquent Career* (Chicago: University of Chicago Press, 1931); Shaw, *Brothers in Crime* (Chicago: University of Chicago Press, 1938); E. H. Sutherland, *The Professional Thief* (Chicago: University of Chicago Press, 1937); and E. C. Hughes, *Men and Their Work* (Glencoe, Ill.: Free Press, 1958). In recent years there has been renewed interest in this approach to the study of deviant careers;

them to judge our appearance, ability, demeanor, knowledge, and conduct in relation to others in the same situation. We rate ourselves and others as more or less successful, good, or praiseworthy in accordance with these socially established standards.[8] Yet there are often significant discrepancies between the criteria which are upheld by the formal ideology of the social order and those which are actually used in making choices, decisions, or judgments—that is, between those criteria which *should* and those which *do* control social evaluations. Even in a democratic society, for example, where the dominant ideology stresses criteria based on social equality, talent, skill, knowledge, and achievement, many competitive selections and judgments take account of such nonuniversalistic criteria as race, religion, family prestige, wealth, social class, and personal friendship.

Data gathered during World War II illustrate the effect of the discrepancy between formal eligibility for advancement and actual or potential achievement on attitudes toward official norms.[9] The research team was interested in discovering relative satisfaction with chance of promotion among soldiers in three different branches of the army, which had quite different promotion rates. To the question "Do you think a soldier with ability has a good chance for promotion?" the soldiers in all three groups were asked to choose among four answers: "a very good chance," "a fairly good chance," "undecided," and "not much or no chance."

In general, the results indicate that those who are eligible for promotion in terms of the formal criteria but who have not

see, *e.g.*, Erving Goffman, "The Moral Career of the Mental Patient," *Psychiatry*, Vol. 22 (May 1959), pp. 123-42. An interesting attempt to apply this perspective systematically to the study of different types of deviant social role is E. M. Lemert, *Social Pathology* (New York: McGraw-Hill, 1951).

8. The institutionalized structure of reference-group orientations and the social and psychological determinants of the comparisons that people make in different situations are subjects that have interested sociologists and psychologists in recent years. For a useful commentary on work in this area, see Merton, *op. cit.*, pp. 281-386.

9. S. A. Stouffer, E. A. Suchman, L. C. DeVinney, Shirley A. Star, and R. M. Williams, Jr., *The American Soldier: Adjustment During Army Life,* Vol. I (Princeton: Princeton University Press, 1949), pp. 250-71.

been advanced tend to be most critical of the system. As one would expect, the lower the rank (holding length of service and education constant), the more critical the opinion about the promotion system. Within the same rank, those with either more education or greater length of service were more critical. When different branches were compared, members of the Air Corps, in which the highest expectations of advancement prevailed, showed the highest proportions of critical judgments about the promotion system.

Another research survey sought to discover what factors determined promotion in the army, in the opinion of the soldiers. A representative cross-section of white enlisted men in the United States in January 1943 was asked: "How do you think the men in your outfit were selected for promotion?" Among the privates and PFC's, the greater the length of service, the greater the stress on "bootlicking or playing politics" rather than "ability" as the basis for promotion; in fact, those with one to three years of service gave bootlicking as the reason more than twice as often as those with less than six months of service (35 per cent as opposed to 15 per cent). Among those enlisted men with one to three years of service, 35 per cent of the privates and PFC's but only 16 per cent of the noncommissioned officers chose bootlicking; 28 per cent of the privates and PFC's as compared with 53 per cent of the noncoms chose ability as the reason for promotion. A survey of American corporals and privates in fighter groups in England in December 1943 showed comparable results; of the college-educated respondents, 64 per cent chose "having an 'in' with the right people" in contrast to 14 per cent who checked "ability on the job" as the most important reason for promotion. The comparable percentages for those with grade-school or some high-school education were 42 and 27 per cent, respectively.

These studies suggest that there are identifiable conditions under which individuals will tend to attribute failure to external factors. Those who appraise themselves as better equipped than their fellows according to the formal criteria of advancement seem inclined to blame the system rather than themselves when their expectations of achievement are not met.

Furthermore, when the better-qualified are denied opportunities to satisfy their expectations for promotion they are much more likely to perceive discrepancies between the formal criteria of evaluation and those which are actually operative. In a system that stresses ability as the basis of advancement, the failures who view themselves as equal in ability to those who succeed tend to feel unjustly deprived of opportunities which on formal grounds should be theirs also. Thus they come to believe that bootlicking and not ability paves the way to promotion.

It is our impression that a sense of being unjustly deprived of access to opportunities to which one is entitled is common among those who become participants in delinquent subcultures. Delinquents tend to be persons who have been led to expect opportunities because of their potential ability to meet the formal, institutionally established criteria of evaluation.[10] Their sense of injustice arises from the failure of the system to fulfill these expectations. Their criticism is not directed inward since they regard themselves in comparison with their fellows as capable of meeting the formal requirements of the system. It has frequently been noted that delinquents take especial delight in discovering hypocrisy in the operation of the established social order. They like to point out that "it's who you know, not what you know" that enables one to advance or gain coveted social rewards. They become convinced that bribery, blackmail, fear-inspiring pressure, special influence, and similar factors are more important than the publicly avowed criteria of merit.

The sense of unjust deprivation can play a significant role in the withdrawal of attributions of legitimacy from official norms. When a system is found deficient in terms of its own

10. There is no evidence, for example, that members of delinquent subcultures are objectively less capable of meeting formal standards of eligibility than are nondelinquent lower-class youngsters. In fact, the available data support the contention that the basic endowments of delinquents, such as intelligence, physical strength, and agility, are the equal of or greater than those of their nondelinquent peers. A convenient summary of the evidence on this point is presented in H. A. Bloch and F. T. Flynn, *Delinquency: The Juvenile Offender in America Today* (New York: Random House, 1956), pp. 115-50.

established criteria, one becomes free not only to criticize it but to withdraw sentiments supporting it. Thus a feeling of unjust deprivation weakens the motivations for accepting the legitimacy of official norms and permits the individual to accept alternative patterns of conduct on grounds of expediency or self-interest. Hard work, perseverance, and honesty may lose their force as norms when there are more persons capable of meeting these criteria than there are opportunities. Furthermore, ultimate success is likely to involve such criteria as race, speech mannerisms, familial ties, and "connections." Many candidates who are capable of meeting the formal criteria cannot meet these supplementary operative criteria. The sense of injustice that arises under such circumstances tends to neutralize the traditional emotional or moral sentiments buttressing acceptance of the officially sponsored models of behavior. It is as if the unjust deprivation cancels out the individual's obligation to the established system—at least in one area of action—and encourages him to emulate other role models on the basis of expediency alone. In this area, the question of the relative moral validity of the new and the old rules of conduct is suspended while the individual seeks compensation for the injustice he has suffered from the officially supported system of norms.

This, at least, is how the situation is likely to appear to the emerging delinquent. For him the process of alienation has its roots in the discrepancy between the formal criteria of evaluation which he feels he can meet and the operative criteria, which allocate limited opportunities to a surplus of eligible candidates. Anticipating that he will be unable to meet these operative criteria, he perceives his failure to gain access to opportunities as an injustice in the system rather than as a deficiency in himself. He thus becomes free to join with others in a delinquent solution to his problem without great concern about the moral validity of his actions. The situation that provokes his sense of injustice provides advance justification for his subsequent acts of deviance.

The discrepancy between formal and operative criteria of

evaluation appears to be inherent in the organization of a democratic society.[11] The democratic ideology of equality of opportunity creates constant pressure for formal criteria of evaluation that are universalistic rather than particularistic, achieved rather than ascribed—that is, for a structure of opportunities that are available to all on an open competitive basis rather than the proprietory right of a select group and that are achieved by one's own effort rather than acquired by the mere fact of birth into a particular race, religion, social class, or family. However, the democratic society, like other types of society, is also characterized by a limited supply of rewards and opportunities. Although many are eligible for success on the basis of formal criteria, relatively few can succeed, even in a rapidly expanding economy. It is therefore necessary to make choices on some basis or other among candidates who are equally eligible on formal grounds.[12] The informal criteria that are invoked in such circumstances are often in conflict, usually covertly, with the publicly declared criteria.

It seems inevitable that such ideologically repudiated criteria will be used most frequently at those places in the social structure where rewards and opportunities are most scarce. Minority groups suffering from discrimination are quick to point out that they are "the last to be hired and the first to be fired." The more clearly the formal standards for career opportunities are stated in terms of achievement, the more the lower-class youngster is led to expect from his own efforts. When he

11. For a relevant discussion of the strains inherent in a social system based on a universalistic-achievement ideology, see Talcott Parsons, *The Social System* (Glencoe, Ill.: Free Press, 1951), pp. 182-91.

12. De Tocqueville pointed out this relationship with characteristic clarity: "The same equality that allows every citizen to conceive . . . lofty hopes renders all the citizens less able to realize them; it circumscribes their powers on every side, while it gives freer scope to their desires. . . . They have swept away the privileges of some of their fellow creatures which stood in their way, but they have opened the door to universal competition; *the barrier has changed its shape rather than its position*" (Alexis de Tocqueville, *Democracy in America*, Vol. 2 [New York: Vintage Books, 1958], p. 146; emphasis added).

fulfills the established standards he expects to be selected. However, the changes in the formal criteria have also increased the number of his peers who share his eligibility—and his expectations—for the limited opportunities available. In this situation, criteria based on race, religion, or class that have been publicly repudiated in favor of achievement standards are informally invoked to eliminate the surplus candidates. Thus the democratization of standards of evaluation tends to increase the competition for rewards and opportunities and hence the discrepancy between the formal and the actual criteria of selection for lower-class youngsters.

It would, of course, be possible to avoid such an effect if opportunities and rewards throughout the social structure kept pace with the increasing emphasis on achievement in the standards of career recruitment. However, the democratization of standards in the direction of universalistic achievement norms appears to result in increasingly stiff requirements of ability, knowledge, and skill.[13] Although more people at all social levels are eligible to compete for various career opportunities, the levels of education and performance required to succeed become ever higher. Thus, although the lower-class adolescent finds more possibilities nominally open to him, the special disadvantages he encounters in attaining educational goals (see Chap. 4) maintain a situation of restricted opportunity.

From this analysis it seems clear that democratizing the criteria of evaluation without at the same time increasing the opportunities available to lower-class youngsters will accentuate

---

13. The relationship between an increasing stress on universalistic achievement norms and higher standards of performance was also observed by De Tocqueville: "As the candidates appear to be nearly alike, and as it is difficult to make a selection without infringing the principle of equality, which is the supreme law of democratic societies, the first idea which suggests itself is to make them all advance at the same rate and submit to the same trials. Thus, in proportion as men become more alike and the principle of equality is more peaceably and deeply infused into the institutions and manner of the country, the rules for advancement become more inflexible, advancement itself slower, the difficulty of arriving quickly at a certain height far greater" (*ibid.*, p. 259).

the conditions that produce feelings of unjust deprivation. The increased stress on achievement norms inflates the expectations and aspirations of the lower-class adolescent. At the same time, it limits the career opportunities available to him, demanding levels of education which he experiences special disadvantages in attaining. In addition, he finds that the career possibilities for which he is qualified have become excessively competitive, so that discriminatory criteria are covertly applied. Under such conditions he is inclined to locate the source of his troubles in the social system rather than in his own shortcomings. His sense of injustice encourages him to withdraw sentiments attributing legitimacy to the dominant social order and to search for a more efficient means to achieve his aspirations.

VISIBILITY OF BARRIERS TO OPPORTUNITY

When external barriers to the achievement of success-goals and their influence on the criteria of evaluation are clearly apparent, it is much more likely that persons who fail to achieve their aspirations will attribute failure to the social order rather than to themselves. For example, a Negro may find it difficult to maintain his faith in the ideology of equality under social conditions which conspicuously bar members of his "race" from access to legitimate opportunities for achieving success. Indeed, Negroes are even at a disadvantage in the illegitimate world, as we shall see in Chapter 8. An increase in the visibility of external barriers to the advancement of Negroes heightens their sense of discrimination and justifies withdrawal of attributions of legitimacy from conventional rules of conduct.

A common strategy of reform groups is to increase the social visibility of discriminatory practices. The discrepancy between the formal and the operative criteria of evaluation can often be reduced if it is exposed and made an issue of broad concern. The consequences of efforts to expose the operation of discriminatory criteria will depend on the types of aspiration held by the lower-class persons who are denied access to opportunities by these criteria. Those who are primarily interested in rising into the middle class—Whyte's "college boys"—are more likely to participate in programs intended to publicize and reform unfair practices. Their efforts are directed toward upward mobility for their group as a whole, since the elimination of discriminatory practices requires a change in the attitude of the discriminators toward all members of the disadvantaged group. For example, the elimination of color as a barrier to employment in certain jobs clears the path for all Negroes and results in a change in the criteria of eligibility. In contrast to the "college boys," those who aspire to material and prestige goals within the lower class itself are more likely to seek illegitimate avenues to success when they are made aware of barriers to legitimate routes. Such persons may be quite sympathetic toward attempts to remove discriminatory obstacles to legitimate achievement. However, as we noted in Chapter 4, these obstacles do not always prevent them from reaching their goals; indeed, they may even attain their goals more expeditiously by illicit means than by adhering to the established rules of conduct. The efforts of reformers to expose discriminatory practices actually furnish such persons with further justification for withdrawing sentiments in support of the legitimacy of the established norms and free them to attribute legitimacy to alternative norms which may be both legally and morally proscribed by the dominant system.

It is interesting to speculate, for example, about the differential effects on lower-class adolescent Negro boys of a recent widely publicized study of discrimination against Negroes in apprenticeship training.

> The report of the National Association for the Advancement of Colored People on "The Negro Wage-Earner and Apprenticeship Training Programs" throws much-needed light on a field of which far too little is publicly known.
>
> It stresses the urgent need for a great expansion of apprenticeship training in general. The supply of apprentices is falling far short of meeting the enormous and growing need for skilled craftsmen which has followed increasing automation and the opening up of employment in new industries. But the greatest contribution of the report is its impressive demonstration of the "almost total

exclusion" of Negroes from apprenticeship training, in spite of the need for such workers.

Figures in the report show that Negroes make up only 1.69 per cent of the total number of apprentices. The proportion of Negroes is actually less than 1 per cent of the apprentice carpenters, electricians, machinists and plumbers. And the situation in the North is not very different from the South; it is nationwide.

Management, of course, is basically responsible. After all, it does the hiring and many practices, as well as employers' attitudes, close doors to Negro opportunity. Unions, too, play a key role in the recruitment of apprentices and in keeping Negroes out, mostly the old-line craft union locals where apprenticeship training has been most widely developed—as has racial bias. While specialized federal and state agencies promote, advise and service apprenticeship activities in private industry and also suggest standards for them, they have no direct responsibility for their operations.

The NAACP challenges all three groups to undertake an anti-bias campaign, as each is able to, and also a concerted effort both to expand and to publicize the apprentice system in general. Employers and unions have the power to do away with racial bars directly. Government agencies can do so indirectly by withholding subsidies and facilities where discrimination exists. Here is a challenge that all concerned should accept.[14]

Thus the NAACP report, according to this New York *Times* editorial, exposes and publicizes a concealed discriminatory practice, defines the extent of discrimination, points out those who are responsible, outlines a program of remedial action, and urges support for reforms. Those adolescents who are interested in achieving middle-class status are likely to respond enthusiastically to the appeal to support reform efforts. However, those who aspire to material or prestige rewards within the lower-class style of life may simply regard the report as further corroboration of the unfairness of the established system and hence additional justification for the use of illegitimate routes to success goals.

If exposing the existence of discriminatory barriers to

---

14. New York *Times,* March 20, 1960. The publication cited in the editorial is *The Negro Wage-Earner and Apprenticeship Training Programs* (New York: National Association for the Advancement of Colored People, 1960).

opportunity can result in the attribution of blame for failure to "the system," it may be that publicizing successful careers can increase the tendency to attribute blame to personal inadequacy. Merton, for example, notes that:

> . . . conspicuously successful individuals who have risen rapidly in a social hierarchy and who are much in the public eye function as models or reference figures testifying to a mobility-system in which, apparently, careers are still open to talent. For some, these success-models are living testimony to the legitimacy of the institutional system and in this comparative context, the individual deflects criticism of the system onto himself.[15]

Indeed, the "rags to riches" story is a common device for bolstering belief in the legitimacy of the established organization of opportunities in an egalitarian society. How effectively it elicits conforming behavior depends on how well it illustrates the absence of discrimination and the operation of criteria of evaluation based solely on ability, skill, knowledge, and achievement.

Collective vs. *Individual Solutions*

THE DEVELOPMENT and maintenance of a delinquent subculture is obviously a collective enterprise. Delinquent norms are a group product and command the allegiance of individuals as members of a group. Yet many youngsters "resolve" their problems of adjustment by developing essentially solitary or individualistic deviant forms of behavior, especially various types of mental illness. Consequently, in attempting to account for the emergence of delinquent norms, we must also consider what conditions tend to encourage the development of collective rather than individual adaptations.

As we have noted, the tendency to withdraw attributions of legitimacy from established social norms depends in part

15. Merton, *op. cit.*, pp. 240-41. See also R. K. Merton, Marjorie Fiske, and Alberta Curtis, *Mass Persuasion* (New York: Harper & Bros., 1946), pp. 152*ff*.

upon whether the individual attributes failure to the social order or himself. It is our hypothesis that collective adaptations are likely to emerge when failure is attributed to the inadequacy of existing institutional arrangements; conversely, when failure is attributed to personal deficiencies, solitary adaptations are more likely.

In our society success and failure are ideologically explained in essentially individualistic terms. Success is formally attributed to ambition, perseverence, talent, and the like; failure, on the other hand, is regarded as a result of a lack of these traits. In explaining occupational achievements or failures, we do not ordinarily refer to the "life chances" or "objective opportunities" of the individual; we tend, rather, to ask whether he has made the most of the chances that he has, whether he has been diligent, industrious, and imaginative in the pursuit of success-goals. This tendency to equate success with ability and failure with personal inferiority helps to ensure the stability and continuity of existing arrangements by deflecting criticism from the institutional order and turning it back upon the self.

Those who attribute failure to their own shortcomings in effect accept the prevailing ideology of the society. They use socially accepted evaluative criteria in explaining their adjustment problems. Such persons are not at odds with society; on the contrary, self-blame is an important index of attitudinal conformity, for it is essentially an affirmation of the fairness and moral validity of the prevailing ideology. Individuals who explain failure in this way then have the problem of coping with the psychic consequences of internalized definitions of themselves as unworthy or inferior. It is unlikely that they will join with others to develop a solution, for they see their adjustment problem as essentially personal. They tend to experience feelings of guilt, shame, and loss of self-esteem which lead them to withdraw from others in seeking to solve their difficulties. Such persons may violate established rules of conduct in reaching their personal solutions, but these "solutions," however deviant, do not necessarily involve repudiation of the legitimacy of the prevailing system. The legitimacy of official norms is in fact asserted by the act of blaming oneself. The individual who violates official norms in these circumstances usually experiences strong feelings of guilt.

The individual who attributes his achievement dilemmas to deficiencies in the prevailing institutional arrangements, on the other hand, is at odds wtih the social order. This alienation generates a great deal of tension in relation to the carriers of the dominant cultural ideology. To some extent, the tension can be relieved if the alienated person can gain the support of others who are in the same position and who share the view that their misfortunes are due to an unjust system of social arrangements. Collective support can provide reassurance, security, and needed validation of a frame of reference toward which the world at large is hostile and disapproving.

The youngster who is motivated by a sense of injustice generally commits his first acts of deviance in a climate of uncertainty and fear of disapproval. The withdrawal of attributions of legitimacy from the dominant social norms is initially tentative and unstable. These first acts are usually minor and often impulsive expressions of resentment against the apparent injustice of the established social order. However, they bring the individual into conflict with the official system and expose him to its arsenal of invidious definitions and punitive sanctions. Members of the conventional community are likely to respond to them with strong efforts at repression, precisely because they recognize the underlying attitude of alienation from the established norms. These early acts of deviance are in effect tentative steps toward the adoption of norms in competition with the official rules. At this stage the deviant needs all the encouragement and reassurance he can muster to defend his position. He finds these by searching out others who have faced similar experiences and who will support one another in common attitudes of alienation from the official system. The deviant who is unable to mobilize such social support will have great difficulty in establishing firm grounds for his defiance of the official system, for he requires not only justifying beliefs but also social validation of the appropriateness of his deviant acts.

The initial contest between the individual and the authorities over the legitimacy of certain social norms and the appropriateness of certain acts of deviance sets in motion a process of definition that marks the offender as different from law-abiding folk. His acts and his person are defined as "evil," and he is caught up in a vicious cycle of norm-violation, repression, resentment, and new and more serious acts of violation. The process of alienation is accelerated, and the chasm between the offender and those who would control and reform him grows wider and deeper. In such circumstances he becomes increasingly dependent on the support of others in his position. The gang of peers forms a new social world in which the legitimacy of his delinquent conduct is strongly reinforced.

Tannenbaum locates the beginning of this alienation process in the innocent, random play activities of youngsters which result in acts that conflict with adult interests and values. The adult response of disapproval defines the acts and subsequently the child himself as "bad." This initiates a process that emphasizes and crystallizes the very behavior that is being proscribed.

In the conflict between the young delinquent and the community there develop two opposing definitions of the situation. In the beginning the definition of the situation by the young delinquent may be in the form of play, adventure, excitement, interest, mischief, fun. Breaking windows, annoying people, running around porches, climbing over roofs, stealing from pushcarts, playing truant—all are items of play, adventure, excitement. To the community, however, these activities may and often do take on the form of nuisance, evil, delinquency, with the demand for control, admonition, chastisement, punishment, police court, truant school. This conflict arises out of a divergence of values. As the problem develops, the attitude of the community hardens definitely into a demand for suppression. There is a gradual shift from the definition of the specific acts as evil to a definition of the individual as evil, so that all his acts come to be looked upon with suspicion. In the process of identification his companions, hangouts, play, speech, income, all his conduct, the personality itself, become subject to scrutiny and question. . . .

Early in his career, then, the incipient professional criminal develops an attitude of antagonism to the regulated orderly life that he is required to lead. This attitude is hardened and crystallized by opposition. The conflict becomes a clash of wills. . . .

The firm dramatization of the "evil" which separates the child out of his group for specialized treatment plays a greater role in making the criminal than perhaps any other experience. It cannot be too often emphasized that for the child the whole situation has become different. He now lives in a different world. He has been tagged. A new and hitherto nonexistent environment has been precipitated out for him.

The process of making the criminal, therefore, is a process of tagging, defining, identifying, segregating, describing, emphasizing, making conscious and self-conscious; it becomes a way of stimulating, suggesting, emphasizing, and evolving the very traits that are complained of. If the theory of relation of response to stimulus has any meaning, the entire process of dealing with the young delinquent is mischievous in so far as it identifies him to himself or to the environment as a delinquent person.[16]

This process tends to isolate the child from constructive adult influences and make him dependent for security on the support and encouragement of others like himself. As Tannenbaum puts it: "The child's isolation forces him into companionship with other children similarly defined, and the gang becomes his means of escape, his security."

We agree with Tannenbaum and others in assigning central importance to the definitional process and peer-group support in the development of delinquent careers. However, our theoretical position differs from Tannenbaum's in two major respects. First, we assign much less importance to rule violations that grow out of the random play activities of children as the starting point of the alienation process. What Tannenbaum calls the "innocent divergence of the child from the straight road" during "play, adventure, excitement," along with unfavorable adult reactions to such "divergence," is experienced by *all* children in the normal course of socialization; yet relatively few children move toward delinquent *careers* after such experiences. In our view, the factor that distinguishes the children who do become delinquent is their withdrawal of attributions of legitimacy from established social norms. Children who continue to accept the conventional rules

16. Frank Tannenbaum, *Crime and the Community* (New York: Columbia University Press, 1938), pp. 17-20.

of conduct as binding are likely to accept adult disapproval as a justifiable response to their rule violations. They frequently feel guilty about their deviance and become motivated to act in more conforming fashion. However, those who question the legitimacy of the dominant norms are likely to resist being defined as morally inferior, which adult disapproval implies. Indeed, this invidious definition only feeds their resentment and encourages further misconduct. For such children, the definitional process that Tannenbaum describes increases alienation from conventional norms and fosters the development of a delinquent career. But this occurs because the young offender has already developed an attitude of alienation from at least some of the required forms of behavior. He is already capable in some measure of viewing his misconduct as justified.

Our second point of difference with Tannenbaum is that we assign an active role in the alienation process to the predispositions of the deviant youngster, whereas Tannenbaum focuses exclusively on the definitions and other responses given by adults to the innocent misconduct of children. The child, to Tannenbaum, is analogous to a pool ball propelled into the pocket of a delinquent career by the definitional thrusts of adults, whatever their intentions.

> The person becomes the thing he is described as being. Nor does it seem to matter whether the valuation is made by those who would punish or those who would reform. In either case the emphasis is upon the conduct that is disapproved of. The parents or the policemen, the older brother or the court, the probation officer or the juvenile institution, in so far as they rest upon the thing complained of, rest upon a false ground. Their very enthusiasm defeats their aim. The harder they work to reform the evil, the greater the evil grows under their hands. The persistent suggestion, with whatever good intentions, works mischief, because it leads to bringing out the bad behavior that it would suppress.[17]

Since, according to Tannenbaum, it is the definitional structure of the adult community that creates delinquency, the solution lies in modifying that structure: "The way out is through a refusal to dramatize the evil. The less said about it the

---

17. *Ibid.*

better. The more said about something else, still better."[18]

Tannenbaum's tendency to overstress the adult response to youthful misconduct is in part a conscious reaction against the tendency of other writers to ascribe "the cause of the unsocial behavior" to "a personal shortcoming of the offender." He states his opposition to this position in strong terms:

> The assumption that crime is caused by any sort of inferiority, physiological or psychological, is here completely and unequivocally repudiated.
>
> This does not mean that morphological or psychological techniques do not have value for the individual. It merely means that they have no greater value in the study of criminology than they would have in the study of any profession.[19]

Once the pressure to adopt a polemical position is removed, it is possible to recognize delinquency as a product of the interaction between certain internalized orientations of the delinquent and the structure of definitions and evaluations with which he is confronted. The adult response to misconduct has different consequences for the youngster who is disposed to question the legitimacy of established norms than for one who is not. Further, we contend, the consequences differ depending upon whether the invidious definitions based on minor acts of misconduct are imposed on those who already view the established order as unjust and deprivational.

Techniques of Defense Against Guilt

PEOPLE who violate rules which they accept as valid are likely to experience strong feelings of guilt, anxiety, or fear, whether or not the rule violations have collective support. With repeated violations, the accumulated anxiety tends to become so intense that the offender gives up his deviant conduct unless he can develop some defense against feelings of guilt. He must find a way of managing the guilt generated by the con-

18. *Ibid.*
19. *Ibid.*, p. 22.

flict between what he does and what he feels he should do before he can accept delinquent conduct as a stable solution to his adjustment problem.

The psychological literature dealing with delinquency has concentrated on identifying the devices by which this guilt is handled.[20] We take a somewhat different approach, by drawing a distinction between the legitimacy of social norms and their moral validity. If an individual withdraws sentiments supporting specific official norms and attributes legitimacy instead to officially prohibited modes of conduct, the guilt problem in regard to the violated norms has been solved in advance of the act. He may then engage in delinquent acts without experiencing acute guilt feelings about them because he has come to believe in the legitimacy of these acts, given the social circumstances in which he is placed. Distinguishing between the question of the legitimacy of norms and the question of their moral validity permits the performance of acts that the actor himself may view as morally inferior to some alternative way of behaving but as nevertheless justified. The problem of guilt does not arise for him so long as the specific attribution of legitimacy can be defended. One does not feel very guilty about violating a rule which one does not view as binding on one's conduct.

In this chapter we have traced the process of alienation by which the potential offender is led to attribute legitimacy to officially disapproved modes of conduct. A person who places blame for failure on the unjust organization of the established social order and who finds support from others for his withdrawal of legitimacy from official norms may be induced to resort to illegitimate means of achieving success-goals as a stable form of adaptation. Having withdrawn his acceptance of officially approved norms, he is psychologically protected against the guilt feelings that would otherwise result

20. See, *e.g.*, August Aichhorn, *Wayward Youth* (New York: Viking Press, 1935); Kate Friedlander, *The Psychoanalytic Approach to Juvenile Delinquency* (New York: International Universities Press, 1944); and K. R. Eisler, ed., *Searchlights on Delinquency* (New York: International Universities Press, 1949).

from violation of those norms. Successful communication and sharing of discontent with others who are similarly situated furnishes social support for and lends stability to whatever pattern of deviant conduct develops.

These steps are accompanied by the growth of a supporting structure of beliefs and values that provide advance justification for deviant conduct. Those who regard the social order as unjust and evaluate themselves as the equal of persons who have been granted access to legitimate opportunities in effect rationalize their deviance before it occurs. Thus they take steps to preserve their sense of personal integrity as they change their allegiance from conforming to prohibited modes of conduct. The emerging deviant subculture acquires a set of beliefs and values which rationalize the shift in norms as a natural response to a trying situation. These beliefs are in the form of descriptions and evaluations of the social world of the delinquent which contradict those held by conforming persons. Armed with these new conceptions of his social situation, the delinquent is able to adhere to the norms of the delinquent subculture with less vulnerability to the invidious definitions of his actions by law-abiding persons.

Recognizing this sequence in the development of delinquent norms and justifying beliefs and values makes it easier to understand the intractable and apparently conscienceless behavior of the fully indoctrinated members of delinquent subcultures. The absence of guilt feelings and a stubborn resistance to correction have earned such offenders the label of "psychopathic personalities." Most attempts to reform them through clinical therapy have been unsuccessful, largely because it is necessary for the "patient" to have guilt feelings before customary treatment procedures leading to psychological reorganization can be brought into play. This difficulty has been extensively documented in the work of Fritz Redl and his associates.[21] In order to create the requisite conditions for effective clinical treatment, they found it necessary to engage in prolonged and continuous assaults on the delinquents'

21. Fritz Redl and David Wineman, *Children Who Hate* (Glencoe, Ill.: Free Press, 1956).

underlying structure of justificatory beliefs and values. The offenders displayed remarkable ingenuity, skill, and determination in defending these cornerstones of their delinquent style of life. The literature contains descriptions of many individual delinquents who experience strong guilt feelings because they continue in some ambivalent fashion to acknowledge the legitimacy of the rules that they have violated. One even finds accounts of fully indoctrinated members of delinquent subcultures who occasionally give evidence of uncertainty about the validity of their justifying beliefs and values. Generally, however, members of delinquent subcultures effectively fight off these challenges and maintain their commitments to delinquent norms in appropriate behavior areas. Of course, even members of the delinquent core group conform to conventional codes of conduct in many of their daily activities. In those behavioral areas which make up the delinquent role, however, they have attributed legitimacy to codes of conduct that compete directly with official norms and they staunchly defend the beliefs and values which support these codes.

Recent interpretations offered by Cohen and by Sykes and Matza differ from the foregoing analysis. Both contend that the delinquent retains a belief in the legitimacy of the official norms, although they differ in estimating the delinquent's awareness of this imputation. "The hallmark of the delinquent subculture," according to Cohen, "is the explicit and wholesale repudiation of middle-class standards and the adoption of their very antithesis."[22] However, he suggests that this repudiation is more apparent than real, for the delinquent maintains a secret and repressed desire for what he openly rejects:

May we assume that when the delinquent seeks to obtain unequivocal status by repudiating, once and for all, the norms of the college-boy culture, these norms really undergo total extinction? Or do they, perhaps, linger on, underground, as it were, repressed, unacknowledged, but an ever-present threat to the adjustment which has been achieved at no small cost? There is much evidence from

22. A. K. Cohen, *Delinquent Boys: The Culture of the Gang* (Glencoe, Ill.: Free Press, 1955), p. 129.

clinical psychology that moral norms, once effectively internalized, are not lightly thrust aside or extinguished.[23]

This assumption of a basic ambivalence which threatens the stability of the delinquent adaptation makes it possible for Cohen to introduce the psychological concept of reaction-formation to explain the "maliciousness" and "negativism" of some delinquent behavior. Apparently the constant internal and external threats to his adjustment lead the delinquent to exaggerate the extent of his alienation from middle-class norms of conduct.

> If a new moral order is evolved which offers a more satisfactory solution to one's life problems, the old order usually continues to press for recognition, but if this recognition is granted, the apple-cart is upset. The symptom of this obscurely felt, ever-present threat is clinically known as "anxiety," and the literature of psychiatry is rich with devices for combatting . . . this threat to a hard-won victory. One such device is reaction-formation. Its hallmark is an "exaggerated," "disproportionate," "abnormal" intensity of response, "inappropriate" to the stimulus which seems to elicit it. . . . The "overreaction" . . . has the function of reassuring the actor against an *inner* threat to his defenses as well as the function of meeting an external situation on its own terms. . . . We would expect the delinquent boy, who, after all, has been socialized in a society dominated by a middle-class morality and who can never quite escape the blandishments of middle-class society, to seek to maintain his safeguards against seduction. Reaction-formation, in his case, should take the form of an "irrational," "malicious," "unaccountable" hostility to the enemy within the gates as well as without: the norms of the respectable middle-class society.[24]

In Cohen's view, then, the delinquent never quite gives up his allegiance to middle-class norms but continues to acknowledge their legitimacy secretly while openly challenging them by his behavior. In fact, the form and content of his behavior are apparently accounted for by this very ambivalence.

Sykes and Matza also see the delinquent as a person who continues to impute legitimacy to the official norms of the society, although they differ from Cohen in believing that this

23. *Ibid.*, p. 132.
24. *Ibid.*, p. 133.

imputation is often quite conscious. As they put it, "The juvenile delinquent frequently recognizes *both* the legitimacy of the dominant social order and its moral rightness."[25] Cohen solves the problem of the discrepancy between the delinquent's conduct and his attribution of legitimacy to middle-class norms by viewing his attachment to these rules as repressed and unconscious. Sykes and Matza solve the problem by citing various techniques which enable the delinquent to escape guilt feelings for his behavior by redefining the applicability of the official norms. The delinquent, they contend, does not repudiate conventional norms; he "neutralizes" them. What makes it possible for him to do this is that accepted rules of conduct "appear as *qualified* guides for action, limited in their applicability in terms of time, place, persons, and social circumstances"[26]—limited, for example, by the forms of justification allowed by the criminal law as defenses against crime. The delinquent subculture simply extends these limitations so as to justify the conduct of its members.

> The individual can avoid moral culpability for his criminal action—and thus avoid the negative sanctions of society—if he can prove that criminal intent was lacking. *It is our argument that much delinquency is based on what is essentially an unrecognized extension of defenses to crimes, in the form of justifications for deviance that are seen as valid by the delinquent but not by the legal system or society at large.*[27]

Thus the delinquent seems to concede the legitimacy of the existing structure of social rules, but he redefines the limitations on their applicability in such a way that his misconduct can be justified, at least to himself and his associates. For example, a street gang whose "turf" is invaded by a rival gang might redefine the situation as analogous to that of nations at war and might behave accordingly toward the invaders. Official representatives of the dominant value system and other conventional adults claim that this is an unwarranted extension

---

25. G. M. Sykes and David Matza, "Techniques of Neutralization: A Theory of Delinquency," *American Sociological Review*, Vol. 22 (Dec. 1957), p. 665.
26. *Ibid.*, p. 666.
27. *Ibid.*

of the code of conduct permissible in time of war. Youngsters claim, however, that this redefinition realistically fits the situation that confronts them.

It must be recognized in evaluating the position of Sykes and Matza that the delinquent's qualifications of official norms generally call for markedly different behavior than is conventionally expected in the situations to which they apply. Some established limitations upon the conditions under which otherwise proscribed conduct is justifiable are indispensable to the stability of the official normative system. By challenging the official definitions of these conditions, delinquent norms do compete with official norms.

In our view, the analyses by Cohen and by Sykes and Matza both fail to make four relevant distinctions: (1) between delinquent norms or rules of conduct (prescriptions), on the one hand, and the structure of beliefs (descriptions) and values (evaluations) on the other; (2) between the attribution of legitimacy to norms and the attribution of moral validity; (3) between the normative and moral problems of delinquents who are members of delinquent subcultures and the comparable problems of those who are not; and (4) between the presence of guilt and its absence in relation to the sequential development of justifying beliefs and delinquent norms.

In both these accounts there is a tendency to use the terms "norm," "belief," and "value" interchangeably, which leads to much confusion.[28] It is quite possible that the norms, beliefs, and values of a subculture develop by quite different processes. Unless these three features of a cultural system are kept analytically distinct, it is impossible to identify such developmental differences, to compare the time sequences in their growth, and to analyze how they become integrated into the system.

Secondly, both the Cohen and the Sykes and Matza

---

28. Examples of this practice can be found in the quotations from Cohen's work cited previously and in the following characteristic passage from Sykes and Matza (*op. cit.*, p. 666): "A basic clue is offered by the fact that social rules or norms calling for valued behavior seldom if ever take the form of categorical imperatives. Rather, values or norms appear as *qualified* guides for action. . . ."

positions tend to treat the problem of the legitimacy of a set of action prescriptions as equivalent to the problem of their moral validity.[29] They fail to perceive that the individual may regard a given norm as a legitimate guide to behavior under a particular set of circumstances even though at the same time he considers that pattern of action morally inferior to some alternative pattern. He may believe that law-abiding conduct is morally right but inappropriate or impossible in a particular situation. As a consequence of their failure to develop this distinction, Cohen and Sykes and Matza seem to be concerned almost exclusively with the moral judgments of delinquents and the way in which offenders handle problems of guilt. Both accounts assume that delinquents consciously or unconsciously impute legitimacy to the norms of the larger society. It is for this reason that Cohen and Short are able to view the work of Sykes and Matza as "an important elaboration of the argument of *Delinquent Boys*."[30] Similarly, both analyses assume that delinquents accept the moral superiority of conventional norms. Cohen and Short, in fact, point to reaction-formation as a mechanism for handling the resulting moral ambivalence and stress the importance of this mechanism in the position of Sykes and Matza as well.

Thirdly, these accounts do not differentiate sufficiently between the problems of members of delinquent subcultures and those of solitary delinquents. Yet this distinction may have strategic theoretical value. For example, it is our impression that the lone delinquent is much more likely to experience feelings of ambivalence toward conventional norms of conduct and moral evaluations. He is therefore more likely to experience severe guilt reactions and to use various psychological mechanisms for controlling them, such as the ones Cohen and Sykes and Matza describe. Further, the withdrawal of sentiments in support of law-abiding norms of conduct and the

29. Although Sykes and Matza recognize the distinction in a footnote commenting on its use by Weber (*ibid.*, p. 665, n. 4), it plays no part in their analytical scheme.

30. A. K. Cohen and J. F. Short, Jr., "Research in Delinquent Subcultures," *Journal of Social Issues*, Vol. 14, No. 3 (1958), p. 21.

imputation of legitimacy to a new set of norms seems much more likely to occur among delinquents who have collective support. It is difficult to see how an individual delinquent could maintain such a shift as a stable form of accommodation to his adjustment problems unless he also managed to acquire a rigid structure of supporting conceptions comparable to the delusional system of a paranoic. Generally speaking, the imputation of legitimacy to a model of conduct that is widely disapproved requires continual reassurance from others in order to persist.

Finally, the question of whether or not guilt feelings become a significant problem depends in large measure on when delinquent norms and justifying beliefs are developed. As we have indicated, the problem of guilt is resolved in advance of the delinquent act when the process of alienation has previously brought about a withdrawal of sentiments from official norms and the collective development of a supporting belief structure that justifies adherence to delinquent norms.[31] Sykes and Matza explicitly recognize this fact:

> These justifications are commonly described as rationalizations. They are viewed as following deviant behavior and as protecting the individual from self-blame and the blame of others after the

---

31. This insistence on the sequential priority of the justificatory beliefs to the development of delinquent norms is similar to Cressey's analysis of the relationship of "rationalizations" and acts of embezzlement. (See D. R. Cressey, *Other People's Money* [Glencoe, Ill.: Free Press, 1953], esp. pp. 93-138.) Cressey assigns a crucial role to the learning of rationalizations which would permit the offender to embezzle without damaging his self-image as a law-abiding person. He insists that these rationalizing beliefs, such as the assertion that one is "only borrowing," are not *post facto* defenses against accusations of dishonesty but mechanisms that facilitate the act in advance of its performance.

Cressey emphasizes the priority of the rationalization to the act more consistently than Sykes and Matza do. However, his usage differs sharply from ours in regard to the attribution of legitimacy. In Cressey's cases, the embezzlers continued to attribute legitimacy to law-abiding norms of conduct and employed rationalizing arguments of their continued adherence to those norms. In contrast, the innovators of delinquent subcultural norms develop beliefs which justify their withdrawal of legitimacy from established norms and their attribution of legitimacy to officially proscribed models of behavior.

act. But there is also reason to believe that they precede deviant behavior and make deviant behavior possible. . . . Disapproval flowing from internalized norms and conforming others in the social environment is neutralized, turned back, or deflected in advance. Social controls that serve to check or inhibit deviant motivational patterns are rendered inoperative, and the individual is freed to engage in delinquency without serious damage to his self-image. In this sense the delinquent both has his cake and eats it too, for he remains committed to the dominant normative system and yet so qualifies its imperatives that violations are "acceptable" if not "right." Thus the delinquent represents not a radical opposition to law-abiding society but sometimes more like an apologetic failure, often more sinned against than sinning in his own eyes. We call these justifications of deviant behavior "techniques of neutralization," and we believe these techniques make up a crucial component of Sutherland's "definitions favorable to the violation of law." It is by learning these techniques that the juvenile becomes delinquent, rather than by learning moral imperatives, values or attitudes standing in direct contradiction to those of the dominant society.[32]

They do not develop the implications of the priority of justifying beliefs to delinquent norms for the presence or absence of guilt. Instead they stress the delinquent's continued attribution of legitimacy to the dominant normative system and his consequent need to manage or neutralize the guilt that results.

The Collective Problem-Solving Process

IN ADDITION TO the motivation to seek support from others who feel alienated from the prevailing social norms, collective solutions require a set of conditions in which communication among alienated persons can take place. If there are serious barriers to communication among the disaffected, the chances for the development of a collective solution will be relatively slight. As Cohen points out, "The crucial condition for the emergence of new cultural norms is the existence, *in effective interaction with one another,* of a number of actors with similar problems of adjustment."[33] However, as Cohen makes clear,

32. Sykes and Matza, *op. cit.,* p. 666.
33. Cohen, *op. cit.,* p. 59.

"The existence of problems of adjustment, even of like problems of adjustment, among a plurality of actors is not sufficient to insure the emergence of a subcultural solution."[34] He calls attention to a variety of social conditions that may impede communication and hence the formation of a subculture:

People with like problems may be so separated by barriers of physical space or social convention that the probability of mutual exploration and discovery is small. Free choice of associates may be regulated by persons in power, as parents may regulate the associates of their children. Where status differences among people with like problems are great, the probability of spontaneous communication relating to private, intimate, emotionally involved matters is small. Where the problems themselves are of a particularly delicate, guilt-laden nature, like many problems arising in the area of sex, inhibitions on communication may be so powerful that persons with like problems may never reveal themselves to one another, although circumstances are otherwise favorable for mutual exploration. Or the problems themselves may be so infrequent and atypical that the probability of running into someone else whose interest would be served by a common solution is negligible.[35]

Cohen has described the collective problem-solving process as a "conversation of gestures" in which each participant gradually stimulates the others to reveal themselves. Through "mutual conversion" a "compromise formation" results to which each participant has contributed.

. . . [H]ow does one *know* whether a gesture toward innovation will strike a responsive and sympathetic chord in others or whether it will elicit hostility, ridicule and punishment? *Potential* concurrence is always problematical and innovation or the impulse to innovate a stimulus for anxiety.

The paradox is resolved when the innovation is broached in such a manner as to elicit from others reactions suggesting their receptivity; and when, at the same time, the innovation occurs by increments so small, tentative and ambiguous as to permit the actor to retreat, if the signs be unfavorable, without having become identified with an unpopular position. Perhaps all social actions have, in addition to their instrumental, communicative and expressed functions, this quality of being *exploratory* gestures. For the actor with problems of adjustment which cannot be resolved within the

34. *Ibid.*, p. 70.
35. *Ibid.*, pp. 70-71.

frame of reference of the established culture, each response of the other to what the actor says and does is a clue to the directions in which change may proceed further in a way congenial to the other and to the direction in which change will lack social support. And if the probing gesture is motivated by tensions common to other participants it is likely to initiate a process of *mutual* exploration and *joint* elaboration of a new solution. My exploratory gesture functions as a cue to you; your exploratory gesture as a cue to me. By a casual, semi-serious, noncommittal or tangential remark I may stick my neck out just a little way, but I will quickly withdraw it unless you, by some sign of affirmation, stick *yours* out. I will permit myself to become progressively committed but only as others, by some visible sign, become likewise committed. The final product, to which we are jointly committed, is likely to be a compromise formation of all the participants to what we may call a cultural process, a formation perhaps unanticipated by any of them. Each actor may contribute something directly to the growing product, but he may also contribute indirectly by encouraging others to advance, inducing them to retreat, and suggesting new avenues to be explored. The product cannot be ascribed to any one of the participants; it is a real "emergent" on a group level.

We may think of this process as one of mutual conversion. The important thing to remember is that we do not first convert ourselves and then others. The acceptability of an idea to oneself depends upon its acceptability to others. Converting the other is part of the process of converting oneself.[36]

This conversation of gestures serves at least four important functions. First, it permits the participants to explore the extent and intensity of one another's alienation from the prevailing cultural norms and to determine how far each is willing to go in developing alternative prescriptions for action. Secondly, it permits them to explore their mutual interest in developing a collective as opposed to an individual solution—to estimate the extent to which they will be able to rely upon one another for support if their solution should take a daring, rebellious, or delinquent path. Thirdly, it gives them an opportunity to elaborate and test various justificatory beliefs and values by means of which problems of moral validity and guilt can be neutralized in anticipation of commitment to a deviant course of action. Finally, it permits them to explore a variety

36. *Ibid.*, pp. 60-61.

of deviant solutions to the common adjustment problem, to assess the merits of each and its chances of success, and to weigh the commitment that the other is willing to undertake to each type of solution. Once they have located the blame for their troubles in the social system and have successfully communicated to one another the extent of their alienation from established norms and their interest in finding an alternative collective solution, the development of delinquent norms and of some type of delinquent subculture becomes possible.

The exploration and adoption of a collective alternative solution are facilitated by the invidious definitions and punitive responses with which the law-abiding adult community reacts to collective acts of deviance. Thus the emerging collectivity is made more acutely aware of its isolation from the conventional community.

> It does not become a gang, however, until it begins to excite disapproval and opposition, and thus acquires a more definite group-consciousness. It discovers a rival or an enemy in the gang in the next block; its baseball or football team is pitted against some other team; parents or neighbors look upon it with suspicion and hostility; "the old man around the corner," the storekeepers, or the "cops" begin to give it "shags" (chase it); or some representative of the community steps in and tries to break it up. This is the real beginning of the gang, for now it starts to draw itself more closely together. It becomes a conflict group.[37]

The group members begin to exhibit a greater cohesiveness and sense of mutual dependence. They learn to define more closely those who are friendly or hostile to their activities. The experience of arrest, court adjudication, and correctional treatment of some members of the group casts a new light on the meaning and consequences of their activities.

> There is a great deal more delinquency practiced and committed by the young groups than comes to the attention of the police. The boy arrested, therefore, is singled out in specialized treatment. This boy, no more guilty than the other members of his group, discovers a world of which he knew little. His arrest suddenly precipitates a series of institutions, attitudes, and experiences

---

37. F. M. Thrasher, *The Gang* (Chicago: University of Chicago Press, 1927), p. 30.

which the other children do not share. For this boy there suddenly appear the police, the patrol wagon, the police station, the other delinquents and criminals found in the police lock-ups, the court with all its agencies such as bailiffs, clerks, bondsmen, lawyers, probation officers. There are bars, cells, handcuffs, criminals. He is questioned, examined, tested, investigated. His history is gone into, his family is brought into court. Witnesses make their appearance. The boy, no different from the rest of his gang, suddenly becomes the center of a major drama in which all sorts of unexpected characters play important roles. And what is it all about? About the accustomed things his gang has done and has been doing for a long time. In this entirely new world he is made conscious of himself as a different human being than he was before his arrest. He becomes classified as a thief, perhaps, and the entire world about him has suddenly become a different place for him and will remain different for the rest of his life.[38]

The development of a delinquent solution thus depends not only on the exploratory gestures that boys direct toward one another but also on their interaction with others in the community. Through its representatives, official and unofficial, its institutions, and its other adolescent collectivities, the community enters into the life of the emerging delinquent gang at every stage. By the definitions it imposes and the opportunities it provides or denies, it helps to shape the final product.

Given conditions favorable for the development of a delinquent subculture, there is still the problem of explaining why different types of delinquent subculture develop. We must identify a new set of variables to explain why certain beliefs, values, and prescriptions for action emerge rather than others. It is to this problem that we turn in the next chapter.

38. Tannenbaum, *op. cit.*, p. 19.

HAROLD BRIDGES LIBRARY
S. MARTIN'S COLLEGE
LANCASTER

CHAPTER 6

Illegitimate Means and Delinquent Subcultures[1]

IN THIS CHAPTER and in Chapter 7, we shall be dealing with the differentiation of delinquent subcultures. Although we have discussed the pressures that give rise to delinquency and the forces that result in collective attempts to meet these pressures, we have yet to consider the question of why delinquent subcultures develop distinctive content. In this chapter, we shall develop a general hypothesis that, we believe, helps to answer this question. In Chapter 7

1. Substantial portions of this chapter have been taken from R. A. Cloward, "Illegitimate Means, Anomie and Deviant Behavior," *American Sociological Review,* Vol. 24, No. 2 (April 1959), pp. 164-76. See also R. K. Merton, "Social Conformity, Deviation, and Opportunity Structures: A Comment on the Contributions of Dubin and Cloward," *idem.,* pp. 177-89.

the specific applicability of this hypothesis to the criminal, conflict, and retreatist subcultures will be discussed in greater detail.

The Availability of Illegitimate Means

SOCIAL NORMS are two-sided. A prescription implies the existence of a prohibition, and *vice versa.* To advocate honesty is to demarcate and condemn a set of actions which are dishonest. In other words, norms that define legitimate practices also implicitly define illegitimate practices. One purpose of norms, in fact, is to delineate the boundary between legitimate and illegitimate practices. In setting this boundary, in segregating and classifying various types of behavior, they make us aware not only of behavior that is regarded as right and proper but also of behavior that is said to be wrong and improper. Thus the criminal who engages in theft or fraud does not invent a new way of life; the possibility of employing alternative means is acknowledged, tacitly at least, by the norms of the culture.

This tendency for proscribed alternatives to be implicit in every prescription, and *vice versa,* although widely recognized, is nevertheless a reef upon which many a theory of delinquency has foundered. Much of the criminological literature assumes, for example, that one may explain a criminal act simply by accounting for the individual's readiness to employ illegal alternatives of which his culture, through its norms, has already made him generally aware. Such explanations are quite unsatisfactory, however, for they ignore a host of questions regarding the *relative availability* of illegal alternatives to various potential criminals. The aspiration to be a physician is hardly enough to explain the fact of becoming a physician; there is much that transpires between the aspiration and the achievement. This is no less true of the person who wants to be a successful criminal. Having decided that he "can't make it legitimately," he cannot simply choose among an array of illegitimate means, all equally available to him. As we have noted earlier, it is assumed in the theory of anomie that access to conventional means is differentially distributed, that some individuals, because of their social class, enjoy certain advantages that are denied to those elsewhere in the class structure. For example, there are variations in the degree to which members of various classes are fully exposed to and thus acquire the values, knowledge, and skills that facilitate upward mobility. It should not be startling, therefore, to suggest that there are socially structured variations in the availability of illegitimate means as well. In connection with delinquent subcultures, we shall be concerned principally with differentials in access to illegitimate means within the lower class.

Many sociologists have alluded to differentials in access to illegitimate means without explicitly incorporating this variable into a theory of deviant behavior. This is particularly true of scholars in the "Chicago tradition" of criminology. Two closely related theoretical perspectives emerged from this school. The theory of "cultural transmission," advanced by Clifford R. Shaw and Henry D. McKay, focuses on the development in some urban neighborhoods of a criminal tradition that persists from one generation to another despite constant changes in population.[2] In the theory of "differential association," Edwin H. Sutherland described the processes by which criminal values are taken over by the individual.[3] He asserted that criminal behavior is learned, and that it is learned in interaction with others who have already incorporated criminal values. Thus the first theory stresses the value systems of different areas; the second, the systems of social relationships that facilitate or impede the acquisition of these values.

Scholars in the Chicago tradition, who emphasized the

---

2. See esp. C. R. Shaw, *The Jack-Roller* (Chicago: University of Chicago Press, 1930); Shaw, *The Natural History of a Delinquent Career* (Chicago: University of Chicago Press, 1931); Shaw *et al.*, *Delinquency Areas* (Chicago: University of Chicago Press, 1940); and Shaw and H. D. McKay, *Juvenile Delinquency and Urban Areas* (Chicago: University of Chicago Press, 1942).

3. E. H. Sutherland, ed., *The Professional Thief* (Chicago: University of Chicago Press, 1937); and Sutherland, *Principles of Criminology*, 4th Ed. (Philadelphia: Lippincott, 1947).

processes involved in learning to be criminal, were actually pointing to differentials in the availability of illegal means—although they did not explicitly recognize this variable in their analysis. This can perhaps best by seen by examining Sutherland's classic work, *The Professional Thief.* "An inclination to steal," according to Sutherland, "is not a sufficient explanation of the genesis of the professional thief."[4] The "self-made" thief, lacking knowledge of the ways of securing immunity from prosecution and similar techniques of defense, "would quickly land in prison; . . . a person can be a professional thief only if he is recognized and received as such by other professional thieves." But recognition is not freely accorded: "Selection and tutelage are the two necessary elements in the process of acquiring recognition as a professional thief. . . . A person cannot acquire recognition as a professional thief until he has had tutelage in professional theft, *and tutelage is given only to a few persons selected from the total population.*" For one thing, "the person must be appreciated by the professional thieves. He must be appraised as having an adequate equipment of wits, front, talking-ability, honesty, reliability, nerve and determination." Furthermore, the aspirant is judged by high standards of performance, for only "a very small percentage of those who start on this process ever reach the stage of professional thief. . . ." Thus motivation and pressures toward deviance do not fully account for deviant behavior any more than motivation and pressures toward conformity account for conforming behavior. The individual must have access to a learning environment and, once having been trained, must be allowed to perform his role. Roles, whether conforming or deviant in content, are not necessarily freely available; access to them depends upon a variety of factors, such as one's socioeconomic position, age, sex, ethnic affiliation, personality characteristics, and the like. The potential thief, like the potential physician, finds that access to his goal is governed by many criteria other than merit and motivation.

4. All quotations on this page are from *The Professional Thief,* pp. 211-13. Emphasis added.

What we are asserting is that access to illegitimate roles is not freely available to all, as is commonly assumed. Only those neighborhoods in which crime flourishes as a stable, indigenous institution are fertile criminal learning environments for the young. Because these environments afford integration of different age-levels of offender, selected young people are exposed to "differential association" through which tutelage is provided and criminal values and skills are acquired. To be prepared for the role may not, however, ensure that the individual will ever discharge it. One important limitation is that more youngsters are recruited into these patterns of differential associations than the adult criminal structure can possibly absorb. Since there is a surplus of contenders for these elite positions, criteria and mechanisms of selection must be evolved. Hence a certain proportion of those who aspire may not be permitted to engage in the behavior for which they have prepared themselves.

Thus we conclude that access to illegitimate roles, no less than access to legitimate roles, is limited by both social and psychological factors. We shall here be concerned primarily with socially structured differentials in illegitimate opportunities. Such differentials, we contend, have much to do with the type of delinquent subculture that develops.

Learning and Performance Structures

OUR USE of the term "opportunities," legitimate or illegitimate, implies access to both learning and performance structures. That is, the individual must have access to appropriate environments for the acquisition of the values and skills associated with the performance of a particular role, and he must be supported in the performance of the role once he has learned it.

Tannenbaum, several decades ago, vividly expressed the point that criminal role performance, no less than conventional role performance, presupposes a patterned set of relationships through which the requisite values and skills are transmitted by established practitioners to aspiring youth:

It takes a long time to make a good criminal, many years of specialized training and much preparation. But training is something that is given to people. People learn in a community where the materials and the knowledge are to be had. A craft needs an atmosphere saturated with purpose and promise. The community provides the attitudes, the point of view, the philosophy of life, the example, the motive, the contacts, the friendships, the incentives. No child brings those into the world. He finds them here and available for use and elaboration. The community gives the criminal his materials and habits, just as it gives the doctor, the lawyer, the teacher, and the candlestick-maker theirs.[5]

Sutherland systematized this general point of view, asserting that opportunity consists, at least in part, of learning structures. Thus "criminal behavior is learned" and, furthermore, it is learned "in interaction with other persons in a process of communication." However, he conceded that the differential-association theory does not constitute a full explanation of criminal behavior. In a paper circulated in 1944, he noted that "criminal behavior is partially a function of opportunities to commit [*i.e.*, to perform] specific classes of crime, such as embezzlement, bank burglary, or illicit heterosexual intercourse." Therefore, "while opportunity may be partially a function of association with criminal patterns and of the specialized techniques thus acquired, it is not determined entirely in that manner, and consequently differential association is not the sufficient cause of criminal behavior."[6]

To Sutherland, then, illegitimate opportunity included conditions favorable to the performance of a criminal role as well as conditions favorable to the learning of such a role (differential associations). These conditions, we suggest, depend upon certain features of the social structure of the community in which delinquency arises.

---

5. Frank Tannenbaum, "The Professional Criminal," *The Century*, Vol. 110 (May-Oct. 1925), p. 577.

6. See A. K. Cohen, Alfred Lindesmith, and Karl Schuessler, eds., *The Sutherland Papers* (Bloomington, Ind.: Indiana University Press, 1956), pp. 31-35.

Differential Opportunity: A Hypothesis

We believe that each individual occupies a position in both legitimate and illegitimate opportunity structures. This is a new way of defining the situation. The theory of anomie views the individual primarily in terms of the legitimate opportunity structure. It poses questions regarding differentials in access to legitimate routes to success-goals; at the same time it assumes either that illegitimate avenues to success-goals are freely available or that differentials in their availability are of little significance. This tendency may be seen in the following statement by Merton:

Several researches have shown that specialized areas of vice and crime constitute a "normal" response to a situation where the cultural emphasis upon pecuniary success has been absorbed, but where there is little access to conventional and legitimate means for becoming successful. The occupational opportunities of people in these areas are largely confined to manual labor and the lesser white-collar jobs. Given the American stigmatization of manual labor *which has been found to hold rather uniformly for all social classes,* and the absence of realistic opportunities for advancement beyond this level, the result is a marked tendency toward deviant behavior. The status of unskilled labor and the consequent low income cannot readily compete *in terms of established standards of worth* with the promises of power and high income from organized vice, rackets and crime. . . . [Such a situation] leads toward the gradual attenuation of legitimate, but by and large ineffectual, strivings and the increasing use of illegitimate, but more or less effective, expedients.[7]

The cultural-transmission and differential-association tradition, on the other hand, assumes that access to illegitimate means is variable, but it does not recognize the significance of comparable differentials in access to legitimate means. Sutherland's "ninth proposition" in the theory of differential association states:

Though criminal behavior is an expression of general needs and

7. R. K. Merton, *Social Theory and Social Structure,* Rev. and Enl. Ed. (Glencoe, Ill.: Free Press, 1957), pp. 145-46.

values, it is not explained by those general needs and values since non-criminal behavior is an expression of the same needs and values. Thieves generally steal in order to secure money, but likewise honest laborers work in order to secure money. The attempts by many scholars to explain criminal behavior by general drives and values, such as the happiness principle, striving for social status, the money motive, or frustration, have been and must continue to be futile since they explain lawful behavior as completely as they explain criminal behavior.[8]

In this statement, Sutherland appears to assume that people have equal and free access to legitimate means regardless of their social position. At the very least, he does not treat access to legitimate means as variable. It is, of course, perfectly true that "striving for social status," "the money motive," and other socially approved drives do not fully account for either deviant or conforming behavior. But if goal-oriented behavior occurs under conditions in which there are socially structured obstacles to the satisfaction of these drives by legitimate means, the resulting pressures, we contend, might lead to deviance.

The concept of differential opportunity structures permits us to unite the theory of anomie, which recognizes the concept of differentials in access to legitimate means, and the "Chicago tradition," in which the concept of differentials in access to illegitimate means is implicit. We can now look at the individual, not simply in relation to one or the other system of means, but in relation to both legitimate and illegitimate systems. This approach permits us to ask, for example, how the relative availability of illegitimate opportunities affects the resolution of adjustment problems leading to deviant behavior. We believe that the way in which these problems are resolved may depend upon the kind of support for one or another type of illegitimate activity that is given at different points in the social structure. If, in a given social location, illegal or criminal means are not readily available, then we should not expect a criminal subculture to develop among adolescents. By the same logic, we should expect the manipulation of violence to become a primary avenue to higher status only in areas

8. *Principles of Criminology, op. cit.*, pp. 7-8.

where the means of violence are not denied to the young. To give a third example, drug addiction and participation in subcultures organized around the consumption of drugs presuppose that persons can secure access to drugs and knowledge about how to use them. In some parts of the social structure, this would be very difficult; in others, very easy. In short, there are marked differences from one part of the social structure to another in the types of illegitimate adaptation that are available to persons in search of solutions to problems of adjustment arising from the restricted availability of legitimate means.[9] In this sense, then, we can think of individuals as being located in two opportunity structures—one legitimate, the other illegitimate. Given limited access to success-goals by legitimate means, the nature of the delinquent response that may result will vary according to the availability of various illegitimate means.[10]

Illegitimate Opportunities and the Social Structure of the Slum

WHEN we say that the form of delinquency that is adopted is conditioned by the presence or absence of appropriate illegitimate means, we are actually referring to crucial differences

9. For an example of restrictions on access to illegitimate roles, note the impact of racial definitions in the following case: "I was greeted by two prisoners who were to be my cell buddies. Ernest was a first offender, charged with being a 'hold-up' man. Bill, the other buddy, was an old offender, going through the machinery of becoming a habitual criminal, in and out of jail. . . . The first thing they asked me was, 'What are you in for?' I said, 'Jack-rolling.' The hardened one (Bill) looked at me with a superior air and said, 'A hoodlum, eh? An ordinary sneak thief. Not willing to leave jack-rolling to the niggers, eh? That's all they're good for. Kid, jack-rolling's not a white man's job.' I could see that he was disgusted with me, and I was too scared to say anything" (Shaw, *The Jack-Roller, op. cit.*, p. 101).

10. For a discussion of the way in which the availability of illegitimate means influences the adaptations of inmates to prison life, see R. A. Cloward, "Social Control in the Prison," *Theoretical Studies of the Social Organization of the Prison*, Bulletin No. 15 (New York: Social Science Research Council, March 1960), pp. 20-48.

in the social organization of various slum areas, for our hypothesis implies that the local milieu affects the delinquent's choice of a solution to his problems of adjustment. One of the principal ways in which slum areas vary is in the extent to which they provide the young with alternative (albeit illegitimate) routes to higher status. Many of the works in the cultural-transmission and differential-association tradition are focused directly on the relationship between deviant behavior and lower-class social structure. By reconceptualizing aspects of that tradition, we hope to make our central hypothesis more explicit.

INTEGRATION OF DIFFERENT AGE-LEVELS OF OFFENDER

In their ecological studies of the urban environment, Shaw and McKay found that delinquency tended to be confined to limited areas and to persist in these areas despite demographic changes. Hence they spoke of "criminal traditions" and of the "cultural transmission" of criminal values.[11] As a result of their observations of slum life, they concluded that particular importance must be assigned to the relationships between immature and sophisticated offenders—which we call the integration of different age-levels of offender. They suggested that many youngsters are recruited into criminal activities as a direct result of intimate associations with older and more experienced offenders:

> Stealing in the neighborhood was a common practice among the children and approved of by the parents. Whenever the boys got together they talked about robbing and made more plans for stealing. I hardly knew any boys who did not go robbing. The little fellows went in for petty stealing, breaking into freight cars, and stealing junk. The older guys did big jobs like stick-ups, burglary, and stealing autos. The little follows admired the "big shots" and longed for the day when they could get into the big racket. Fellows who had "done time" were the big shots and looked up to and gave the little fellows tips on how to get by and pull off big jobs.[12]

11. See esp. Shaw *et al., Delinquency Areas, op. cit.,* Chap. 16.
12. Shaw, *The Jack-Roller, op. cit.,* p. 54.

Thus the "big shots"—conspicuous successes in the criminal world—become role-models for youth, much more important as such than successful figures in the conventional world, who are usually socially and geographically remote from the slum area. Through intimate and stable associations with these older criminals, the young acquire the values and skills required for participation in the criminal culture. Further, structural connections between delinquents, semimature criminals, and the adult criminal world, where they exist, provide opportunities for upward mobility; where such integrative arrangements do not exist, the young are cut off from this alternative pathway to higher status.

INTEGRATION OF CONVENTIONAL AND DEVIANT VALUES

Shaw and McKay were describing deviant learning structures—that is, alternative routes by which people seek access to the goals that society holds to be worthwhile. Their point was that access to criminal roles and advancement in the criminal hierarchy depend upon stable associations with older criminals from whom the necessary values and skills may be learned. Yet Shaw and McKay failed to give explicit recognition to the concept of illegitimate means and the socially structured conditions of access to them—probably because they tended to view slum areas as "disorganized." Although they consistently referred to illegitimate *activities* as "organized," they nevertheless tended to label high-rate delinquency *areas* "disorganized" because the values transmitted were criminal rather than conventional. Hence they sometimes made statements which we now perceive to be internally inconsistent, such as the following:

> This community situation was not only disorganized and thus ineffective as a unit of control, but it was characterized by a high rate of juvenile delinquency and adult crime, not to mention the widespread political corruption which had long existed in the area. Various forms of stealing and many organized delinquent and criminal gangs were prevalent in the area. These groups exercised a powerful influence and tended to create a community spirit

which not only tolerated but actually fostered delinquent and criminal practices.[13]

Sutherland was among the first to perceive that the concept of social disorganization tends to obscure the stable patterns of interaction which exist among carriers of criminal values: "the organization of the delinquent group, which is often very complex, is social disorganization only from an ethical or some other particularistic point of view."[14] Like Shaw and McKay, he had observed that criminal activities in lower-class areas were organized in terms of a criminal value system, but he also observed that *this alternative value system was supported by a patterned system of social relations.* That is, he recognized the fact that crime, far from being a random, unorganized activity, is often an intricate and stable system of arrangements and relationships. He therefore rejected the "social disorganization" perspective: "At the suggestion of Albert K. Cohen, this concept has been changed to differential group organization, with organization for criminal activities on one side and organization against criminal activities on the other."[15]

William F. Whyte, in his classic study of an urban slum, carried the empirical description of the structure and organization of illegal means a step further. Like Sutherland, Whyte rejected the position of Shaw and McKay that the slum is *dis*organized simply because it is organized according to principles different from those in the conventional world:

It is customary for the sociologist to study the slum district in terms of "social disorganization" and to neglect to see that an area such as Cornerville has a complex and well-established organization of its own. . . . I found that in every group there was a hierarchical structure of social relations binding the individuals to one another and that the groups were also related hierarchically to one another. Where the group was formally organized into a politi-

13. Shaw, *The Natural History of a Delinquent Career, op. cit.*, p. 229.

14. Cohen, Lindesmith, and Schuessler, eds., *op. cit.*, p. 21.

15. *Ibid.*

cal club, this was immediately apparent, but for informal groups it was no less true.[16]

But Whyte's view of the slum differed somewhat from Sutherland's in that Whyte's emphasis was not on "differential group organization"—the idea that the slum is composed of two discrete systems, conventional and deviant. He stressed, rather, the way in which the occupants of various roles in these two systems become integrated in a single, stable structure which organizes and patterns the life of the community. Thus Whyte showed that individuals who participate in stable illicit enterprises do not constitute a separate or isolated segment of the community but are closely integrated with the occupants of conventional roles. He noted, for example, that "the rackets and political organizations extend from the bottom to the top of Cornerville society, mesh with one another, and integrate a large part of the life of the district. They provide a general framework for the understanding of the actions of both 'little guys' and 'big shots.' "[17]

In a recent article, Kobrin has clarified our understanding of slum areas by suggesting that they differ in the *degree* to which deviant and conventional value systems are integrated with each other. This difference, we argue, affects the relative accessibility of illegal means. Pointing the way to the development of a "typology of delinquent areas based on variations in the relationship between these two systems," Kobrin describes the "polar types" on such a continuum. The integrated area, he asserts, is characterized not only by structural integration between carriers of the two value systems but also by reciprocal participation by carriers of each in the value system of the other. Thus, he notes:

Leaders of [illegal] enterprises frequently maintain membership in such conventional institutions of their local communities as churches, fraternal and mutual benefit societies and political parties. . . . Within this framework the influence of each of the two value systems is reciprocal, the leaders of illegal enterprise par-

16. W. F. Whyte, *Street Corner Society*, Enl. Ed. (Chicago: University of Chicago Press, 1955), p. viii.

17. *Ibid.*, p. xii.

ticipating in the primary orientation of the conventional elements in the population, and the latter, through their participation in a local power structure sustained in large part by illicit activity, participating perforce in the alternate, criminal value system.[18]

The second polar type consists of areas in which the relationships between carriers of deviant and conventional values break down because of disorganizing forces such as "drastic change in the class, ethnic, or racial characteristics of [the] population." Kobrin suggests that in such slums "the bearers of the conventional culture and its value system are without the customary institutional machinery and therefore in effect partially demobilized with reference to the diffusion of their value system." At the same time, areas of this type are "characterized principally by the absence of systematic and organized adult activity in violation of the law, despite the fact that many adults in these areas commit violations." Thus both value systems remain implicit, but the fact that neither is "systematic and organized" precludes the possibility of effective integration.

How does the accessibility of illegal means vary with the relative integration of conventional and criminal values in a given area? Although Kobrin does not take up this problem explicitly, he does note that the integrated area apparently constitutes a "training ground" for the acquisition of criminal values and skills. Of his first polar type he says:

> The stable position of illicit enterprise in the adult society of the community is reflected in the character of delinquent conduct on the part of children. While delinquency in all high-rate areas is intrinsically disorderly in that it is unrelated to official programs for the education of the young, in the [integrated community] boys may more or less realistically recognize the potentialities for personal progress in local society through access to delinquency. In a general way, therefore, delinquent activity in these areas constitutes a training ground for the acquisition of skill in the use of violence, concealment of offense, evasion of detection and arrest, and the purchase of immunity from punishment. Those who come to excel in these respects are frequently noted and valued by adult leaders in the rackets who are confronted, as are the leaders of

18. Solomon Kobrin, "The Conflict of Values in Delinquency Areas," *American Sociological Review,* Vol. 16 (Oct. 1951), pp. 657-58.

all income-producing enterprises, with problems of the recruitment of competent personnel.[19]

Kobrin makes no mention of the extent to which learning structures and opportunities for criminal careers are available in the unintegrated area. Yet the fact that neither conventional nor criminal values are articulated in this type of area as he describes it suggests that the appropriate learning structures—principally integration of different age-levels of offenders—are not available. Furthermore, Kobrin's description of adult violative activity in such areas as "unorganized" suggests that illegal opportunities are severely limited. Even if youngsters were able to secure adequate preparation for criminal roles, the social structure of such neighborhoods would appear to provide few opportunities for stable criminal careers. Kobrin's analysis—as well as that of Whyte and others before him—supports our conclusion that *illegal opportunity structures tend to emerge only when there are stable patterns of accommodation between the adult carriers of conventional and of deviant values.* Where these two value systems are implicit, or where the carriers are in open conflict, opportunities for stable criminal-role performance are limited. Where stable accommodative relationships exist between the adult carriers of criminal and conventional values, institutionalized criminal careers are available. The alienated adolescent need not rely on the vagaries of private entrepreneurship in crime, with the attendant dangers of detection and prosecution, imprisonment, fluctuations in income, and the like. Instead, he may aspire to rise in the organized criminal structure and to occupy a permanent position in some flourishing racket. Secure in such a position, he will be relatively immune from prosecution and imprisonment, can expect a more or less stable income, and can look forward to acceptance by the local community—criminal and conventional.

Some urban neighborhoods, in short, provide relief from pressures arising from limitations on access to success-goals by legitimate means. Because alternative routes to higher status are made available to those who are ambitious, diligent, and

19. *Ibid.*

meritorious, the frustrations of youth in these neighborhoods are drained off. Where such pathways do not exist, frustrations become all the greater.

Slum Organization and Subcultural Differentiation

BEFORE we turn to a discussion of the relationship between particular forms of slum organization and the differentiation of subcultural content, it might be useful to note a recent article by Cohen and Short pertaining to subcultural differentiation.[20] These authors assert that delinquency is basically "non-utilitarian, malicious, negativistic, versatile, and characterized by short-run hedonism and group-autonomy"—a position consistent with Cohen's earlier point of view, as expressed in *Delinquent Boys*. But the recent work of Cohen and Short also notes the existence of different types of delinquent subculture—principally of the criminal, conflict, and drug-use varieties. How, then, do they reconcile this conclusion about subcultural differentiation with their assertion that delinquency is "basically" non-utilitarian, malicious, and the like?

The point they make is that subcultural content varies depending on the age-level of the participants. Among younger delinquents, they suggest, a universal or generic form of subculture emerges which is *independent* of its specific social milieu. This subcultural form is characterized by a diffuse agglomeration of cultural traits, including an orientation toward the "kick," a "conflict" orientation, and an orientation toward the illegal acquisition of money or goods. These traits or orientations, some of which are more or less incompatible with others, can nevertheless coexist because the subculture is loosely organized and thus capable of considerable cultural versatility. As the participants mature, however, additional (un-

20. A. K. Cohen and J. F. Short, Jr., "Research in Delinquent Subcultures," *Journal of Social Issues*, Vol. 14, No. 3 (Summer 1958), pp. 20-37.

specified) forces intervene which intensify the latent conflict between these orientations. Cliques within the subculture may then break away and form a more specialized sub-subculture which tends to value one orientation more than others (*e.g.*, disciplined theft rather than indiscriminate violence and destruction). If a particular cultural orientation comes to be widely diffused through the group, the generic culture as a whole may tend to become specialized. In either case, Cohen and Short believe that the process of subcultural differentiation occurs at later stages in the age cycle.

We question the validity of this point of view, for it rests upon what we consider an unwarranted premise; namely, that the social milieu influences the content of subcultural solutions at some points in the age cycle but not at other points. We prefer to make a quite different assumption; namely, that *the social milieu affects the nature of the deviant response whatever the motivation and social position* (i.e., *age, sex, socioeconomic level*) *of the participants in the delinquent subculture.* We assume that the local cultural and social structure impinges upon and modifies deviant responses from the very outset. The delinquent subculture may or may not be fully specialized at first, but we should not expect it to manifest all three delinquent orientations to the same extent, even at an early stage of development. In other words, we should expect the content of delinquent subcultures to vary predictably with certain features of the milieu in which these cultures emerge. And we should further expect these predominant traits to become all the more articulated and specialized as the subcultures become stabilized and integrated with their respective environments. With these notions in mind, we turn now to a discussion of the three types of subculture and their relationship to features of slum social structure.

CHAPTER 7

Subcultural Differentiation

WE COME NOW to the question of the specific social conditions that make for the emergence of distinctive delinquent subcultures. Throughout this analysis, we shall make extensive use of the concepts of social organization developed in the preceding chapter: namely, integration of different age-levels of offenders, and integration of carriers of conventional and deviant values. Delinquent responses vary from one neighborhood to another, we believe, according to the articulation of these structures in the neighborhood. Our object here is to show more precisely how various forms of neighborhood integration affect the development of subcultural content.

The Criminal Subculture

THE CRIMINAL SUBCULTURE, like the conflict and retreatist adaptations, requires a specialized environment if it is to flourish. Among the environmental supports of a criminal style of life are integration of offenders at various age-levels and close integration of the carriers of conventional and illegitimate values.

INTEGRATION OF AGE-LEVELS

Nowhere in the criminological literature is the concept of integration between different age-levels of offender made more explicit than in discussions of criminal learning. Most criminologists agree that criminal behavior presupposes patterned sets of relationships through which the requisite values and skills are communicated or transmitted from one age-level to another. What, then, are some of the specific components of systems organized for the socialization of potential criminals?

Criminal Role-Models—The lower class is not without its own distinctive and indigenous illegitimate success-models. Many accounts in the literature suggest that lower-class adults who have achieved success by illegitimate means not only are highly visible to young people in slum areas but often are willing to establish intimate relationships with these youth.

"Every boy has some ideal he looks up to and admires. His ideal may be Babe Ruth, Jack Dempsey, or Al Capone. When I was twelve, we moved into a neighborhood with a lot of gangsters. They were all swell dressers and had big cars and carried "gats." Us kids saw these swell guys and mingled with them in the cigar store on the corner. Jack Gurney was the one in the mob that I had a fancy to. He used to take my sis out and that way I saw him often. He was in the stick-up rackets before he was in the beer rackets, and he was a swell dresser and had lots of dough. . . . I liked to be near him and felt stuck up over the other guys because he came to my home to see my sis."[1]

Just as the middle-class youth, as a consequence of intimate relationships with, say, a banker or a businessman, may aspire to *become* a banker or a businessman, so the lower-class youth may be associated with and aspire to become a "policy

1. C. R. Shaw, "Juvenile Delinquency—A Group Tradition," *Bulletin of the State University of Iowa*, No. 23, N. S. No. 700, 1933, p. 8.

king": " 'I want to be a big shot. . . . Have all the guys look up to me. Have a couple of Lincolns, lots of broads, and all the coppers licking my shoes.' "[2] The crucial point here is that success-goals are not equally available to persons in different positions in the social structure. To the extent that social-class lines act as barriers to interaction between persons in different social strata, conventional success-models may not be salient for lower-class youth. The successful criminal, on the other hand, may be an intimate, personal figure in the fabric of the lower-class area. Hence one of the forces leading to rational, disciplined, crime-oriented delinquency may be the availability of criminal success-models.

Age-grading of Criminal Learning and Performance—The process by which the young acquire the values and skills prerequisite for a stable criminal career has been described in many studies. The central mechanism in the learning process is integration of different age-levels of offender. In an extensive study of a criminal gang on the Lower East Side of New York City, Bloch and Niederhoffer found that

> . . . the Pirates [a group of young adults] was actually the central organizing committee, the party headquarters for the youthful delinquents in the area. They held regular conferences with the delegates from outlying districts to outline strategy. . . . The younger Corner Boys [a gang of adolescents in the same vicinity] who . . . were trying to join with the older Pirates . . . were on a probationary status. If they showed signs of promise, a couple of them were allowed to accompany the Pirates on tours of exploration to look over the terrain around the next "job."[3]

At the pinnacle of this age-graded system stood an adult, Paulie.

> Paulie had real prestige in the gang. His was the final say in all important decisions. Older than the other members [of the Pirates] by seven or eight years, he maintained a certain air of mystery. . . . From talks with more garrulous members, it was learned that Paulie was the mastermind behind some of the gang's most impressive coups.[4]

---

2. *Ibid.*, p. 9.
3. H. H. Bloch and Arthur Niederhoffer, *The Gang: A Study in Adolescent Behavior* (New York: Philosophical Library, 1958), pp. 198-99.
4. *Ibid.*, p. 201.

The basis of Paulie's prestige in the gang is apparent in the following account of his relationship with the full-fledged adult criminal world:

From his contacts, information was obtained as to the most inviting locations to burglarize. It was he who developed the strategy and outlined the major stages of each campaign of burglary or robbery. . . . Another vital duty which he performed was to get rid of the considerable loot, which might consist of jewelry, clothing, tools, or currency in large denominations. His contact with professional gangsters, fences, bookies, made him an ideal choice for this function.[5]

Learning alone, as we have said, does not ensure that the individual can or will perform the role for which he has been prepared. The social structure must also support the actual performance of the role. To say that the individual must have the opportunity to discharge a stable criminal role as well as to prepare for it does not mean that role-preparation necessarily takes place in one stage and role-performance in a succeeding stage. The apprentice may be afforded oportunities to play out a particular role at various points in the learning process.

When we were shoplifting we always made a game of it. For example, we might gamble on who could steal the most caps in a day, or who could steal in the presence of a detective and then get away. This was the best part of the game. I would go into a store to steal a cap, by trying one on when the clerk was not watching, walk out of the store, leaving the old cap. With the new cap on my head I would go into another store, do the same thing as in the other store, getting a new hat and leaving the one I had taken from the other place. I might do this all day. . . . It was the fun I wanted, not the hat. I kept this up for months and *then began to sell the things to a man on the West Side. It was at this time that I began to steal for gain.*[6]

This quotation illustrates how delinquent role-preparation and role-performance may be integrated even at the "play-group" stage of illegitimate learning. The child has an opportunity to actually perform illegitimate roles because such activity finds

5. *Ibid.*
6. Shaw, *op. cit.*, p. 3. Emphasis added.

support in his immediate neighborhood milieu. The rewards—monetary and other—of successful learning and performance are immediate and gratifying at each age level.

INTEGRATION OF VALUES

Unless the carriers of criminal and conventional values are closely bound to one another, stable criminal roles cannot develop. The criminal, like the occupant of a conventional role, must establish relationships with other categories of persons, all of whom contribute in one way or another to the successful performance of criminal activity. As Tannenbaum says, "The development of the criminal career requires and finds in the immediate environment other supporting elements in addition to the active 'criminal gangs'; to develop the career requires the support of middlemen. These may be junk men, fences, lawyers, bondsmen, 'backers,' as they are called."[7] The intricate systems of relationship between these legitimate and illegitimate persons constitute the type of environment in which the juvenile criminal subculture can come into being.[8]

An excellent example of the way in which the content of a delinquent subculture is affected by its location in a particular milieu is afforded by the "fence," a dealer in stolen goods who is found in some but not all lower-class neighborhoods. Relationships between such middlemen and criminals are not confined to adult offenders; numerous accounts of lower-class life suggest not only that relationships form between fences and youngsters but also that the fence is a crucial element in the structure of illegitimate opportunity. He often caters to and encourages delinquent activities among the young. He may even exert controls leading the young to orient their stealing in the most lucrative and least risky directions. The same point

7. Frank Tannenbaum, *Crime and the Community* (New York: Columbia University Press, 1938), p. 60.

8. In this connection, see R. A. Cloward, "Social Control in the Prison," *Theoretical Studies of the Social Oragnization of the Prison,* Bulletin No. 15 (New York: Social Science Research Council, March 1960), pp. 20-48, which illustrates similar forms of integration in a penal setting.

may be made of junk dealers in some areas, racketeers who permit minors to run errands, and other occupants of illegitimate or semilegitimate roles.

As the apprentice criminal passes from one status to another in the illegitimate opportunity system, we should expect him to develop an ever-widening set of relationships with members of the semilegitimate and legitimate world. For example, a delinquent who is rising in the structure might begin to come into contact with mature criminals, law-enforcement officials, politicians, bail bondsmen, "fixers," and the like. As his activities become integrated with the activities of these persons, his knowledge of the illegitimate world is deepened, new skills are acquired, and the opportunity to engage in new types of illegitimate activity is enhanced. Unless he can form these relationships, the possibility of a stable, protected criminal style of life is effectively precluded.

The type of environment that encourages a criminal orientation among delinquents is, then, characterized by close integration of the carriers of conventional and illegitimate values. The *content* of the delinquent subculture is a more or less direct response to the local milieu in which it emerges. And it is the "integrated" neighborhood, we suggest, that produces the criminal type of delinquent subculture.

STRUCTURAL INTEGRATION AND SOCIAL CONTROL

Delinquent behavior generally exhibits a component of aggressiveness. Even youth in neighborhoods that are favorable learning environments for criminal careers are likely to engage in some "bopping" and other forms of violence. Hence one feature of delinquency that must be explained is its tendency toward aggressive behavior. However, aggressiveness is not the primary component of all delinquent behavior; it is much more characteristic of some delinquent groups than of others. Therefore, we must also concern ourselves with the conditions under which the aggressive component becomes ascendant.

The importance of assessing the relative dominance of

expressive and instrumental components in delinquent patterns is often overlooked. Cohen, for example, stresses the aggressive or expressive aspect of delinquent behavior, remarking that "it is non-utilitarian, malicious and negativistic," although he also asserts that these traits may not characterize all delinquency. Cohen's tendency to neglect relatively nonaggressive aspects of delinquency is related to his failure to take into account the relationships between delinquent behavior and adult criminality. However, *depending upon the presence or absence of those integrative relationships,* behavior that appears to be "non-utilitarian" in achieving access to conventional roles may possess considerable utility for securing access to criminal roles. Furthermore, these integrated systems may have important consequences for social control.

To the extent that delinquents take as their primary reference group older and more sophisticated gang boys, or even fully acculturated criminals or racketeers, dramatic instances of "malicious, negativistic" behavior may represent efforts to express solidarity with the norms of the criminal world. Delinquents who so behave in an attempt to win acceptance by older criminals may be engaging in a familiar sociological process; namely, overconformity to the norms of a group to which they aspire but do not belong. By such overconformity to the norms of the criminal world, delinquents seek to dramatize their eligibility for membership. To an observer oriented toward conventional values, aggressive behavior of this kind might appear to be purposeless. However, from the perspective of the carriers of deviant values, conspicuous defiance of conventional values may validate the "rightness" of the aspirant. Once he has been defined as "right," he may then be selected for further socialization and preparation for mature criminal activity.

Once the delinquent has successfully demonstrated his eligibility for acceptance by persons higher in the criminal structure, social controls are exerted to suppress undisciplined, expressive behavior; there is no place in organized crime for the impulsive, unpredictable individual. A dramatic illustration of the emphasis upon instrumental performance is offered by the case of Murder, Inc. Abe Reles, a former member of the syndicate who turned state's evidence, made certain comments about Murder, Inc. which illustrate perfectly Max Weber's famous characterization of the norms governing role performance and interpersonal relationships in bureaucratic organizations: *"Sine ira et studio"* ("without anger or passion").

> The crime trust, Reles insists, never commits murder out of passion, excitement, jealousy, personal revenge, or any of the usual motives which prompt private, unorganized murder. It kills impersonally, and solely for business considerations. Even business rivalry, he adds, is not the usual motive, unless "somebody gets too balky or somebody steps right on top of you." No gangster may kill on his own initiative; every murder must be ordered by the leaders at the top, and it must serve the welfare of the organization. . . . The crime trust insists that that murder must be a business matter, organized by the chiefs in conference and carried out in a disciplined way. "It's a real business all the way through," Reles explains. "It just happens to be that kind of business, but nobody is allowed to kill from personal grievance. There's got to be a good business reason, and top men of the combination must give their okay."[9]

The pressure for rational role performance in the adult criminal world is exerted downward, we suggest, through interconnected systems of age-graded statuses. At each point in this illegitimate hierarchy, instrumental rather than expressive behavior is emphasized. In their description of the Pirates, for example, Bloch and Niederhoffer observe that Paulie, the adult mastermind of the gang, avoided expressive behavior: "The younger Pirates might indulge in wild adolescent antics. Paulie remained aloof."[10] Paulie symbolized a mode of life in which reason, discipline, and foresight were uppermost. To the extent that younger members of the gang identified with him, they were constrained to adopt a similar posture. Rico, the leader of a gang described in a recent book by Harrison Salisbury, can be characterized in much the same way:

---

9. Joseph Freeman, "Murder Monopoly: The Inside Story of a Crime Trust," *The Nation,* Vol. 150, No. 21 (May 25, 1940), p. 648. This is but one of many sources in which the bureaucratization of crime is discussed.

10. Bloch and Niederhoffer, *op. cit.,* p. 201.

This youngster was the most successful kid in the neighborhood. He was a dope pusher. Some weeks he made as much as $200. He used his influence in some surprising ways. He persuaded the gang members to stop bopping because he was afraid it would bring on police intervention and interfere with his drug sales. He flatly refused to sell dope to boys and kicked out of the gang any kid who started to use drugs. He sold only to adults. With his money he bought jackets for the gang, took care of hospital bills of members, paid for the rent on his mother's flat, paid most of the family expenses and sometimes spent sixty dollars to buy a coat as a present for one of his boys.[11]

The same analysis helps to explain a puzzling aspect of delinquent behavior; namely, the apparent disregard delinquents sometimes exhibit for stolen objects. Some theorists have concluded from this that the ends of stealing are not utilitarian, that delinquents do not steal because they need or want the objects in question or for any other rational reason. Cohen, for example, asserts that "were the participant in the delinquent subculture merely employing illicit means to the end of acquiring economic goods, he would show more respect for the goods he has thus acquired."[12] Hence, Cohen concludes, the bulk of stealing among delinquents is "for the hell of it" rather than for economic gain. Whether stealing is expressive or instrumental may depend, however, on the social context in which it occurs. Where criminal opportunities exist, it may be argued that stealing is a way of expressing solidarity with the carriers of criminal values and, further, that it is a way of acquiring the various concrete skills necessary before the potential criminal can gain full acceptance in the group to which he aspires. That is, a certain amount of stealing may be motivated less by immediate need for the objects in question than by a need to acquire skill in the arts of theft. When practice in theft is the implicit purpose, the manner of disposing of stolen goods is unimportant. Similarly, the status accruing to the pickpocket who can negotiate a "left-front-breech" derives not so much

---

11. H. E. Salisbury, *The Shook-up Generation* (New York: Harper & Bros., 1958), p. 176.

12. A. K. Cohen, *Delinquent Boys: The Culture of the Gang* (Glencoe, Ill.: Free Press, 1955), p. 36.

from the immediate profit attaching to this maneuver as from the fact that it marks the individual as a master craftsman. In other words, where criminal learning environments and opportunity structures exist, stealing beyond immediate economic needs may constitute anticipatory socialization. But where these structures do not exist, such stealing may be simply an expressive act in defiance of conventional values.

Shaw pointed to a related aspect of the social control of delinquent behavior. Noting the prestige ordering of criminal activities, he commented on the way in which such definitions, once internalized, tend to regulate the behavior of delinquents:

> It is a matter of significance to note . . . that there is a general tendency among older delinquents and criminals to look with contempt upon the person who specializes in any form of petty stealing. The common thief is not distinguished for manual dexterity and accomplishment, like the pickpocket or mobsman, nor for courage, ingenuity and skill, like the burglar, but is characterized by low cunning and stealth—hence the term "sneak thief." . . . It is possible that the stigma attaching to petty stealing among members of older delinquent groups is one factor which gives impetus to the young delinquent's desire to abandon such forms of petty delinquency as stealing junk, vegetables, breaking into freight cars . . . and to become identified with older groups engaged in such crimes as larceny of automobiles and robbery with a gun, both of which are accredited "rackets" among older delinquents. . . .[13]

To the extent that an area has an age-graded criminal structure in which juvenile delinquents can become enmeshed, we suggest that the norms governing adult criminal-role performance filter down, becoming significant principles in the life-organization of the young. The youngster who has come into contact with such an age-graded structure and who has won initial acceptance by older and more sophisticated delinquents will be less likely to engage in malicious, destructive behavior than in disciplined, instrumental, career-oriented behavior. In this way the adult criminal system exerts controls over the behavior of delinquents. Referring to urban areas characterized by integration of different age-levels of offender,

---

13. Shaw, *op. cit.*, p. 10.

Kobrin makes an observation that tends to bear out our theoretical scheme:

> . . . delinquency tends to occur within a partial framework of social controls, insofar as delinquent activity in these areas represents a tolerated means for the acquisition of an approved role and status. Thus, while delinquent activity here possesses the usual characteristics of violence and destructiveness, there tend to develop effective limits of permissible activity in this direction. Delinquency is, in other words, encompassed and contained within a local social structure, and is marginally but palpably related to that structure.[14]

In summary, the criminal subculture is likely to arise in a neighborhood milieu characterized by close bonds between different age-levels of offender, and between criminal and conventional elements. As a consequence of these integrative relationships, a new opportunity structure emerges which provides alternative avenues to success-goals. Hence the pressures generated by restrictions on legitimate access to success-goals are drained off. Social controls over the conduct of the voung are effectively exercised, limiting expressive behavior and constraining the discontented to adopt instrumental, if criminalistic, styles of life.

The Conflict Subculture

BECAUSE youngsters caught up in the conflict subculture often endanger their own lives and the lives of others and cause considerable property damage, the conflict form of delinquency is a source of great public concern. Its prevalence, therefore, is probably exaggerated. There is no evidence to suggest that the conflict subculture is more widespread than the other subcultures, but the nature of its activities makes it more visible and thus attracts public attention. As a consequence, many people

14. Solomon Kobrin, "The Conflict of Values in Delinquency Areas," *American Sociological Review,* Vol. 16 (Oct. 1951), p. 657.

erroneously equate "delinquency" and "conflict behavior." But whatever its prevalence, the conflict subculture is of both theoretical and social importance, and calls for explanation.

Earlier in this book, we questioned the common belief that slum areas, because they are slums, are necessarily disorganized. We pointed to forms of integration which give some slum areas unity and cohesion. Areas in which these integrative structures are found, we suggested, tend to be characterized by criminal rather than conflict or retreatist subcultures. But not all slums are integrated. Some lower-class urban neighborhoods lack unity and cohesiveness. Because the prerequisites for the emergence of stable systems of social relations are not present, a state of social disorganization prevails.

The many forces making for instability in the social organization of some slum areas include high rates of vertical and geographic mobility; massive housing projects in which "site tenants" are not accorded priority in occupancy, so that traditional residents are dispersed and "strangers" re-assembled; and changing land use, as in the case of residential areas that are encroached upon by the expansion of adjacent commercial or industrial areas. Forces of this kind keep a community off balance, for tentative efforts to develop social organization are quickly checked. Transiency and instability become the overriding features of social life.

Transiency and instability, in combination, produce powerful pressures for violent behavior among the young in these areas. First, an unorganized community cannot provide access to legitimate channels to success-goals, and thus discontent among the young with their life-chances is heightened. Secondly, access to stable criminal opportunity systems is also restricted, for disorganized neighborhoods do not develop integration of different age-levels of offender or integration of carriers of criminal and conventional values. The young, in short, are relatively deprived of *both* conventional and criminal opportunity. Finally, social controls are weak in such communities. These conditions, we believe, lead to the emergence of conflict subcultures.

SOCIAL DISORGANIZATION AND OPPORTUNITY

Communities that are unable to develop conventional forms of social organization are also unable to provide legitimate modes of access to culturally valued success-goals. The disorganized slum is a world populated with failures, with the outcasts of the larger society. Here families orient themselves not toward the future but toward the present, not toward social advancement but toward survival. The adult community, being disorganized, cannot provide the resources and opportunities that are required if the young are to move upward in the social order.

Just as the unintegrated slum cannot mobilize legitimate resources for the young, neither can it provide them with access to stable criminal careers, for illegitimate learning and opportunity structures do not develop. The disorganized slum, populated in part by failures in the conventional world, also contains the outcasts of the criminal world. This is not to say that crime is nonexistent in such areas, but what crime there is tends to be individualistic, unorganized, petty, poorly paid, and unprotected. This is the haunt of the small-time thief, the grifter, the pimp, the jackroller, the unsophisticated "con" man, the pickpocket who is all thumbs, and others who cannot graduate beyond "heisting" candy stores or "busting" gas stations. Since they are unorganized and without financial resources, criminals in these areas cannot purchase immunity from prosecution; they have neither the money nor the political contacts to "put in the fix." Hence they are harassed by the police, and many of them spend the better part of their lives in prison. The organized criminal world is generally able to protect itself against such harassment, prosecution, and imprisonment. But professional crime and organized rackets, like any business enterprise, can thrive only in a stable, predictable, and integrated environment. In this sense, then, the unintegrated area does not constitute a promising launching site for lucrative and protected criminal careers. Because such areas fail to develop criminal learning environments and opportunity structures, stable criminal subcultures cannot emerge.

SOCIAL DISORGANIZATION AND SOCIAL CONTROL

As we have noted, social controls originate in both the conventional and the illegitimate sectors of the stable slum area. But this is apparently not the case in the disorganized slum. The basic disorganization of the conventional institutional structure makes it impossible for controls to originate there. At the same time, Kobrin asserts, "Because adult crime in this type of area is itself unorganized, its value system remains implicit and hence incapable of generating norms which function effectively on a groupwide basis." Hence "juvenile violators readily escape not merely the controls of conventional persons in the community but those of adult violators as well." Under such conditions,

> . . . [the] delinquencies of juveniles tend to acquire a wild, untrammelled character. Delinquents in this kind of situation more frequently exhibit the personality traits of the social type sometimes referred to as the hoodlum. Both individually and in groups, violent physical combat is engaged in for its own sake, almost as a form of recreation. Here groups of delinquents may be seen as excluded, isolated conflict groups dedicated to an unending battle against all forms of constraint. The escape from controls originating in any social structure, other than that provided by unstable groupings of the delinquents themselves, is here complete.[15]

Unlike Kobrin, we do not attribute conflict behavior in unorganized urban areas to the absence of controls alone. The young in such areas are also exposed to acute frustrations, arising from conditions in which access to success-goals is blocked by the absence of any institutionalized channels, legitimate or illegitimate. They are deprived not only of conventional opportunity but also of criminal routes to the "big money." In other words, precisely when frustrations are maximized, social controls are weakened. Social controls and channels to success-goals are generally related: where oppor-

15. *Ibid.*, p. 658.

tunities exist, patterns of control will be found; where opportunities are absent, patterns of social control are likely to be absent too. The association of these two features of social organization is a logical implication of our theory.

SOCIAL DISORGANIZATION AND VIOLENCE

Those adolescents in disorganized urban areas who are oriented toward achieving higher position but are cut off from institutionalized channels, criminal as well as legitimate, must rely upon their own resources for solving this problem of adjustment. Under these conditions, tendencies toward aberrant behavior become intensified and magnified. These adolescents seize upon the manipulation of violence as a route to status not only because it provides a way of expressing pent-up angers and frustrations but also because they are not cut off from access to violent means by vicissitudes of birth. In the world of violence, such attributes as race, socioeconomic position, age, and the like are irrelevant; personal worth is judged on the basis of qualities that are available to all who would cultivate them. The principal prerequisites for success are "guts" and the capacity to endure pain. One doesn't need "connections," "pull," or elaborate technical skills in order to achieve "rep." The essence of the warrior adjustment is an expressed feeling-state: "heart." The acquisition of status is not simply a consequence of skill in the use of violence or of physical strength but depends, rather, on one's willingness to risk injury or death in the search for "rep." A physically immature boy may find a place among the warrior elite if, when provoked, he will run such risks, thus demonstrating "heart."

As long as conventional and criminal opportunity structures remain closed, violence continues unchecked. The bulk of aggressive behavior appears to be channeled into gang warfare; success in street combat assures the group that its "turf" will not be invaded, that its girls will not be molested, that its members will otherwise be treated deferentially by young and old in the local community. *If new opportunity structures are opened, however, violence tends to be relinquished.* Indeed, the success of certain efforts to discourage violent, aggressive behavior among warrior gangs has resulted precisely from the fact that some powerful group has responded deferentially to these gangs. (The group is powerful because it can provide, or at least hold out the promise of providing, channels to higher position, such as jobs, education, and the like.) The most dramatic illustration of this process may be seen in programs conducted by social group workers who attach themselves to street gangs. Several points should be noted about the results of these programs.

First, violent behavior among street gangs appears to diminish rapidly once a social worker establishes liaison with them. Reporting on the outcome of detached-worker programs in Boston, for example, Miller notes, "One of the earliest and most evident changes . . . was that groups worked with directly [by social workers] relinquished active participation in the [established] network of conflict groups. . . ."[16] The reduction in conflict may reflect the skill of the social workers, but another explanation may be that *the advent of the street-gang worker symbolized the end of social rejection and the beginning of social accommodation.* To the extent that violence represents an effort to win deference, one would logically expect it to diminish once that end has been achieved.

Secondly, a detached-worker program, once initiated, tends to give rise to increased violence among groups to which workers have *not* been provided. In the Boston experience, to the extent that they interpreted having a street-club worker as an act of social deference, gangs came to compete for this prestigeful symbol. As Miller notes, "During later phases of the Program [there was] an upsurge in gang fights involving Program groups. . . . These conflicts did not involve Program groups fighting one another but represented for the most part attacks on Program groups by corner groups in adjacent areas which did not have an area worker." Miller suggests that such

16. This quotation and those that follow are from W. B. Miller, "The Impact of a Community Group Work Program on Delinquent Corner Groups," *Social Service Review,* Vol. 31, No. 4 (Dec. 1957), pp. 390-406.

attacks took place in part because "the outside groups knew that Program groups were given a social worker in the first place because they were troublesome; so they reasoned, 'They were bad, and they got a social worker; if we're bad enough now, we'll get a social worker, too.' " An attack by an outside gang on a Program gang was not, therefore, simply an expression of the traditional hostility of one gang toward another but an attempt on the part of the non-Program gang to win "rep." Thus Miller is led to observe, "A program aiming to 'clean up' the gang situation in a single section of the city cannot count on limiting its influence to that section but must anticipate the fact that its very successes in its home district may increase difficulties in adjacent areas." This suggests that programs aimed at curbing violence constitute a new opportunity structure in which gangs compete for social deference from the conventional world.

Finally, a resurgence of violent behavior may be observed when the liaison between the street worker and the gang is terminated if the members of the gang have not been successfully incorporated in a conventional opportunity system. Continuing to lack conventional economic opportunity, the gang fears the loss of the one form of recognition it has achieved from conventional society, symbolized by the street worker. Hence the group may reassert the old patterns of violence in order to retain the social worker. Under these conditions, the conventional society will continue to accommodate to the group for fear that to do otherwise would result in renewed violence, as indeed it so often does. A successful street-gang program, in short, is one in which detached workers can create channels to legitimate opportunity; where such channels cannot be opened up, the gang will temporize with violence only as long as a street worker maintains liaison with them.

In summary, severe limitations on both conventional and criminal opportunity intensify frustrations and position discontent. Discontent is heightened further under conditions in which social control is relaxed, for the area lacking integration between age-levels of offender and between carriers of conventional and criminal values cannot generate pressures to contain frustrations among the young. These are the circumstances, we suggest, in which adolescents turn to violence in search of status. Violence comes to be ascendant, in short, under conditions of relative detachment from all institutionalized systems of opportunity and social control.

The Retreatist Subculture

THE CONSUMPTION of drugs—one of the most serious forms of retreatist behavior—has become a severe problem among adolescents and young adults, particularly in lower-class urban areas. By and large, drug use in these areas has been attributed to rapid geographic mobility, inadequate social controls, and other manifestations of social disorganization. In this section, we shall suggest a hypothesis that may open up new avenues of inquiry in regard to the growing problem of drug use among the young.

PRESSURES LEADING TO RETREATIST SUBCULTURES

Retreatism is often conceived as an isolated adaptation, characterized by a breakdown in relationships with other persons. Indeed, this is frequently true, as in the case of psychotics. The drug-user, however, must become affiliated with others, if only to secure access to a steady supply of drugs. Just as stable criminal activity cannot be explained by reference to motivation alone, neither can stable drug use be fully explained in this way. Opportunity to use drugs must also be present. But such opportunities are restricted. As Becker notes, the illegal distribution of drugs is limited to "sources which are not available to the ordinary person. In order for a person to begin marihuana use, he must begin participation in some group through which these sources of supply become available to him."[17]

---

17. H. S. Becker, "Marihuana Use and Social Control," *Social Problems,* Vol. 3, No. 1 (July 1955), pp. 36-37.

Because of these restrictions on the availability of drugs, new users must become affiliated with old users. They must learn the lore of drug use, the skills required in making appropriate "connections," the controls which govern the purchase of drugs (*e.g.,* drugs will not generally be made available to anyone until he is "defined as a person who can safely be trusted to buy drugs without endangering anyone else"), and the like. As this process of socialization proceeds, the individual "is considered more trustworthy, [and] the necessary knowledge and introductions to dealers [then become] available to him." According to Becker, the "processes by which people are emancipated from the larger set of controls *and become responsive to those of the subculture*" are "important factors in the genesis of deviant behavior."[18] The drug-user, in other words, must be understood not only in terms of his personality and the social structure, which create a readiness to engage in drug use, but also in terms of the new patterns of associations and values to which he is exposed as he seeks access to drugs. The more the individual is caught in this web of associations, the more likely that he will persist in drug use, for he has become incorporated in a subculture that exerts control over his behavior.

Despite these pressures toward subcultural formation, it is probably also true that the resulting ties among addicts are not so solidary as those among participants in criminal and conflict subcultures. Addiction is in many ways an individualistic adaptation, for the "kick" is essentially a private experience. The compelling need for the drug is also a divisive force, for it leads to intense competition among addicts for money. Forces of this kind thus limit the relative cohesion which can develop among users.

"DOUBLE FAILURE" AND DRUG USE

We turn now to a discussion of the social conditions which give rise to retreatist reactions such as drug use among adolescents. According to Merton,

18. *Ibid.,* p. 35. Emphasis added.

> Retreatism arises from continued failure to near the goal by legitimate measures and from an inability to use the illegitimate route because of internalized prohibitions, this process occurring while the supreme value of the success-goal has not yet been renounced. The conflict is resolved by abandoning both precipitating elements, the goals and the norms. The escape is complete, the conflict is eliminated and the individual is asocialized.[19]

Thus he identifies two principal factors in the emergence of retreatist adaptations: (1) continued failure to reach culturally approved goals by legitimate means, and (2) inability to employ illegitimate alternatives because of internalized prohibitions. We take it that "internalized prohibitions" have to do with the individual's attitudes toward norms. Retreatists, according to Merton, do not call into question the legitimacy of existing institutional arrangements—a process which might then be followed by the use of illegitimate alternatives. Rather, they call into question their own adequacy, locating blame for their dilemma in personal deficiencies. One way of resolving the intense anxiety and guilt which ensue is to withdraw, to retreat, to abandon the struggle.

This definition of the processes giving rise to retreatist behavior is useful in connection with some types of retreatism, but it does not, we believe, fit the facts of drug use among lower-class adolescents. It is true that some youthful addicts appear to experience strong constraints on the use of illegitimate means; the great majority of drug-users, however, had a history of delinquency before becoming addicted. In these cases, unfavorable attitudes toward conventional norms are evident. Hence we conclude that internalized prohibitions, or

---

19. R. K. Merton, *Social Theory and Social Structure,* Rev. and Enl. Ed. (Glencoe, Ill.: Free Press, 1957), pp. 153-54. For discussions of drug use among juveniles, see D. L. Gerard and Conon Kornetsky, "Adolescent Opiate Addiction—A Study of Control and Addict Subjects," *Psychiatric Quarterly,* Vol. 29 (April 1955), pp. 457-86; Isidor Chein *et al., Studies of Narcotics Use Among Juveniles* (New York University, Research Center for Human Relations, mimeographed, Jan. 1956); Harold Finestone, "Cats, Kicks, and Color," *Social Problems,* Vol. 5, No. 1 (July 1957), pp. 3-13; and D. M. Wilmer, Eva Rosenfeld, R. S. Lee, D. L. Gerard, and Isidor Chein, "Heroin Use and Street Gangs," *Criminal Law, Criminology and Police Science,* Vol. 48, No. 4 (Nov-Dec. 1957), pp. 399-409.

favorable attitudes toward conventional norms, may not be a necessary condition for the emergence of retreatist behavior.

If internalized prohibitions are not a necessary component of the process by which retreatism is generated, then how are we to account for such behavior? We have noted that there are differentials in access both to illegitimate and to legitimate means; not all of those who seek to attain success-goals by prohibited routes are permitted to proceed. There are probably many lower-class adolescents oriented toward success in the criminal world who fail; similarly, many who would like to acquire proficiency in the use of violence also fail. We might ask, therefore, what the response would be among those faced with failure in the use of *both* legitimate and illegitimate means. We suggest that persons who experience this "double failure" are likely to move into a retreatist pattern of behavior. That is, retreatist behavior may arise as a consequence of limitations on the use of illegitimate means, whether the limitations are internalized prohibitions or socially structured barriers. For our purpose, the two types of restriction are functional equivalents. Thus we may amend Merton's statement as follows:

> Retreatism arises from continued failure to near the goal by legitimate measures and from an inability to use the illegitimate route because of internalized prohibitions *or socially structured barriers,* this process occurring while the supreme value of the success-goal has not yet been renounced.

This hypothesis permits us to define two general classes of retreatist: those who are subject to internalized prohibitions on the use of illegitimate means, and those who seek success-goals by prohibited routes but do not succeed. If we now introduce a distinction between illegitimate opportunity structures based on the manipulative use of violence and those based on essentially criminal means, such as fraud, theft, and extortion, we can identify four classes of retreatist.

Types I and II both arise in the manner described by Merton—that is, as a consequence of internalized restrictions on the use of illegitimate means. The two types differ only with respect to the content of the internalized restraints. In type II, it is the use of criminal means that is precluded; in type I, it is the use of violence. Resort to illegitimate means, violent or criminal, apparently evokes extreme guilt and anxiety among persons in these categories; such persons are therefore effectively cut off from criminal or violent routes to higher status. For persons of types III and IV, access to illegitimate routes is limited by socially structured barriers. They are not restrained by internal prohibitions; they would employ illegitimate means if these were available to them.

Retreatist Adaptations

Basis of Illegitimate Opportunity Structure	*Restrictions on Use of Illegitimate Means* Internalized Prohibitions	Socially Structured Barriers
Violence	I	III
Criminal Means	II	IV

Generally speaking, it has been found that most drug addicts have a history of delinquent activity prior to becoming addicted. In Kobrin's research, conducted in Chicago, "Persons who become heroin users were found to have engaged in delinquency *in a group-supported and habitual form* either prior to their use of drugs or simultaneously with their developing interest in drugs."[20] And from a study of drug addicts in California, "A very significant tentative conclusion [was reached]: namely, that the use of drugs follows criminal activity and criminal association rather than the other way around,

20. Solomon Kobrin, *Drug Addiction Among Young Persons in Chicago* (Illinois Institute for Juvenile Research, Oct. 1953), p. 6. Harold Finestone, in a study of the relationship between addicts and criminal status, comments: "The impression gained from interviewing . . . was that these addicts were petty thieves and petty 'operators' who, status-wise, were at the bottom of the criminal population of the underworld" ("Narcotics and Criminality," *Law and Contemporary Problems,* Vol. 22, No. 1 [Winter 1957], pp. 69-85).

which is often thought to be the case."[21] In other words, adolescents who are engaged in group-supported delinquency of the criminal or conflict type may eventually turn to drug use. Indeed, entire gangs sometimes shift from either criminal or conflict to retreatist adaptations.

We view these shifts in adaptation as responses to restrictions on the use of illegitimate means. Such restrictions, as we have seen, are always operative; not all who would acquire success by violence or criminal means are permitted to do so. It is our contention that retreatist behavior emerges among some lower-class adolescents because they have failed to find a place for themselves in criminal or conflict subcultures. Consider the case of competition for membership in conflict gangs. To the extent that conflict activity—"bopping," street-fighting, "rumbling," and the like—is tolerated, it represents an alternative means by which adolescents in many relatively disorganized urban areas may acquire status. Those who excel in the manipulation of violence may acquire "rep" within the group to which they belong and respect from other adolescent groups in the vicinity and from the adult world. In areas which do not offer criminal opportunities, the use of violence may be the only available avenue to prestige. But prestige is, by definition, scarce—just as scarce among adolescents who seek to acquire it by violence as it is elsewhere in the society. Not only do juvenile gangs compete vigorously with one another, but within each gang there is a continual struggle for prestigeful positions. Thus some gangs will acquire "rep" and others will fail; some persons will become upwardly mobile in conflict groups and others will remain on the periphery.

If the adolescent "failure" then turns to drugs as a solution to his status dilemma, his relationships with his peers become all the more attenuated. Habitual drug use is not generally a valued activity among juvenile gangs. Ordinarily the drug-user, if he persists in such behavior, tends to become completely disassociated from the group. Once disassociated, he may develop an even greater reliance upon drugs as a solution to

21. *Narcotics in California* (Board of Corrections, State of California, Feb. 18, 1959), p. 9.

status deprivations. Thus adolescent drug-users may be "double failures" who are restrained from participating in other delinquent modes of adaptation because access to these illegitimate structures is limited.

Our hypothesis states that adolescents who are double failures are more vulnerable than others to retreatist behavior; it does not imply that *all* double failures will subsequently become retreatists. Some will respond to failure by adopting a law-abiding lower-class style of life—the "corner boy" adaptation. It may be that those who become retreatists are incapable of revising their aspirations downward to correspond to reality. Some of those who shift to a corner-boy adaptation may not have held high aspirations initially. It has frequently been observed that some adolescents affiliate with delinquent groups simply for protection in gang-ridden areas; they are motivated not by frustration so much as by the "instinct of self-preservation." In a less hostile environment, they might simply have made a corner-boy adjustment in the first place. But for those who continue to exhibit high aspirations under conditions of double failure, retreatism is the expected result.

SEQUENCES OF ADAPTATION

Access to success-goals by illegitimate means diminishes as the lower-class adolescent approaches adulthood. Illegitimate avenues to higher status that were available during early adolescence become more restricted in later adolescence. These new limitations intensify frustration and so create pressures toward withdrawal or retreatist reactions.

With regard to criminal means, late adolescence is a crucial turning point, for it is during this period that the selection of candidates for stable adult criminal roles takes place. It is probably true that more youngsters are exposed to criminal learning environments during adolescence than can possibly be absorbed by the adult criminal structure. Because of variations in personality characteristics, criminal proficiency, and capacity to make "the right connections," or simply because of luck, some persons will find this avenue to higher status open and some will find it closed off. In effect, the latter face a dead end. Some delinquents, therefore, must cope with abrupt discontinuity in role-preparation and role-performance which may lead to retreatist responses.

In the case of conflict patterns, a similar process takes place. As adolescents near adulthood, excellence in the manipulation of violence no longer brings high status. Quite the contrary, it generally evokes extreme negative sanctions. What was defined as permissible or tolerable behavior during adolescence tends to be sharply proscribed in adulthood. New expectations are imposed, expectations of "growing up," of taking on adult responsibilities in the economic, familial, and community spheres. The effectiveness with which these definitions are imposed is attested by the tendency among fighting gangs to decide that conflict is, in the final analysis, simply "kid stuff": "As the group grows older, two things happen. Sports, hell raising, and gang fights become 'kid stuff' and are given up. In the normal course of events, the youthful preoccupations are replaced with the more individual concerns about work, future, a 'steady' girl, and the like."[22] In other words, powerful community expectations emerge which have the consequence of closing off access to previously useful means of overcoming status deprivations. Strains are experienced, and retreatist behavior may result.

As we have noted, adolescents who experience pressures leading to retreatist reactions are often restrained by their peers. Adolescent gangs usually devalue drug use (except on an experimental basis or for the sake of novelty) and impose negative sanctions upon those who become "hooked." The very existence of the gang discourages the potential user:

> The activities of the gang offer a measure of shared status, a measure of security and a sense of belonging. The boys do not have to face life alone—the group protects them. Escape into drugs is not necessary as yet.[23]

In the post-adolescent period, however, the cohesiveness

---

22. Wilmer *et al., op. cit.*, p. 409.
23. *Ibid.*

of the peer group usually weakens. Those who have the requisite skills and opportunities begin to make the transition to adulthood, assuming conventional occupational and kinship roles. As the solidarity of the group declines, it can no longer satisfy the needs or control the behavior of those who continue to rely upon it. These members may try to reverse the trend toward disintegration and, failing this, turn to drugs:

> This group organized five years ago for self-protection against other fighting groups in the area. Recently, as the majority grew cool to bopping, a group of three boys broke off in open conflict with the president; *soon after, these three started using heroin and acting "down with the cats."* They continue making efforts to get the gang back to fights. . . . The three users are still out and it is unlikely that they will be readmitted.[24]

For some adolescents, the peer group is the primary avenue to status as well as the primary source of constraints on behavior. For these youngsters, the post-adolescent period, during which the group may disintegrate or shift its orientation, is one in which social controls are weakened precisely when tensions are heightened.

Whether the sequence of adaptations is from criminal to retreatist or from conflict to retreatist, we suggest that limitations on legitimate and illegitimate opportunity combine to produce intense pressures toward retreatist behavior. When both systems of means are simultaneously restricted, it is not strange that some persons become detached from the social structure, abandoning cultural goals and efforts to achieve them by any means.

---

24. *Ibid.*, p. 405. Emphasis added.

CHAPTER 8

Persistence and Change in Delinquent Subcultures

WE COME NOW to a discussion of persistence and change in delinquent subcultures, the final class of questions delineated in Chapter 2. For analytical purposes, such questions must be distinguished from questions of how subcultures arise. Forces that bring about the emergence of a subculture may continue to operate, thus contributing to the persistence of the subculture. However, new forces may also intervene, exerting pressure for either persistence or change.

This chapter is divided roughly into two parts. In the first part, we take up several problems pertaining to stability or persistence in delinquent subcultures; in the second, we attempt to analyze various historical aspects of change in delinquent subcultures. The range of problems that might be considered in either of these sections is, of course, very wide. Therefore, we have made no effort to be comprehensive but have focused on problems that seem to us of special importance and that illustrate the viability of the system of ideas developed in earlier chapters.

Patterns of Persistence in Delinquent Subcultures

AMONG THE FACTORS determining the relative stability of a delinquent subculture is the extent to which it can attract new recruits and the extent to which it can become integrated with other groups in its immediate social environment. This section focuses upon these two aspects of the problem of persistence.

RECRUITMENT OF NEW MEMBERS

Once a delinquent subculture has been formed, its continuance depends upon the recruitment of new members. Throughout this book we have argued that the principal function of a delinquent subculture is to provide alternative channels of opportunity. Its "core" members are persons who experience a marked discrepancy between socially induced aspirations and the possibilities of achievement. But once a subculture has come into being, it then exists as a force in the neighborhood and may attract persons for whom it promises to serve a wide range of needs and motives. Except for the existence of the subculture, these persons might never have adopted a delinquent style of life at all. For some, the subculture may offer the possibility of rewarding peer relationships, of participation in what appear to be exciting activities, or of "protection":

A boy moves into a gang or club gradually through his years of association with others in the neighborhood. He early learns that his movements in the neighborhood, his recreation, and his play with other children are restricted by the fact that play groups are organized and one must be a member to join in the fun. Furthermore, he learns that he has to rely on his associates for his personal defense. Life in Eastville is said to be "tough," and boys and girls who belong to some kind of group find that this assures them of protection from the aggression of others.[1]

As the recruit's links to the group solidify, however, he may become fully caught up in the life of the subculture, conforming to its norms and internalizing its central beliefs and values. On this point, we are much in accord with Cohen:

> A subculture owes its existence to the fact that it provides a solution to certain problems of adjustment shared among a community of individuals. However, it does not follow that for every individual who participates these problems provide the sole or sufficient source of motivation. Indeed, there may be some participants to whose motivation these problems contribute very little. Consider first that membership, as such, in a social group may yield all sorts of benefits and satisfactions sufficient to motivate people to want to belong. The distinctive creed of such a group may be a matter of indifference to a particular individual; it is not the creed but the other benefits of membership which attract him to the group. . . . In such a case, the motivation for his participation in the subculture may throw little light on the reasons for its distinctive content. Conversely, the needs and problems which make intelligible this distinctive content may have little to do with why this particular individual has taken it over.[2]

Whatever the forces motivating diverse persons to join an ongoing delinquent subculture, their affiliation as such contributes to its stability. Although these recruits may have had nothing to do with the formation of the subculture, they exert a pressure for its persistence simply because it is capable of satisfying their needs as well as the needs of the "core" members.

DIFFERENTIAL INTEGRATION

In previous chapters, we stated that different forms of neighborhood integration result in different types of delinquent

---

1. Elena Padilla, *Up from Puerto Rico* (New York: Columbia University Press, 1958), p. 229.

2. A. K. Cohen, *Delinquent Boys: The Culture of the Gang* (Glencoe, Ill.: Free Press, 1955), pp. 148-49.

subculture. Systems of integration also affect the relative stability of subcultures. In this section, we shall discuss integration between age-levels of offender and between subcultures.

Integration of Different Age-Levels—Delinquent subcultures vary considerably in the range of age-levels that come to be integrated with one another. Integration of a wide range of age-groups contributes to the stability of the subculture; limited integration results in instability.

Delinquents in criminal subcultures, as we have noted, tend to be highly integrated with older offenders, including adults. In fact, these connections between age-levels are the most distinctive structural feature of the criminal subculture. Such integration gives unity and coherence to the subculture, facilitates illegitimate learning, provides illegitimate opportunity, and is a source of social control. The integration of age-levels, as we have noted, is a function of integration between adult carriers of criminal and conventional values. This integration between the criminal and conventional worlds lends great stability to criminal groups. Many conventional groups have an interest in seeing to it that criminal activities are maintained; thus integration encourages the persistence of criminal subcultures. The "take" from racketeering operations often finds its way into political campaign chests; police often find that cooperating with racketeers is a much more effective way of preserving order than attempting to suppress crime; and for such men as the fence and the bail bondsman, the criminal activity of others is a necessary source of income.

Evidence on retreatist subcultures, limited though it is, also reveals that a wide range of age-levels is typically integrated. Because access to drugs is limited, the addict must establish connections with suppliers. This, in turn, requires him to affiliate with other addicts, from whom he learns the lore of drug use, the skills to make appropriate connections, and the norms that govern the purchase of drugs. Because the addict must undergo these learning processes in order to obtain access to supplies of drugs, a continuous pressure for the integration of age-levels is exerted.

Pressure for integration also arises from the fact that many users become peddlers in order to support their habits. Successful sellers must constantly find new customers. Younger persons who are ready to experiment or who already are occasional users represent a readily exploitable market; hence mature users tend to become linked to these younger persons. The older user provides access both to learning and to drugs; the younger provides a ready market for drug sales. Because of these reciprocal functions, some integration of different age-levels takes place.

The narrowest range of ages are integrated in the conflict subculture. Adults generally have no interest in the maintenance of conflict groups. Consequently, powerful pressures are exerted upon the participant to relinquish this mode of adjustment as he approaches adulthood. The conflict role is abruptly discontinuous and hence unstable.

Integration Between Subcultures—There is considerable variation in the degree to which the various types of delinquent subculture and their adult counterparts, if any, are linked to one another. Generally speaking, such integration produces stability. The isolated subculture tends to be unstable and vulnerable to change.

In criminal groups, as we have noted, considerable control is exercised over the behavior of members to discourage irrational, undisciplined acts. Street fighting and other forms of violent, expressive behavior are at least nonfunctional if not dysfunctional for this subculture. Hence there is little basis for integration between the criminal and conflict subcultures. This is not to say that youngsters who participate in criminal groups do not occasionally engage in violence, or that members of conflict cultures never steal or engage in other illegitimate income-producing activities. However, there are strong pressures working to disassociate these types of group from each other.

The conflict culture also tends to be disassociated from the retreatist culture. As we have pointed out, gang norms do not generally support addiction. The use of drugs is not fully prohibited; they may be consumed for experimental or social reasons. However, a member of a conflict group is not supposed to become "hooked." If he does become addicted, he is usually relegated to a peripheral position in the group if not expelled from it.

The retreatist subculture and some criminal subcultures tend to become partially merged. Addicts frequently turn to illegal activity in order to support their habits, "pushing," robbery, burglary, and prostitution being the most common forms. Through these activities, they come into contact with various members of the criminal world. They are also in contact with organized criminal subcultures, at least with the lower echelons, through peddlers, runners, and others in the employ of drug rings. The two cultures stand in relation to each other as consumer and distributor, even during late adolescence. Furthermore, the criminal, as distributor, often attempts to expand his market by fostering drug addiction among potential users. He seeks to maintain and expand the drug culture by such means as providing free drugs to potential users for experimentation and organizing "shooting parties" at which they are introduced to drugs on a "social basis." Since they are dependent upon each other, the two cultures partially merge, and, through their integration, each adds to the stability of the other.

Our analysis leads us to conclude that the criminal subculture typically exhibits the greatest resistance to change, since it is integrated with one other delinquent subculture and is characterized internally by considerable integration of different age-levels of participant. The retreatist subculture is moderately resistant to change, for it is somewhat integrated internally and with the criminal subculture. The conflict subculture appears to be integrated in neither of these respects and therefore is the most susceptible to outside influences for change. This analysis may account for the success of many attempts to bring about a reduction in violence among conflict groups and for the frequent failure of attempts to modify retreatist and criminal adaptations.

Patterns of Change in Delinquent Subcultures

IN THIS SECTION, we shall examine, first, the sequence of delinquent adaptations that generally accompanies various stages of assimilation among immigrant groups. We shall then consider the apparent trend toward increasingly violent modes of delinquent behavior during the past decade. These two problems by no means exhaust the change phenomena that might be discussed. They are, however, significant, and they show how our general theory can be employed to account for patterns of change in delinquent subcultures.

In Chapters 6 and 7, we suggested that the content of a delinquent subculture is influenced in crucial ways by the social characteristics of the neighborhood in which it emerges, particularly the institutionalization of legitimate and illegitimate opportunity systems and the effectiveness of systems of social control. Criminal subcultures, we said, tend to arise in integrated slums, conflict subcultures in unintegrated environments. But just as delinquent adaptations vary from one neighborhood to another, so they vary from one time to another in a given neighborhood. We should expect, in terms of our theory, to find that such variations through time reflect changes in the social organization of the slum, especially changes in the relative availability of legitimate and illegitimate opportunities and in the effectiveness with which social controls are exercised. In this section, we focus upon these historical changes in the structure of lower-class areas and the accompanying changes in delinquent subcultures.

Our approach in this chapter entails one departure from the scheme of analysis set out in Chapters 6 and 7. In those chapters, we took differences among neighborhood social systems as given; we did not ask, for example, how integrated and unintegrated systems came into being. We simply asked how, once formed, they impinged upon developing delinquent subcultures and shaped their content. Now, however, we are interested in accounting for changing patterns of subcultural behavior; to the extent that these changes reflect changes in neighborhood social organization, we are obliged to take the milieu as problematical rather than given. In the concluding pages of this book, therefore, we shall direct our attention to forces that bring about important modifications of slum organization, and we shall suggest some implications of these changes for delinquency.

THE IMMIGRANT, THE MIGRANT, AND THE SLUM

The immigrant has been the principal constituent of the American slum. Successive waves of ethnic and nationality groups have come to our shores, settled in the slums of large cities, and eventually become assimilated in the middle classes. There are, we think, three more or less distinct stages in this assimilation process, characterized by differences in access to legitimate and illegitimate opportunity systems and therefore by different forms of delinquent adaptations.

Stages in Assimilation—On their arrival in the United States, most immigrant groups have faced formidable barriers to legitimate systems of opportunity. They have been relegated to the slums and to the lower reaches of the occupational structure. Often for several generations, descendants of the immigrants struggled to make some adjustment to the host culture. During this period, marked by acute personal and social disorganization, the young were subjected to acute frustrations stemming from limitations upon legitimate opportunity while they were relatively unrestrained by community controls. They found few paths to status except through violence. This was generally a period of intense rivalry between gangs of the same or different ethnic and nationality backgrounds, each seeking—principally by force—to establish dominance over a particular neighborhood. Asbury has described some of the great gang battles among the Irish of the pre-Civil War period:

> For many years the Bowery Boys and the Dead Rabbits [both Irish gangs] waged a bitter feud, and a week seldom passed in

which they did not come to blows either along the Bowery, in the Five Points section, or in the ancient battleground of Bunker Hill, north of Grand Street. The greatest gang conflicts of the early nineteenth century were fought by these groups. . . . Sometimes the battles raged for two or three days without cessation, while the streets of the gang area were barricaded with carts and paving stones, and the gangsters blazed away at each other with musket and pistol, or engaged in close work with knives, brickbats, bludgeons, teeth, and fists.[3]

Delinquency in this era closely paralled the behavior of the adult gangs:

. . . in 1850 . . . all of the great brawling, thieving gangs . . . had their sycophantic gangs of youngsters. There were the Forty Little Thieves, the Little Dead Rabbits, and the Little Plug Uglies, the members of which emulated their elders in speech and deed, and as far as possible in appearance. And in the Fourth Ward, along the waterfront, were the Little Daybreak Boys, composed of lads from eight to twelve years of age who were almost as ferocious as the older gangsters whose name they adopted and whose crimes they strove mightily to imitate.[4]

Coincident with patterns of violence was a great deal of petty theft, robbery, burglary, and the like. But crime in this stage was unorganized and relatively unprotected. As succeeding waves of newcomers swelled the ranks of immigrant gangs, however, they were increasingly able to establish dominance over their neighborhood. At this juncture, they began to develop alliances with political elements. Integration between marauding gangs and political groups generally marked the beginning of a second stage in assimilation: one characterized by the growth of organized crime and political power. Referring again to the era before the Civil War, Asbury remarks on the coalition that developed between Irish gangs and Irish elements in Tammany Hall:

The political geniuses of Tammany Hall were quick to see the practical value of the gangsters, and to realize the advisability of providing them with meeting and hiding places, that their favor might

3. Herbert Asbury, *The Gangs of New York: An Informal History of the Underworld* (New York: Alfred A. Knopf, 1927-28), p. 29.
4. *Ibid.,* p. 239.

be curried and their peculiar talents employed on election day to assure government of, by, and for Tammany. . . . The underworld thus became an important factor in politics. . . .[5]

One of the principal means of bringing these criminal and political elements together was the social and athletic club:

These organiaztions were patterned after, and in many instances controlled and supported by, the political associations which had been formed in large numbers by the Tammany district leaders, who thereby strengthened their hold upon the voting masses. Such societies had been an important source of Tammany's power since the early days of New York politics, but it was not until the nineties that they approached the full flower of perfection. . . .It was usually through these organizations . . . that arrangements were made with the gang leaders for thugs to blackjack voters at the polls, act as repeaters and, on occasion, remove opponents who had made themselves obnoxious and dangerous.[6]

The gangsters and racketeers contributed greatly to the coffers of political parties and were rewarded with immunity from prosecution for their various illegal activities. As the political power of the ethnic or nationality group increased, access to legitimate opportunities became enlarged and assimilation facilitated. Indeed, as Bell observes, the coalition of crime and politics has been a crucial factor in the assimilation of many immigrant groups during the past century. Blocked from legitimate access to wealth, the immigrant feels mounting pressures for the use of illegal alternatives. This has resulted in the progressive encroachment by the descendants of each new immigrant group upon the rackets structures established by preceding ethnic or nationality groups.

Excluded from the political ladder—in the early 30's there were almost no Italians on the city payroll in top jobs, nor in the books of the period can one find discussion of Italian political leaders—[and] finding few open routes to wealth, some turned to illicit ways. In the children's court statistics of the 1930's, the largest group of delinquents was the Italian. . . . [In time, however] men of Italian origin [have come to occupy] most of the leading roles in the high drama of gambling and mobs, just as twenty years ago

5. *Ibid.*, p. 37.
6. *Ibid.*, pp. 268-69.

the children of East European Jews were the most prominent figures in organized crime, and before that individuals of Irish descent were similarly prominent.[7]

During this stage the integrated slum organization comes into being. Alliances develop between racketeers and police, politicians, and other legitimate elements of the community. The power of the politician grows, partly financed by the newly won and enlarging wealth of the racketeer. Increased political power makes it possible for the racketeer not only to gain entry to "respectable" ruling groups within the larger urban structure but also to open channels of legitimate ascent for others. Thus illegal activity contributes to social mobility by legitimate as well as illegitimate channels.

In all their activities, legal or illegal, the racketeers perform the important function of providing employment for a large number of men. Most of the employees have no background of experience and skill to prepare them for jobs in private industry. Furthermore, it is widely believed in Cornerville, and not without considerable evidence, that a Cornerville Italian is discriminated against when he applies for a job. The corner boys do not fit into the socially approved economic organization, and in the depression the rackets provided them with jobs which were difficult to find by other means. . . .

The racketeers also provide investment capital for new enterprises. One story will serve as an example. Tom Leonardi was a young Cornerville man who worked for a large corporation. Tom learned the business well and saw opportunities for profits if he started out for himself. . . . City investment bankers would hardly be interested in backing an unknown young Italian who was entering the competition with firmly entrenched corporations. Tom approached several Italian racketeers, and they agreed to invest. With their capital, he was able to buy the plant and equipment necessary for the expansion of his business. . . . This is not an isolated example. The support of racket capital has helped a number of able men to rise to positions otherwise unattainable.[8]

During this stage, we should expect delinquent subcul-

---

7. Daniel Bell, "Crime as an American Way of Life," *Antioch Review*, Vol. 13 (Summer 1953), pp. 146-51.

8. W. F. Whyte, *Street Corner Society: The Social Structure of an Italian Slum*, Enl. Ed. (Chicago: University of Chicago Press, 1955), p. 145.

o

tures to take the form of apprenticeship to organized crime. Unnecessary violence and wanton destruction would be repressed, by the illegitimate elements as well as by the conventional elements of the community. Whyte's description of an Italian community in Boston during the late 1930's contains only one reference to gang fighting, and even here the emphasis on physical injury and lethal weapons is clearly minimized, as "Doc" (one of Whyte's principal informants) takes pains to note:

"We didn't have many rallies [fights] between gangs. There was a lot of mutual respect. . . . We didn't go out to kill them. We didn't want to hurt anybody. It was just fun. . . . I don't remember that anybody ever got hit on the head with a bottle. Maybe on the leg or in the back, but not on the head. The only time anybody ever got hurt was when Charlie got that tin can in his eye. We were rallying the King Streets on the playground. We charged and Charlie got ahead of us. When he got into King Street, somebody threw this can, and the open end caught him right in the eye. . . . We took Charlie home. I remember his screaming while the doctor worked on his eye. That made an impression on us. It never occurred to us before that somebody might get permanently injured in a rally. . . . After that, there weren't any more rallies."[9]

Most of those who negotiate passage to a higher socioeconomic position by either legitimate or illegitimate routes eventually move away from the neighborhood of their origin. The successful racketeer or businessman generally takes up residence in the suburbs rather than continue to live in the slum of his youth:

The early Italian gangsters were hoodlums—rough, unlettered, and young. (Al Capone was only twenty-nine at the height of his power.) Those who survived learned to adapt. By now they are men of middle age or older. They learned to dress conservatively. Their homes are in respectable suburbs. They sent their children to good schools and had sought to avoid publicity.[10]

---

9. *Ibid.*, p. 6.

10. Bell, *op. cit.*, p. 151. The emphasis among successful racketeers upon becoming "respectable" is sometimes taken as evidence that delinquency and crime are a response to prestige deprivations. This position supports the hypothesis that lower-class delinquency is a result of limited access to middle-class status. We have suggested, however, that most lower-class youngsters who become delinquents

As this process of out-migration goes forward, the slum community enters upon a third stage—one of progressive deterioration and disorganization. What remains in the community is a residual of "failures"—persons who have not succeeded in the search for higher socioeconomic status. The old forms of social organization begin to break down, and with them opportunities for upward mobility diminish. Indeed, a new ethnic or nationality group may be invading the community, encroaching upon the old structures, and establishing a claim to dominance of the principal avenues of mobility, both legitimate and illegitimate. Thus a new cycle of community integration and deterioration is initiated. Once again the young find themselves both cut off from avenues to higher status and free from external restraint. This is a period, then, in which we should expect a resurgence of violent modes of delinquent adaptation. In the last stage of assimilation, the conflict adaptation may once again become the principal form of delinquency.

Ethnic and Nationality Sequences—If these notions have any merit, they should enable us to predict changes in delinquent adaptations from one time period to another. The case of Negroes who have migrated from a Southern rural area to such Northern cities as New York provides an illustration. Delinquency among urban Negroes has been largely conflict-oriented, but there is reason to think that this may change in the next decade or two. Apparently the political and rackets structures in the Negro communities of New York City are now

---

are drawn from groups which stress economic achievement rather than movement into the middle class as such (see Chap. 4). How, then, can we account for the pressure toward "respectability" which many criminals exhibit? Our hypothesis is that persons moving upward in the criminal opportunity structure exhibit a sequence of aspirations. In the lower echelons of organized crime, success is defined principally in economic terms. With upward movement, the criminal's contacts with respected members of the middle-class world—lawyers, politicians, industrialists, etc.—become wider and more frequent. Through "differential association" with persons who follow a middle-class style of life, the criminal may take over middle-class criteria for defining success. His attempts to achieve respectability may thus represent a response to his changing position in the social structure. We hypothesize, in short, that *changes in social position will be accompanied by changes in success-goals.*

dominated principally by Italians and Jews; most Negroes have been relegated to minor roles in these structures although they aspire to rise. There is evidence, however, that the Negro has been making a concerted bid for power. Recently, for example, Negroes have charged that the police are systematically discriminating against them in raiding Harlem policy operations by arresting a greater proportion of independent Negro "bankers" than of Italian and Jewish syndicate "bankers" and by harassing the lower-echelon Negro functionaires in syndicated operations dominated by Italians and Jews. The clear implication is that the police are acting in behalf of the Italian and Jewish syndicate. If these charges are true, one of the effects of such arrests would be to forestall attempts by Negroes to win greater control of the policy racket in Harlem. Indeed, this is implied in the recent remarks of Adam Clayton Powell, a Negro Congressman from Harlem, in connection with the arrests:

"I am against numbers in any form. But until the day when numbers is wiped out in Harlem—I hate to say this from the pulpit—I am going to fight for the Negro having the same chance as an Italian."[11]

Powell charged that these arrests were an attempt to stop Negroes who were trying to set up operations independent of the Italian and Jewish syndicate or who were struggling for power within the syndicate. He declared that "every Negro numbers banker had been 'put out of business' "[12] but that

"At this time, no arrests have been made in East Harlem, the center of Italian and syndicate activity. Until action begins in that area and higher up, it is apparent that . . . arrests are an attempt to embarrass the Negro community while continuing the policy of allowing the higher-ups to go scot-free."[13]

The police would not disclose figures on the relative proportions of Negroes, Italians, and Jews who had been arrested, claiming that to "issue crime statistics by race or creed" was contrary to departmental policy: "We are not interested in a

11. New York *Times*, Jan. 4, 1960.
12. *Ibid.*, Jan. 10, 1960.
13. *Ibid.*, Jan. 7, 1960.

criminal's color, only his crime."[14] The New York *Times,* however, estimated that "more than 90 per cent" of the several hundred persons who were arrested were Negro, all of them "suspected runners and players."[15] No reports have been issued by the police department indicating that any top figure in the policy racket has been apprehended.

In connection with this controversy, it should be noted that the game is being played for big stakes. Policy is said to be one of Harlem's major industries, and control of its proceeds would greatly enhance the political position of the Negro.

Harlem experts estimate that more than 100,000 players dreaming of a big hit—600 to 1 if they get three numbers right in a row, or 8 to 1 on a single-number play—put down $2,000,000 to $4,000,000 a month in Harlem and the Bedford-Stuyvesant section of Brooklyn. More than 10,000 persons reportedly make a living from the game.[16]

* * *

From the gross play, a banker, nowadays generally an outsider [*i.e.,* a white rather than a Negro], takes perhaps 65 per cent, out of which he pays the wins—perhaps 20 to 25 per cent of the play. A controller, in the middle, takes 35 per cent. From this he pays runners, lawyers, bondsmen—and also, rumors say, the police for as much as 15 per cent at low echelons of the department. Thus [the] argument is that 50 per cent of the play—derived from wages, pensions, relief checks—flows out of the [Negro] community in a monthly total of at least $1,000,000.[17]

Yet, Congressman Powell claimed:

"There is not operating in Harlem, a single Negro banker. . . . The entire operation is totally in the hands of people who do not reside nor are connected with this community. Here we find a community lower in income than any other in the city. And yet we spend $50,000,000 a year to support Italian and Jewish policy bankers."[18]

The likelihood is great that the Negro will eventually win his struggle for control of the rackets and for a greater voice

14. *Ibid.,* Jan. 4, 1960.
15. *Ibid.,* Jan. 6, 1960.
16. *Ibid.,* Jan. 11, 1960.
17. *Ibid.,* Jan. 6, 1960.
18. *Ibid.,* Jan. 10, 1960.

in urban politics. If our analysis is correct, drastic changes may be imminent in the character of Negro delinquency, not only in Harlem but also in many other urban centers where the Negro's power is beginning to be felt. The growth of illegal wealth and political power will probably lead to the types of neighborhood integration that provide opportunities for legitimate as well as illegitimate social ascent. We may expect, therefore, that violence will diminish in Negro neighborhoods and that criminal modes of delinquency will increase. In addition, such defeatist adaptations as widespread drug use may be on the wane. However, our analysis suggests that delinquency in *residual* neighborhoods, such as Italian East Harlem in New York City, will increasingly take the forms of conflict and retreatism as criminal opportunities lessen.

We must note, however, that important structural changes are taking place in some large urban areas. As a result, the experience of the Negroes may not directly parallel that of other groups before them. Present conditions of urban life are different in certain significant respects from those of an earlier time, when the Italian immigrant occupied a status similar to that of the Negro today. Vast changes have taken place in urban politics, organized crime, and the general character of lower-class life. For the most part, these changes have resulted in the disorganization of slums, restricted opportunity, and lessened social control. Thus the pattern of ascent to illegal wealth and political power by Negroes may be somewhat different from the pattern that was followed by Italian and other groups. The next sections discuss the current and anticipated effects of these changes.

FUTURE TRENDS IN DELINQUENT ADAPTATIONS

Basic changes are taking place in lower-class social structure. In combination, these changes are resulting in greater restrictions upon legitimate and illegitimate opportunities and greatly reduced systems of social control. The imminent decline that we have predicted for Italian slum communities has probably occurred already in the older slum communities of the

Irish and the East European Jew. The Negro, a relative newcomer to urban life, is a deviant case, for he is winning increasing access to illegal wealth and political power at a time when most residual slum groups are diminishing in size, wealth, and power. With this major exception, the urban lower class is coming to be composed of a more or less permanent residual of the vast immigrations of earlier eras. Great proportions of those immigrant groups have been absorbed into the middle classes; what remains in the slum areas are those who have been unable to find a channel of social ascent.

On the basis of the theory developed in this book, we predict that delinquency will become increasingly aggressive and violent in the future as a result of the disintegration of slum organization. Indeed, there is some evidence that conflict behavior is already beginning to increase, although, as we have mentioned, its prevalence is probably overestimated. Observers of the lower-class scene—settlement-house personnel, street-gang workers, police officials, and others—generally agree that violence and aggression are on the upsurge among urban slum youth. In 1952, for example, the New York City Youth Board reported,

> During the past decade many teen-age groups in large urban areas, particularly New York, Chicago, Los Angeles, Cleveland and Detroit, have developed . . . an intense, hostile manner which has erupted into violent gang warfare involving the use of lethal weapons and resulting in serious injury and death to an appreciable number of teen-age boys.[19]

19. J. E. McCarthy and J. S. Barbara, "Redirecting Teen-age Gangs," *Reaching the Unreached* (New York City Youth Board, 1952), p. 99. We do *not* say that violent forms of delinquency are necessarily more prevalent today than formerly. What we are suggesting is that rates of participation in such modes of delinquent behavior have varied from one time to another depending on variations in the basic features of urban neighborhood social structure. It is our view, for example, that violence is probably a prevailing delinquent motif among most immigrant groups in both the early and the late stages of assimilation. Any comparison of contemporary and past forms of delinquency must therefore be couched in highly specific terms: it must deal with particular groups at a particular location in the social structure at a particular stage of assimilation. Gross comparisons of the present and past obscure these distinctions and therefore are probably not very useful.

But why are urban slums becoming disorganized? There are several reasons. Throughout this book, we have stressed the important social functions that crime performs directly for the integration of urban neighborhoods and indirectly for the patterning of delinquent subcultures. But crime is not a static, unchanging phenomenon. "As a society changes," Bell has noted, "so does, in lagging fashion, its type of crime."[20] And as crime changes, we might add, so does its impact upon the patterning of delinquent adaptations. One of the principal changes in criminal activity during the past several decades has been the emergence of syndicated gambling as the major source of illegal revenue. Previously crime was less well organized, consisting principally of small groups of entrepreneurs, many of them marauding and predatory in character. Indeed, the decline of the industrial rackets in the 1930's and the end of Prohibition signalized the passing of the old-style "gangster" in American life. In his stead, a new figure emerged—the semi-respectable professional gambler—who differed greatly from his predecessor in crime. Although his origins may have been in the small, locally based predatory gang of a dying era, he had gained experience in large-scale organization during the days of Prohibition and had thus begun to take on the ways of the organization man. For gambling, as distinct from prostitution, traffic in drugs and liquor, industrial rackets, protection rackets, and the like, exhibits a high degree of economic rationalization and organization.

As American society became more "organized," as the American businessman became more "civilized" and less "buccaneering," so did the American racketeer. And just as there were important changes in the structure of business enterprise, so the "institutionalized" criminal enterprise was transformed too. . . . In the America of the last fifty years the main drift of society has been toward the rationalization of industry, the domestication of the crude self-made captain of industry into the respectable man of manners, and the emergence of a mass-consumption economy. The most significant transformation in the field of "institutionalized" crime was the increasing relative importance of gambling as against other kinds of illegal activity. And, as a multi-billion-dollar busi-

20. Bell, *op. cit.*, p. 131.

ness, gambling underwent a transition parallel to the changes in American enterprise as a whole. This parallel was exemplified in many ways: in gambling's industrial organization (*e.g.*, the growth of complex technology such as the national racing wire service and the minimization of risks by such techniques as lay-off betting). . . .[21]

The passing of the gangster and the emergence of syndicated gambling have had great impact upon the social organization of the slum. This impact is symbolized in Whyte's account of the conflict between Mario Serrechia, a notorious Cornerville gangster, and T.S., an "outsider" who was taking over the rackets of Cornerville.[22]

"Mario began his career as a holdup man" during the Prohibition era but shortly moved into bootlegging, small policy operations, and extortion from other racketeers. "He was the rugged individualist of the rackets. As long as he was alive, he was a threat to any comprehensive organization [of the rackets] that was attempted . . . [for his] undisciplined actions made him a menace to too many people." He was subsequently shot to death, presumably by hired assassins. "He was," Whyte observes, "the last of his kind in Cornerville. A new era of racket organization came in with his death."

This new era of racket organization is symbolized in the career of a man known as "T.S." Like Mario, T.S. began as a gangster, and his early activities in Cornerville paralleled those of Mario. He first established himself as the dominant figure in a powerful local gang which controlled illegal traffic in liquor and other rackets. In the struggle for control, he "eliminated" a number of his competitors. However, T.S. differed from men like Mario in that "he displayed superior organizing ability and business sense." Shortly after taking over control of the liquor traffic, he moved in on the local gambling operations, which had previously been managed by local entrepreneurs on a small-business basis. He merged all the independent "policy banks" into one organization and subsequently "became one

21. *Ibid.*, pp. 133-34.

22. The quotations that follow are from Whyte, *op. cit.*, pp. 113-15.

of the members of the syndicate when it was formed to control the [policy] business throughout the city and in other towns and cities." The formation of the syndicate, Whyte observes, "brought about a reign of peace and order in the Cornerville rackets, which has lasted to the present day [about 1940]."

From the standpoint of our theory, one of the principal points to be made about the rationalization of criminal enterprise is that it restricts traditional routes to stable criminal roles. In a fully bureaucratized operation, the local "numbers bank" or "race drop" is little more than a branch office of a far-flung organizational network. In many neighborhoods, the gambling business has become as distant and impersonal as the local store in a supermarket chain. The private entrepreneur has disappeared; local crime is managed by functionaires of a large, bureaucratically organized enterprise. The top figures are distant, perhaps unknown to most people in the neighborhood. Illegitimate figures become no less obscure as role-models to lower-class youth than the role-models of the legitimate world of finance and corporate enterprise. Under such conditions, illegitimate learning is more difficult to acquire.

> The contrast between Mario Serrechia and T. S. illustrates the development of the rackets. Mario was a colorful and romantic figure; to Cornerville he was "the Great Gangster." T. S. works quietly in the background so that *few Cornerville people can present a very definite picture of his personality.* Mario was powerfully built and, using fists or a gun, did his own fighting. T. S. fought when he had to, but he built up an organization which cut violence to a minimum. Mario was the pirate; T. S. is a businessman.[23]

The independent policy bankers whose operations T.S. absorbed were important local figures, widely known throughout Cornerville society; T.S. was more remote.

Restricted access to stable illegitimate roles also results from changes in the criteria of recruitment and selection that have accompanied the transition from small, private criminal enterprise to large corporate enterprise. When crime was on a local scale, delinquency was a way of acquiring the skills and

---

23. *Ibid.*, p. 115. Emphasis added.

attitudes needed for participation in the adult criminal structure. Where it was linked through age-grading with adult criminal occupations, the delinquent subculture was a first stage in access to systems of illegitimate opportunity. But there is considerable reason to doubt whether these same functions are performed by the delinquent subculture in an era of syndicated crime. The illegal corporate enterprise, like its counterpart in the legitimate world, requires highly specialized skills in public relations, finance, business management, and law. The delinquent subculture can no longer perform the educational functions that once made it so vital a force in the continuity of criminal enterprises; it has become obsolete. Illegal channels of social ascent are thus closed off, and pressures for conflict forms of delinquency mount.

Another factor that has contributed greatly to the disintegration of lower-class neighborhoods is the decline of the urban political machine. As a result of the gradual absorption of the immigrant masses into the middle classes and of certain radical changes in the structure of the economy, the locus of political power has shifted from the local neighborhood to the state and national arenas. With the decline of the neighborhood-based political machine, the urban lower class has lost an important integrating structure and a significant channel for social ascent.

It is paradoxical that the very success of the urban political machine in bringing about certain social changes has contributed greatly to its demise. As we have noted, the political machine has helped to facilitate the assimilation of immigrant groups into the society at large. As more and more immigrants became assimilated, their dependence upon the political machine lessened. The political machine also played a strategic part in the process by which crime, especially gambling, was made rational and bureaucratic. But with the progressive rationalization of crime and the integration of its leaders with city, state, and national politicians, the dependence of syndicate operators upon neighborhood political organizations has diminished. Hence local political groups can no longer count upon the financial largesse of illegal enterprises as a stable source of income. Perhaps the greatest paradox of all is the fact that the growth of the welfare state has undermined the importance of the urban political machine, for it was the power mobilized in the large urban machine that made the New Deal possible. "Ironically," Merton observes,

> in view of the close connection of Roosevelt with the large urban political machines, it is a basic structural change in the form of providing services, through the rationalized procedures of what some call "the welfare state," that largely spelled the decline of the political machine. It would be figuratively but essentially true to say that it was the system of "social security" and the growth of more or less bureaucratically administered scholarships which, more than direct assaults of reformers, have so greatly reduced the power of the political machine.[24]

It is of course true that the "welfare state"—through its income-maintenance programs, such as home relief, aid to dependent children, and old-age security—has taken over a function once performed much less adequately by the political machine. But to say that the structure of state welfare services effectively supplants the traditional political machine is to overlook many other functions that the machine performed for lower-class persons. In a comparison of the two structures, it is important to note, as Merton suggests, "not only that aid *is* provided but *the manner in which it is provided*":

> The machine welds its links with ordinary men and women by elaborate networks of personal relations. Politics is transformed into personal ties. . . . In our prevailingly impersonal society, the machine, through its local agents, fulfills the important social function of *humanizing and personalizing all manner of assistance* to those in need. . . . [Furthermore] it is clearly the machine politician who is better integrated with the groups which he serves than the impersonal, professionalized, socially distant and legally constrained welfare worker. And since the politician can at times influence and manipulate the official organization for the dispensation of assistance, whereas the welfare worker has practically no influence on the political machine, this only adds to [the politician's] greater effectiveness.[25]

---

24. R. K. Merton, *Social Theory and Social Structure,* Rev. and Enl. Ed. (Glencoe, Ill.: Free Press, 1957), pp. 193-94.

25. *Ibid.,* pp. 74-75.

One of the principal differences between aid dispensed by welfare agencies and similar assistance given by political machines is that the latter brings about neighborhood social integration while the former does not. The recipient of public aid occupies the highly segmentalized role of "client." Interaction between client and social-welfare personnel does nothing to enhance the client's integration in the local community or otherwise to relate him to social structures that provide him with some semblance of control over his destiny. In effect, the client is treated as if detached from his milieu. To receive aid from the political machine, however, is to become related to a significant social, financial, and power structure.

It is in this sense that the growth of bureaucratically administered welfare services and the decline of the urban political machine are resulting in the progressive breakdown in the cohesion of urban slums, with the possible exception of the Negro community. Income-maintenance programs have greatly improved the standard of living of depressed families, but this positive result has been accompanied by a breakdown in lower-class social organization. And, as we have noted, patterns of delinquent behavior are greatly influenced by the extent of community cohesion; typically, violence among adolescents comes to be widespread in the unintegrated community that lacks both structures of social control and channels of social ascent.

We would be remiss if, in this brief account of the forces that are bringing about the disorganization of slums, we failed to mention the demoralizing effect of the massive slum-clearance programs which have recently been undertaken in many large urban areas. Most low-income housing programs destroy whatever vestiges of social organization remain in the slum community, in part because they fail to give priority in reoccupancy to site tenants. As a result, traditional residents are displaced and dispersed to other areas of the city, while persons who are strangers to one another are assembled in the housing project. Thus the residents of the housing project find themselves in a community that is not only new and alien but lacking in patterns of social organization to which they may link themselves and through which they might develop a stake in community life.

The divisive influence of public-housing programs is intensified by the attitudes of at least some project managers toward the efforts of tenants to develop social groups. A divided, unorganized body of tenants is more easily managed and less likely to exert pressures for change of one kind or another in housing practices. Thus Salisbury reports that housing managers sometimes actively discourage tenant organizations:

> [Housing] projects are political deserts. The precinct bosses have been wiped out with the slum. They do not seem to come back. No one cares whether the new residents vote or not. There is no basket at Thanksgiving. No boss to fix it up when Jerry gets in trouble with the police. The residents have no organization of their own and are discouraged from having any. "We don't want none of them organizers in here!" one manager told me. "All they do is stir up trouble. Used to be some organizers around here. But we cleaned them out good. . . . Communists . . . that's what they were."[26]

Whether or not this view is shared by most housing managers, the fact is that social organization is difficult to resurrect in communities where social institutions have been so completely demolished.

These are the terms, then, in which we trace the decline of social organization in lower-class neighborhoods. Were Whyte to return today to the Cornervilles of America, he would probably find much less evidence of what he called "highly organized and integrated" patterns of slum life. And these are the conditions—limited access to legitimate and illegitimate opportunities and decreasing social control—that we believe are likely to produce more subculturally patterned violence and retreatism among slum youth.

This account of the interrelationships between social structure and delinquent subcultures should provide, if only implicitly, some guidelines to the control and prevention of de-

26. H. E. Salisbury, *The Shook-up Generation* (New York: Harper & Bros., 1958), pp. 80-81.

linquency. We hope that we have at least made it clear that services extending to delinquent individuals or groups cannot prevent the rise of delinquency among others. For delinquency is not, in the final analysis, a property of individuals or even of subcultures; it is a property of the social systems in which these individuals and groups are enmeshed. The pressures that produce delinquency originate in these structures, as do the forces that shape the content of specialized subcultural adaptations. The target for preventive action, then, should be defined, not as the individual or group that exhibits the delinquent pattern, but as the social setting that gives rise to delinquency.

It is our view, in other words, that the major effort of those who wish to eliminate delinquency should be directed to the reorganization of slum communities. Slum neighborhoods appear to us to be undergoing progressive disintegration. The old structures, which provided social control and avenues of social ascent, are breaking down. Legitimate but functional substitutes for these traditional structures must be developed if we are to stem the trend toward violence and retreatism among adolescents in urban slums.

Index

aberrant behavior
  definition of by Merton, 83 (*see also* delinquent behavior; deviant behavior)
absolute-liability offenses, 15
acculturation, 75-76
addiction (*see* drug addiction)
adolescent groups (*see* delinquent subcultures; nondelinquent groups)
adolescent-transition crisis, as explanation of delinquency, 45, 48, 54-64
  by Bloch and Niederhoffer, 55-56
  inadequacies of, 56-64
adolescents, lower-class (*see* lower-class adolescents)
adolescents, male
  delinquency among, 30, 39
  "ganging" tendencies of, 55
  pressures on, toward deviant behavior
    adolescent-transition crisis, 54-56
    masculine-identification crisis, 48-50
    vulnerability to, 106-07
adult status, 55 (*see also* adolescent-transition crisis)
age-levels, integration of, 147-48
  in criminal subculture, 10-11, 153-54, 162-65, 170-71, 190
  in retreatist subculture, 190-91
aggressive behavior, 166
  control of, in criminal subculture, 167-71, 191 (*see also* social control)
  as result of "masculine protest," 49-50
  (*see also* conflict subcuture)
Aichhorn, August, 131*n.*
alienation from conventional norms, 19-20, 108-09
  beginnings of, according to Tannenbaum, 127-29
  causes of, 104-06
    discrepancy between formal and operative criteria, 118
    "dramatization of evil," 127-29
    failure attributed to social injustice, 110-13, 126

alienation (*Cont'd.*)
predisposition of deviant, 129
by Negroes, 121
process of, 110-24
American Bar Foundation, 6*n.*
anomie
definition of, 78
source of
according to Durkheim, 78-82
according to Merton, 82-86
theory of, 146, 150, 151
Asbury, Herbert, 194-96
aspirations
and achievements, discrepancy between (*see* failure)
class distribution of
absolute, 87-89
relative, 89-90
economic crises and, 79-80
limited of Americans, 83-84
and opportunity, discrepancy between, 108-09
types of, 90-91
unlimited, results of (*see* anomie)
of youth, for adult status, 54-56
(*see also* goals)
assimilation, 45-46, 194-99
attitudes, of delinquent
vs. behavior, 15, 16
toward official norms, 133-36, 137 (*see also* alienation)
of gang members toward addict, 183-84, 185-86, 191-92
autonomy, as lower-class value, 67

"bad manners," social control of, 3
Barbara, J. S., 203*n.*
Barron, Milton L., 35
Becker, Howard S., 109*n.*, 178-79
Bell, Daniel, 197*n.*, 198*n.*, 204
Bendix, Reinhard, 87*n.*, 97-98, 102
Bernstein, Walter, 24*n.*
big "score," 10, 22
"big shot" (*see* criminal role-models)
Bloch, H. A., 5*n.*, 117*n.*
Bloch, Herbert H., 38*n.*, 55-64, 90, 163, 168
Broom, Leonard, 17*n.*
"bopper," 24-25

"cat," 25-27
Chein, Isidor, 180*n.*
"Chicago school," 35-36, 146-55 (*see also* McKay; Shaw; Sutherland)
"class bias" in law enforcement, 3-4, 12
Cloward, R. A., 85-86*n.*, 144*n.*, 152*n.*, 165*n.*
Cohen, A. K., 12*n.*, 37-38, 42, 50-52, 90-92, 95-96, 133-34, 136-37, 139-41, 149*n.*, 155, 159-60, 167, 169, 189
collective adaptations
vs. individual solutions, 124-30
sequences of, 184-86
(*see also* delinquent subcultures; nondelinquent groups; *specific subcultures*)
"college boys"
as lower-class type, 90-91, 94, 95-96
participation of, in reform programs, 122-23
Comanche, "delinquent" activity among, 63-64
communication, 139-43
community
disorganized, 157, 170-71, 175-78 (*see also* social disorganization)
integrated, 156-58, 166-71 (*see also* slum)
compulsive masculinity (*see* masculine-identification crisis)
conflict pattern, 24-25
conflict role-model (*see* "bopper")
conflict subculture, 1, 20, 42-43, 171-78
distribution of, 29, 30
instability of, 44, 45, 185-86, 191, 192
prevalence of, 171-72
relations of, with adult world, 24-25
social disorganization and, 171-78
(*see also* "bopper"; violence)
conversation of gestures, 140-42
conformity, 37-38
"cool" (*see* "cat"; retreatist subculture)
"corner boys," 90-93, 97, 184
Cottrell, L. S., 17*n.*
Crawford, P. C., 24*n.*
Cressey, D. R., 138*n.*
criminal behavior
learning, 146-47, 148-49
Sutherland's "ninth proposition" on, 150-51
criminal career, 10-11
criminal pattern, 22-23, 42

criminal role-models, 23, 61, 154, 162-65
criminal subculture, 1, 20, 21, 161-71
distribution of, 29
integration of age-levels in, 44, 162-65, 190
integration of values in, 165-66
and retreatist subculture, 192
stability of, 44, 45, 192
social control in, 166-71
criminology (*see* "Chicago school"; *specific criminologists,* e.g., Bloch; Cohen; Kobrin)
criteria of evaluation
formal *vs.* operative, 114-21
among members of criminal subculture, 22
among members of conflict subculture, 24-25
cultural structure, according to Merton, 82-83
cultural-transmission theory (*see* "Chicago school"; McKay; Shaw)
culture-conflict theory
as explanation of delinquency, 65-76 (*see also* lower-class values)
Curtis, Alberta, 124*n.*

"debs," 30
delinquency (*see* delinquent behavior)
delinquent act, 9-10, 11-12, 70
delinquent behavior
adult response to (*see* "dramatization of evil"; officials of criminal justice)
classification of, 7-10
collective *vs.* individual, 41-42, 124-30, 137-38 (*see also* delinquent subcultures)
definitions of
by authors, 2-3
by Miller, 69
"official," 3-7
statutory, in New York, 4-5
distribution of, 51-52, 56-57, 61-62, 70
in industrial societies, 79
origin of pressures toward
adolescent-transition crisis, 54-64
culture conflict, 65-76
masculine-identification crisis, 48-54
psychological explanation of, 64
range of, 33
rationalizations of, 138-39
delinquent child, 128-29
attitudes of
res. behavior, 15, 16
toward official norms, 133-36, 137
basic endowments of, 117*n.*
as characterized by Cohen, 91
as characterized by Elliott and Merrill, 37-38
clinical treatment of, 132-33
delinquent group (*see* delinquent subcultures)
delinquent norms, 9, 13-20, 77-107
acquisition of, by new members, 74-75
as collective product, 124-30
conformity to, 37
and delinquent subcultures, 37, 53, 57
emergence of, 20, 41, 104-06, 109, 118, 126, 142 (*see also* alienation)
res. official norms, 14-15, 19-20
persistence of, 74-76
regulation of, 82-86
delinquent subcultures, 1, 9, 32, 42, 60, 65, 107, *passim*
change in, 45-46, 193-211
current theories of, 47-76
definition of, 7
by Cohen, 91
vs. delinquent acts, 9-10, 11-12, 70
distribution of, 27-30, 33-34, 70
class, according to Bloch and Niederhoffer, 56-57, 58-59
elements of, 13-14 (*see also* delinquent norms)
evolution of, 40-43, 53, 60, 71-72, 108*ff.*
formation of, 53, 78
impediments to, 140
illegitimate means and, 144-60
members of
"core," 188
fully indoctrinated, 132
newly recruited, 188-89
persistence of, 44-45, 188-92
and slum organization, 159-60, 161
social costs of, 10-12
stability of, 189
types of, 20-27, 42-43, 159-60, 161-86
integration between, 191
(*see also* conflict subculture; criminal subculture; retreatist subculture)

democratic ideology, 84-86, 108, 115, 119-21
deprivation, 113-21
destructive behavior, 63
detached-worker programs, 25, 176-77
deviant behavior. 36-37, 126
  and conformity, 38
  delinquent behavior and, 2-3
  individual and collective, 41-42, 129
  justification of, 118-19, 132
  pressures toward, 34-40, 86, 90, 96, 106
  social functions of, 46*n.*, 197-98
DeVinney, L. C., 115*n.*
Dietrick, D. C., 91, 92*n.*
differential - association theory (*see* "Chicago school"; Sutherland)
"differential group organization," 155-56
differential opportunity, 150-52
"double failure," and drug use, 179-84
"dramatization of evil," 21-22*n.*, 128-30
drug addiction, 10
  causes of, 88-89
  of gang members, 183-84, 185-86, 191-92
  among Negro adolescents, 89
  (*see also* drug users)
drug subcultures (*see* retreatist subculture)
drug use, "double failure" and, 179-84
drug users, 10
  attitudes of, toward norms, 180-81
  previous delinquency of, 180, 182-83
  relationships of, with peers, 183-84, 185-86, 191-92
  (*see also* "cat")
Dumpson, J. R., 24*n.*
Durkheim, Emile, 35*n.*, 78-83

economic crises, 79-80
education
  differential availability of, 85, 97-103, 120
  differentials in attitude toward
    class, 98-99
    ethnic, 99-101
Eisler, K. R., 131*n.*
Elliott, Mabel A., 37
Empey, L. T., 88-89
entertainment, as field of occupation, 104
environment
  for learning criminal roles, 146-48
  (*see also* slum)
evaluation, criteria of (*see* criteria of evaluation)
excitement, as lower-class value, 66
expectations
  and unjust deprivation, 113-21
  (*see also* aspirations; goals)
expressive behavior (*see* aggressive behavior; conflict subculture; instrumental behavior)

failure
  attribution of
    by Negroes, 121-22
    to self, 111-13, 125-26
    to social order, 110-13, 126
  "double," and drug use, 179-84
family (*see* kinship system)
fate, as related to lower-class values, 67
female-centered households, 48
  class distribution of, 51-52
  and masculine-identification crisis
    according to Miller, 72
    according to Parsons, 49-50
"fence," 23, 165
Finestone, Harold, 26, 89, 180*n.*, 182*n.*
Fiske, Marjorie, 124*n.*
Flynn, F. T., 5*n.*, 117*n.*
Freeman, Joseph, 168*n.*
Freedlander, Kate, 131*n.*

gambling, 200-01, 204-06
"ganging," 48
gangs
  evolution of, 142
  (*see also* conflict subculture)
Gerard, D. L., 88, 180*n.*
G. I. Bill of Rights, 103
Glane, Sam, 24*n.*
Glazer, Daniel, 12*n.*, 85*n.*
goals
  regulation of
    according to Durkheim, 78-82
    according to Merton, 82-86
    (*see also* aspirations)
Goffman, Erving, 114*n.*
guilt, 126, 129
  techniques of defense against, 130-39
  (*see also* failure)

Handlin, Oscar, 106*n.*
Havighurst, R. J., 102*n.*
Heider, Fritz, 112*n.*
Henderson, A. M., 16*n.*
"heart," 175
"hipster" cults, 25-27, 95-96
Hollingshead, A. B., 103*n.*
Hughes, E. C., 114*n.*
Hunt, D. E., 112*n.*
Hyman, H. H., 87-89, 98

illegitimate means, availability of, 145-48, 150-52
  decreasing, 184-86
  restrictions on, by race, 152*n.*
  slum social structure and, 152-59
immigrant, and types of delinquency, 45-46, 194-99
industrial society, anomie in, 79-82
instrumental behavior, 167, 169 (*see also* aggressive behavior; social control)
integration
  of age-levels of offender, 148, 153-54, 162-65, 170-71, 190-91
  of conventional and deviant values, 154-59, 165-66
  between subcultures, 191-92
Irish
  in organized crime, 196-97
  violence among, before Civil War, 194-96
Italians
  attitude of, toward education, 99-101
  gang warfare among, 198
  in organized crime, 196-98, 199-201

James, W. H., 112*n.*
Jews
  attitude of, toward education, 99-101
  in organized crime, 196-197, 199-201
Jones, S. V., 24*n.*
justifying beliefs, 126, 132, 133, 138-39, 141 (*see also* delinquent norms; guilt)

Kardiner, Abraham, 63
Karr, Madeline, 24*n.*
"kick," the, 10, 20, 26-27 (*see also* "cat")
kinship system
  and learning of occupational skills, 80-82
  and masculine-identification crisis, 49, 50
Kitsuse, J. I., 91, 92*n.*
Kobrin, Solomon, 156-58, 171, 174, 182
Kornatsky, Conon, 88, 180*n.*
Kornhauser, Ruth R., 93*n.*
Kotinsky, Ruth, 10*n.*
Kramer, Dale, 24*n.*
Kvaracous, W. C., 65*n.*, 69*n.*, 71, 92*n.*

latency period, 50
"law norms," 18-19
lawlessness (*see* anomie)
learning structures, 148-49, 154, 158, 163-64
Lee, R. S., 180*n.*
legitimacy
  attribution of
    to proscribed norms (*see* delinquent norms)
    reasons for, 16-17
    withdrawal of (*see* alienation)
  definition of, 16
  as distinct from moral validity, 17-20, 109, 131, 136-37
legitimate means, availability of, 146, 152
  according to theory of anomie, 150
  according to Chicago school, 150-51
  barriers to, 97-103
Lemart, E. M., 115*n.*
Lindesmith, Alfred, 149*n.*, 155*n.*
Lipset, S. M., 17*n.*, 87*n.*, 97, 98, 102
Loeb, M. B., 102*n.*
lower-class adolescents
  aggressive behavior among, 50-51
  aspirations of, 60-62, 87-93
  attitudes of
    toward education, 98-99
    toward middle-class values, 96-97
  delinquency among, 12, 28
  orientation of, 94-96
  retreatist behavior among, 183
  socialization of, and mobility, 99*n.*
  typology of, 72-73
  (*see also* "college boys"; "corner boys")
lower-class values, 65-67, 71, 74-75*n.*
  and criminal behavior, 22-23 (*see also* "Chicago school")
  vs. middle-class values, 65-76 (*see*

lower-class values (*Cont'd.*)
also culture-conflict theory)
as persisting immigrant values, 99-101
Lunt, P. S., 93*n.*

McCarthy, J. E., 203
McCord, Joan, 6*n.*
McCord, William, 6*n.*
McKay, H. D., 22*n.*, 35-36, 75*n.*, 146, 153-55
Malamud, D. I., 24*n.*
Manus, 63
masculine-identification crisis
as explanation of delinquency, 48-54
among lower-class youth, according to Miller, 72-73
"masculine protest" (*see* masculine-identification crisis)
mass media, 71
Matza, David, 18*n.*, 133-39
Merrill, F. E., 37
Merton, R. K., 17*n.*, 35*n.*, 82-85, 105, 113, 115, 124, 144, 150, 179-80, 208
middle-class adolescents
aggressive behavior among, 51
delinquency among, 12-13
frustrations among, 59
socialization of, and mobility, 99*n.*
middleman (*see* "fence")
Miller, Walter B., 50-51, 52, 65-75, 92, 93, 176-77
mobility, 99*n.*, 172
money, as criterion of social rank, 93-94
"moral norms," 18-19
Mulligan, R. A., 103
Murder, Inc., 168
Murphy, F. J., 6*n.*
Murray, H. A., 112*n.*
Myers, C. K., 24*n.*

NAACP, 122-23
National Youth Administration, 103
Negroes
adolescent
awareness of color distinctions by, 86*n.*
drug addiction among, 89
reaction of, to study of discrimination, 122-23
delinquency among, 199-202
female-centered households among, 49
and Harlem policy racket, 200-02
withdrawal of legitimacy by, 121
New York *Times,* 123, 200-01
neutralization of official norms, 18, 135-36
techniques of, 139
Niederhoffer, Arthur, 38*n.*, 55-58, 59*n.*, 60-64, 90, 163, 168
nondelinquent groups, 56, 58, 60, 69-70
"normal" child, 37-38
norms
commitment to 15, 118
criminal, transmission of, 170
definition of, 13, 168
delinquent (*see* delinquent norms)
legitimacy of *vs.* moral validity, 17-20, 109, 131, 136-37
official (*see* official norms)
(*see also* "law norms"; "moral norms")
Nye, F. I., 6*n.*

occupational system, 80-82
and adolescent-transition crisis, 54-55
and masculine-identification crisis, 49
official norms
attitude toward, of delinquents, 133-36, 127
and delinquent norms, 14-15
neutralization of, 18, 135-36, 139
repudiation of (*see* alienation)
violation of, 14, 19, 126 (*see also* guilt)
officials of criminal justice, 2-7
Olson, V. J., 6*n.*
opportunity, 175-77
aspirations and discrepancies between, 108-09
differential, 150-52
social disorganization and, 173-74
(*see also* illegitimate means; legitimate means)

Padilla, Elena, 188-89
Parsons, Talcott, 16*n.*, 17*n.*, 49-50, 52, 119*n.*
peer group
attitude of
toward drug addiction of members, 183-84, 186-86, 191-92
toward neurotic and psychotic

youth, 9-10
support of, for deviant conduct, 11, 28, 126-28
performance structures, 148-49, 164-65
Petrullo, Luigi, 112*n.*
physical needs, according to Durkheim, 78
Pirates, 61, 163-64, 168
policy, 200-01, 205-06
political machines, 195-97, 207-09
Porterfield, A. L., 6*n.*
position discontent, 82, 89-90
Powell, Adam Clayton, 200-01
prescriptions (*see* norms)
pressures toward deviance, 34-40, 86, 90, 96, 106
prestige (*see* "rep"; status)
prestige ordering of criminal activities, 152*n.*, 170
problems of adjustment, 34-40, 51, 70-71
and deviance, 38-39
distribution of, 39, 86
origins of
adolescent-transition crisis, 54-64
conformity, 38
culture conflict, 65-76
masculine-identification crisis, 48-54
social system, 108-09
permanence of, 40
significance of, 40
professional thief, achieving status as, 147
prosperity, and juvenile crime, 84*n.*-85*n.*
psychopathic personalities, 132

rationalizations, 138-39 (*see also* guilt, techniques of defense against)
reaction-formation
as explanation of "malicious" delinquency, 92, 95, 134
in masculine-identification theory, 50
recruitment, 188-89
Redfield, Robert, 109*n.*
Redl, Fritz, 10*n.*, 132
regulation of goals (*see* anomie)
Reiss, A. J., 102
Reles, Abe, 168
"rep," 10, 20, 183 (*see also* conflict subculture; status)
retreatist pattern, 25-27
retreatist role-model (*see* "cat")
retreatist subculture, 20, 25-27, 42, 152, 178-86
and criminal subculture, 192
distribution of, 29
integration of age-levels in, 190-91
pressures leading to, 178-79
stability of, 45, 192
Rhodes, A. L., 102
Rice, Kent, 85*n.*
"right guy," 23
role-model (*see* "bopper"; "cat"; criminal role-models; sex identification)
role performance, 45
Rosenfeld, Eva, 180*n.*
Rosenzweig, S., 112*n.*
Rotter, J. B., 112*n.*

Salisbury, Harrison, 24*n.*, 30*n.*, 168-69, 210
school, resentment of, by "corner boys," 96-97
Schroder, H. M., 112*n.*
Schuessler, Karl, 149*n.*, 155*n.*
Seeman, Melvin, 110*n.*
Sellin, Thorsten, 68
sex identification (*see* masculine-identification crisis)
Shaw, Clifford R., 22*n.*, 35-36, 41, 42*n.*, 75*n.*, 114*n.*, 146, 152*n.*, 153-55, 162, 164, 170*n.*
Shirley, M. M., 6*n.*
Short, J. F., Jr., 6*n.*, 12*n.*, 137, 159-60
Sibley, Elbridge, 102
Simpson, George, 35*n.*, 78*n.*
Sklare, Marshall, 99*n.*
slum, social structure of, 152-60
and delinquency, 149
illegitimate opportunities and, 152-59
and subcultural differentiation, 151-52, 159-60
slum clearance, effects of, 209-10
"smartness," as lower-class value, 66
social change, 45-46
social control
of aggressive behavior, 167-71
social disorganization and, 174-75
social disorganization
causes of, 172
and conflict subcultures, 172-78
and criminal learning, 154-56
and drug use, 178
social needs, 78

social structure
according to Merton, 82-83
of slum (*see* integration; slum)
Sorokin, P. A., 18-19
Spaulding, J. A., 35*n.*, 78
sports, as field of occupation, 104
stability
of delinquent subcultures, 189, 190-92
of social system, 18
of society, 78-79, 83
of various subcultural types, 44
"stable lower class," 72-73
stable society
according to Durkheim, 78-79
according to Merton, 83
Star, Shirley A., 115*n.*
status
competition for, 82
problems of, and delinquent subculture, 91, 93 (*see also* position discontent)
search for, 73
adult (*see* adolescent-transition crisis)
by "corner boys," 93
by immigrants, 194-96
through manipulation of violence, 20, 24, 175
middle-class, 95-96
by retreatist, 27
stealing, 169 (*see also* criminal behavior)
Stouffer, S. A., 115*n.*
street-gang workers (*see* detached-worker programs)
subcultural differentiation, 161-86
illegitimate opportunities and, 151-52
slum organization and, 151-52, 159-60
(*see also* delinquent subcultures, types of; *specific subcultures*)
success-goals, 82, 86*ff.*
alternative avenues to, 104-07
and democratic ideology, 84-86
differential availability of, 85-86, 163, 184
success symbols, 96
Suchman, E. A., 115*n.*
Sutherland, Edwin H., 22*n.*, 35-36, 75*n.*, 114*n.*, 146-48, 149, 150-51, 155, 156
Sykes, G. M., 18*n.*, 133, 134-39

Tagiuri, Renata, 112*n.*
Tannenbaum, Frank, 21*n.*, 127-28, 129-30, 142-43, 148-49, 165
Tappan, P. W., 4*n.*
"techniques of neutralization," 139
thief, 10
Thrasher, F. M., 142
Toby, Jackson, 99-101
Tocqueville, Alexis de, 83-84, 119*n.*, 120*n.*
toughness, as lower-class value, 66
"trouble," concern over, as feature of lower-class culture, 66

unemployment and crime rates, 84*n.*-85*n.*
upward mobility, 146, 154
utilitarian delinquency (*see* instrumental behavior)

value-conflict theory (*see* culture-conflict theory)
values
conventional and deviant, integration of, 127, 154-60, 165-66, 171
lower-class (*see* culture-conflict theory; lower-class values)
violence
detached-worker programs and, 176-77
among immigrant groups, 46, 194-95, 198, 199
increase in, 45, 202
in Negro neighborhoods, 199, 202
social disorganization and, 175-78, 199
as source of "rep," 10, 20

Wakefield, Dan, 24*n.*
Warner, W. L., 93*n.*, 102, 103
Weber, Max, 16*n.*, 168
welfare state, 208
Whyte, William F., 90, 92, 101*n.*, 122, 155-56, 197-98, 205-06
Williams, R. M., Jr., 115*n.*
Wilmer, D. M., 180*n.*, 185*n.*
Wineman, David, 132*n.*
Wirth, Louis, 67
Witmer, Helen, 6*n.*
withdrawal of support (*see* alienation)

"youth culture" (*see* nondelinquent groups)

Zetterberg, H. L., 13*n.*
Zola, Irving, 6*n.*
Zuok, G. F., 102*n.*